YORK

YORK
A STUDY IN
CONSERVATION

Report to the Minister of Housing and Local
Government and York City Council by
Viscount Esher, MA, D Litt, PPRIBA, FILA, DistTP

London Her Majesty's Stationery Office 1968

Typography by HMSO : J. Saville, MSIA/D. M. Challis

Printed in England for Her Majesty's Stationery Office by
St Clements Fosh & Cross Limited, London

SBN 11 750042 9

Preface

This is one of four reports on the historic towns of Bath, Chester, Chichester and York. They were commissioned jointly by the Minister of Housing and Local Government and the City and County Councils concerned in 1966.

The purpose of the studies has been to discover how to reconcile our old towns with the twentieth century without actually knocking them down. They are a great cultural asset, and, with the growth of tourism, they are increasingly an economic asset as well.

The Civic Amenities Act 1967, sponsored by Mr Duncan Sandys, gave recognition for the first time to the importance of whole groups of architectural or historic value and required local planning authorities to designate 'conservation areas' and to pay special attention to enhancing their character or appearance. While the Act was in preparation, the Government decided that studies should be commissioned to examine how conservation policies might be sensibly implemented in these four historic towns. There were two objectives ; to produce solutions for specific local problems, and to learn lessons of general application to all our historic towns.

At the same time my predecessor (Mr Crossman) asked Lord Kennet, the Joint Parliamentary Secretary to the Ministry, to convene a Preservation Policy Group. Its terms of reference are :

(i) To co-ordinate the conservation studies and to consider the results.

(ii) To review experience of action to preserve the character of other historic towns.

(iii) To consider measures adopted in other countries for preserving the character of historic towns and villages, and their effects.

(iv) To consider what changes are desirable in current legal, financial and administrative arrangements for preservation, including the planning and development aspects, and to make recommendations.

Its membership is : J. S. Berry, BSc (Eng), AMICE, MIStructE, MIHE ; H. J. Buck, MTPI, FRICS ; Theo Crosby, ARIBA, FSIA ; A. Dale, FSA ; Prof. Alan Day, BA ; Miss J. Hope-Wallace, CBE ; R. H. McCall ; Prof. N. B. L. Pevsner, CBE, PhD, FSA, Hon FRIBA ; B. D. Ponsford ; H. A. Walton, B Arch, Dip CD(L'pool), ARIBA, MTPI ; S. G. G. Wilkinson (succeeded by V. D. Lipman) ; A. A. Wood, Dipl Arch, Dipl TP, FRIBA, MTPI ; and Lord Kennet as Chairman.

I should like to take this opportunity of thanking very warmly the members of the Group and particularly Lord Kennet. His deep knowledge of historic buildings and enthusiasm for their safety have greatly contributed to the Group's work. This has fallen into two parts.

The first, concluded in the Spring of 1967, consisted of identifying those changes in the law which would improve our national system for the conservation of historic buildings and towns. The views of the Group were taken into account by the Government during the passage of the Civic Amenities Act 1967 and in devising Part V of the Town and Country Planning Bill. The latter provides a much improved system of controlling alteration or demolition of historic buildings, and makes other important amendments to the law.

The second part of the Group's work, that is considering the recommendations of the consultants, begins with the publication of these reports.

The recommendations the consultants make in these reports are numerous and diverse ; with help from the Preservation Policy Group the Government and the local councils concerned will need to consider them carefully. The councils are not committed to adopt any recommendations of specifically local application, nor is the Government committed to adopt the various suggestions of more general application.

We shall now discuss the reports with the councils concerned and with the local authorities of other towns as well. The Preservation Policy Group will co-ordinate these discussions and study their results. Only then will the full value of these reports be seen.

Meanwhile I commend the reports to everyone concerned with the well-being of our old towns, and express the Government's warm thanks to the consultants who produced them.

Minister of Housing and Local Government

Contents

*This much is certain:
the town has no
room for the citizen—
no meaning at all—
unless he is gathered
into its meaning.
As for architecture;
it need do no more
than assist man's
homecoming.* **Aldo van Eyck**

Introduction

In terms of the old army thought-pattern, this report is laid out as follows:

Information	Chapter 1.	The city in history
	Chapter 2.	The walled city to-day
	Chapter 3.	Activities I
Objectives	These are stated on page 41	
Intentions	Chapter 4.	Activities II
	Chapter 5.	Traffic
	Chapter 6.	General problems of conservation
	Chapter 7.	Conservation in detail
	Chapter 8.	York renewed
Method	Chapter 9.	Costs and returns
	Chapter 10.	Realisation

Thus the first two chapters (with Appendix B) describe the physical structure of the walled city and the third (with Appendices C and D) the life that is lived in it. The fourth and fifth (with Appendices E and F) propose which activities should be encouraged and which withdrawn, and the sixth seventh and eighth visualise the physical effects of such action on the built environment. Finally the last two (with Appendix G) examine the money cost of achieving these effects and its implications in policy.

At Appendix A will be found the names, recorded as best we could, of all those who have collaborated in the work. Here I wish particularly to mention my partner Harry Teggin and his assistant Pamela Ward, who co-ordinated the teams in my office and in York, to express my thanks to the officers of the Corporation for their willing co-operation and to the York Civic Trust for their generosity, and to salute the devoted work of my professional consultants, namely:

Mr Philip Booth, AAI,
of Messrs. Bernard Thorpe & Partners — valuations
Mr W. J. Fussell FRICS, FIArb
of Messrs. Davis, Belfield & Everest — construction costing
Mr Geoffrey Powell, FRICS — shopping survey and
of Messrs. Gerald Eve and Partners — financial analysis
Professor Nathaniel Lichfield, Bsc, PhD, — economics of
PPTPI, FRICS, CEng, AMIMunE — conservation

It seemed natural, with so many of us involved, to write in the first person plural, a style with which I think most architects and planners anyhow feel happier, and this we do from now on.

Esher

Scales and orientation
This is the orientation given to all diagrams
with the exception of the two traffic analysis
maps in chapter 5

1:10000   500
        0

1:5000   500
        0

1:2500   500
        0

1:1250
        0

1:500   100
        0

1   West End of Minster with St. Michael-le- Belfrey

1 The City in history

2 Bootham Bar, York. 1827 W. H. Bartlett

1.1   Of the smaller historic cities of western Europe few have a more varied history or a richer legacy of buildings of all periods than York. The story starts in A.D. 71 with the foundation of the Roman legionary fortress on the N.E. bank of the navigable Ouse, with its customary rectangular structure, evident in the present walls to the N.E. and N.W., and in the alignment of Petergate and Stonegate. But even at that date a substantial suburb or 'colonia' grew up across the river, indicating that the city already had a commercial as well as a purely military significance.

1.2   With the withdrawal of the legions the city if anything increased in importance, not only as the capital of the North and second city in population after London, but as the centre of the astonishing 8th century Renaissance in Northumbria, with the finest library in western Europe. Its triple role as Court, Minster and Market was already emerging. Geographically exposed to the Danish invasions, York soon absorbed its conquerors in large numbers ; and it was in their age that most of the familiar 'medieval' streets, winding through and beyond the Roman rectangle, came into existence.* But the Norman conquest and the destruction of the city and all its treasures by fire in 1069 ensured that no building should survive of the greatest period in the city's cultural history.

1.3   The rebirth of York in the middle ages was a slow process. The rebuilding of the Minster did not get under way until the 13th century and took 250 years to complete.

1.4   By that time the little walled city housing a population of about 10,000 on its 257 acres, (the size and density of a postwar New Town neighbourhood unit) had built or rebuilt as well as the largest cathedral in England, three great abbeys, 40 parish churches and 14 other religious foundations, hospitals and almshouses. Its crenellated walls, gates and barbicans entirely surrounded it except to the north-east where the marsh of the Foss was sufficient defence. Crowding close up to its single stone bridge, itself encrusted with buildings, little ships lined its quays, carrying Yorkshire wool and York cloth to the low Countries and other English ports. The Castle was rebuilt in stone and with St. Mary's Abbey west of the Minster provided head-quarters for the Scottish wars and an alternate seat of government to London.

1.5   Yet even at the peak of its medieval prosperity in the mid 14th century the city was congested, its narrow and noisome alleys over-hung with wooden houses presented a permanent risk of fire and plague, and hundreds of pigs and 'paupers' infested its unpaved streets.

*The suffix 'gate' derives from the Scandinavian 'gat' = street.

1

1.6 In the later middle ages, with the gradual loss of overseas trade to Hull, there was some decline of population, yet the city continued to build. The Guildhall, the Merchant Adventurers' Hall, St. Anthony's Hall, St. William's College, a dozen churches and most of the city's finest stained glass date from these years of gradual economic recession. It was a city of exquisite architecture rising out of a midden.

1.7 In the 16th and 17th centuries York's cloth industry and seaborne trade continued to decline in face of competition from the West Riding towns and the port of Hull. The city which in 1334 had been second in population and wealth to London was by 1524 only 15th in population and had only a fifth of the wealth of Norwich. With the Dissolution the monastic houses became stone quarries, notably St. Mary's Abbey, part of which became the King's Manor and the seat of the King's Council of the North. Sixteen of the parish churches were demolished in a union of parishes and there was much stripping and sale of lead. In compensation the city acquired a graceful new bridge, rivalling the Rialto as one of the longest single spans in Europe, the little church of St. Michael le Belfrey below the Minster, and no doubt a wealth of old oak, recently much prized. Sanitation improved only gradually, and repeated epidemics kept the population below its medieval peak until the late 18th century. The city's economy was now entirely a 'service' one. *The urbs amplissima et metropolis of* the 12th century had become a county town. In 1701 it put up its first classical building—a debtor's prison.

1.8 With Georgian prosperity, improved agriculture and communications and the fashion for country-house life, the 18th century saw a transformation in the character of York society and in the architectural scene. As the only important town within reach of a great number of country estates both large and small, its market prospered, its tradesmen rebuilt their frontages in the new red brick style, and a number of country gentry erected handsome town houses in streets like Mickle-

3 Part of Stonegate. H. Cave 1813

4 Part of Low Ouse Gate. H. Cave 1813

5 Ouse Bridge and St. William's Chapel–
Published and engraved by J. Halfpenny

gate, Petergate and Castlegate and outside the walls in Bootham and Blossom Street. The Corporation set a splendid example with the Mansion House (1725) and Lord Burlington's Assembly Rooms (1730), and John Carr (1723-1807), the city's one native-born architect of national standing, was later employed to build the twin handsome civic buildings in the Castle Yard (1773), as well as the racecourse grandstand and a number of private houses. The city also planted the avenues of trees in Lord Mayor's Walk and the New Walk along the river bank, widened and paved a number of streets and tightened up its sanitary and fire regulations. But there was no Georgian town planning in York, and at the turn of the century, as the population began at last to expand, the city was still medieval in scale and structure.

1.9 York's population growth in the 19th century, which averaged 14 per cent per decade, was close to the national average and nowhere near the explosions which took place in the manufacturing towns; but it was enough to create severe congestion and a new form of squalor in the walled city, a quarter of which had until then consisted of gardens and orchards. Now small workshops and service industries of all kinds jammed themselves up against the back windows of handsome Georgian houses in Micklegate and Petergate, as their owners sold up and moved to London. By 1825 contemporaries had noted a relapse in the smartness of York society and of York buildings, and it was suggested that a university might help to raise the declining city 'to its proper rank in the national account'. The coming of the railway, which many hoped would restore the city's fortunes, brought several thousand impoverished and hungry Irish immigrants. The Walmgate area degenerated into a slum, with one of the highest infant mortality rates in the country. As late as 1886, with 8,000 privies, York was described as 'essentially a midden town', and the Rowntrees were to find in 1936 one third of the population living in 'poverty'. The city was never without its dark side.

3

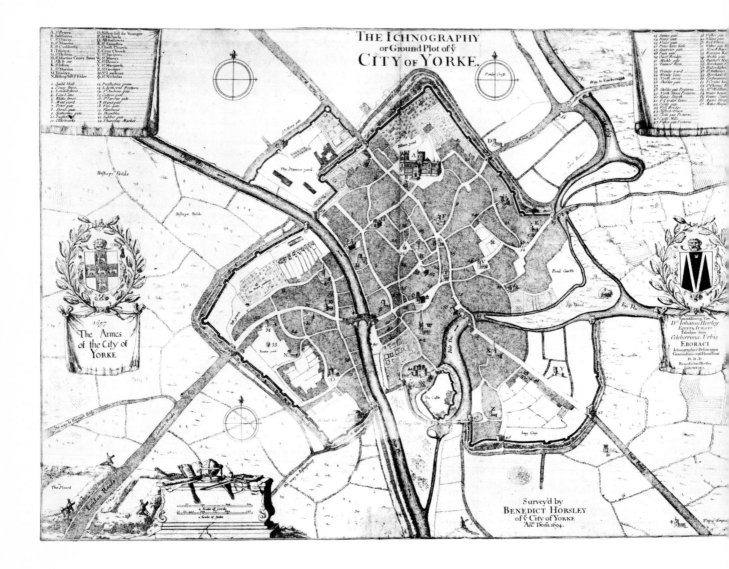

1.10 What the railway did do was to give employment eventually to over 5,000 men, largely through the enterprise of George Hudson in securing the NER Headquarters and its wagon and carriage works for York. And by the fifties it was already carrying the advance guard of the tourist trade, to which York's increasingly decayed and picturesque appearance was a powerful attraction. For female labour the railways were complemented by confectionery. Quakers had started chocolate making in St. Helen's Square in 1767 and in Castlegate in 1785. By the end of the Victorian era Terry's and Rowntrees had about 2,000 employees, by 1939 over 12,000.

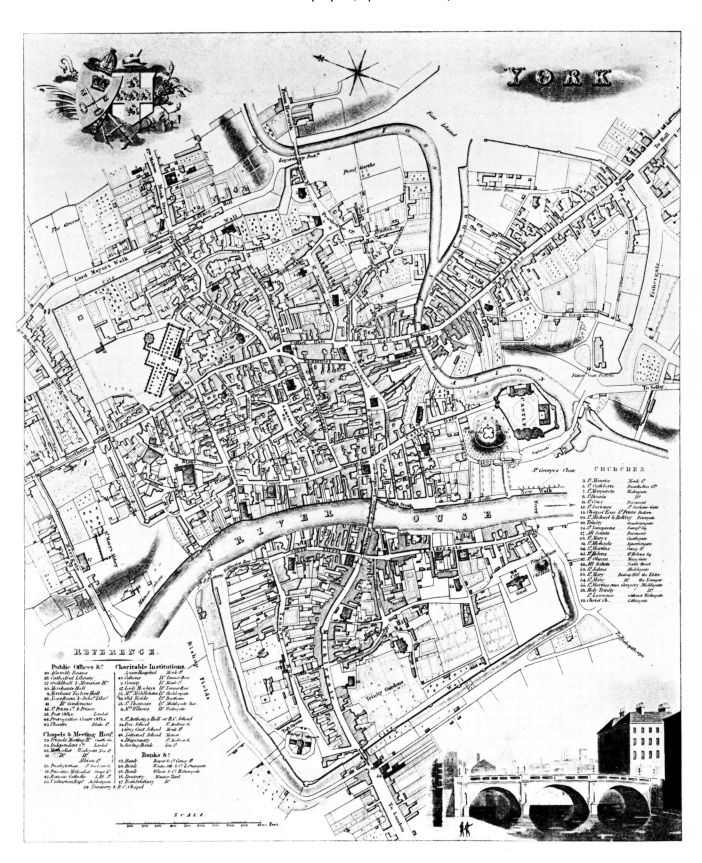

8 A reconstruction of fifteenth century York by Ridsdale Tate

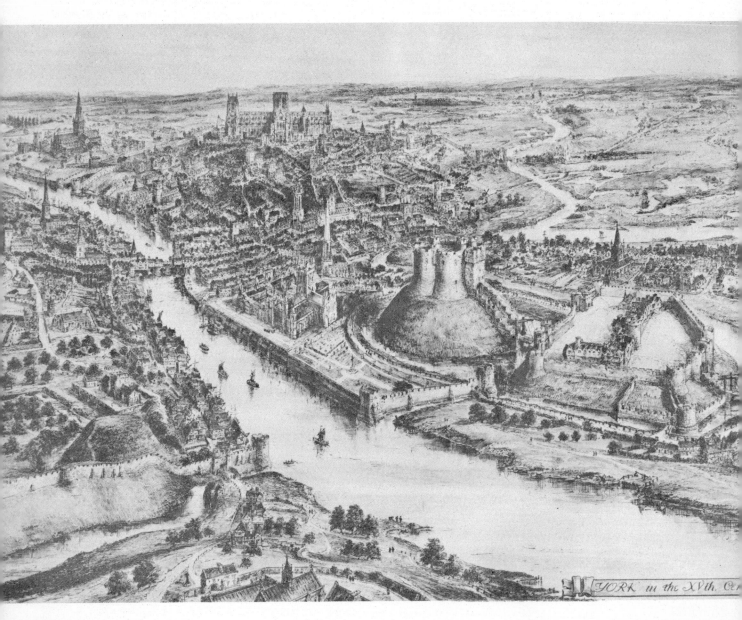

YORK in the XVth Ce

1.11   Nineteenth century civic improvements were on a suitably modest scale. Ouse Bridge was rebuilt (1810), St. Leonard's Terrace (1825) and Parliament Street (1835) were cleared and built up, and later in the century Museum Street and Duncombe Place were improved and Clifford Street broken through, each furnished with what were thought to be appropriately solemn buildings. Probably the most attractive Victorian building in York is Andrew's Yorkshire Insurance Building in St. Helen's Square (1846).

1.12   The walled city contains two twentieth-century streets, Piccadilly (1912) and Stonebow (1960), and their visual characteristics are sufficient commentary on the national loss of touch which has led to the need for this Report. Individual twentieth-century buildings are noticed in their place in Appendix B. On the scale of the city in history, the most important event so far this century has been the foundation of the University.

10 The Royal Commission on Historical Monuments' version of the 1851 Ordnance Survey map

11 Vertical air photograph of historic core of York : scale 1/5000

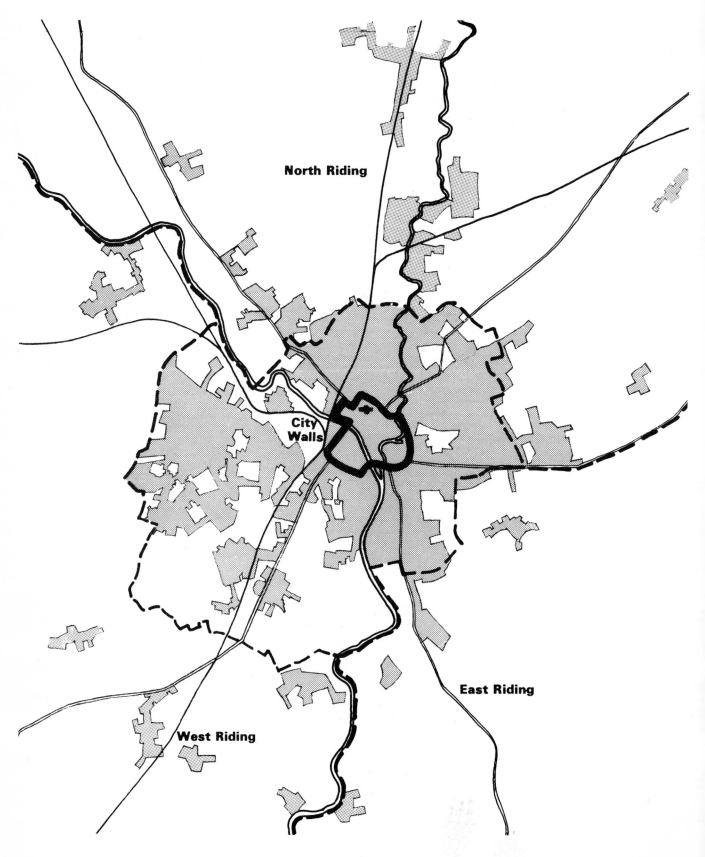

North Riding

City
Walls

East Riding

West Riding

2 The walled City today

12   The walled city in relation to the built up area of York
Scale : 1 mile to the inch

2.1   The walls of York are unspectacular, but they identify the historic core as effectively as the walls of a room which one enters through a choice of doors. Outside, all makes for the centre. No sooner inside than there is an unmistakable change of atmosphere which makes certain kinds of buildings and vehicles and noises seem like intruders.

2.2   At Appendix B is an alphabetical street gazetteer which takes the city to pieces and describes its components. This section attempts to put it together again and to see it as a whole.

2.3   Micklegate Bar, which stands at the crest of what seems a considerable hill, is only 40 feet above the banks of the Ouse, and the Minster precinct 13 feet lower. So topographically the Minster gets no help, and in fact in spite of its immensity it by no means dominates the historic core; it stands back in its Victorian precinct, is glimpsed at the end of narrow streets or above rooftops and is seldom seen from ground level except fragmentarily. The visual wealth of York is in the secular city itself, one of the richest and most complex townscapes in the world. It is the most medieval in feeling of all English cities, a city of streets rather than spaces, and its streets are narrow and bent to close all vistas and lead the walker round corners—so that the only wide and straight ones (Parliament Street and Piccadilly) seem alien both in name and nature. Curves are free and non-geometrical with the sole and therefore striking exception of St. Leonard's Place. The scale is minuscule and pedestrian, and exaggerates the size of vehicles; it conspicuously enhances the importance of man. Materials are dark and rich—York stone, slabs, cobbles, timber and crimson brick, blackened or (where cleaned) ochrous limestone, vermilion and black pantiles, bravely lettered walls, shining slate roofs.

2.4   It is a city of silhouettes, but at close range. Beyond the walls where the city sprawls unconfined across the plain, distance soon diminishes the Minster, and even within them the sharp rise of Bishophill is so tightly built up that only glimpses of the towers and spires are caught between buildings and trees. But there is a splendid variety of middle-distance features, among which the Minster towers, the cone of the Chapter-House, the spires of St. Mary's Castlegate and All Saints North Street, the lanterns of All Saints, Pavement and St. Martin's Coney Street, the cooling tower, the Foss Warehouse, Clifford's Tower and the turrets of the Law Courts are the most prominent. Closer still, gables and pediments and chimneys diversify the skyline, with the occasional long horizontal of the Minster ridge or a modern office block. None of the latter are as yet high enough to damage the silhouette, whatever damage they may do to the streets, where hitherto unified ranges of buildings larger in scale than the Victorian bye-law terrace have been rare; the essence of York is still the single-family house or house-cum-shop grouped together in infinite variety of form and period. It is this smallness of the

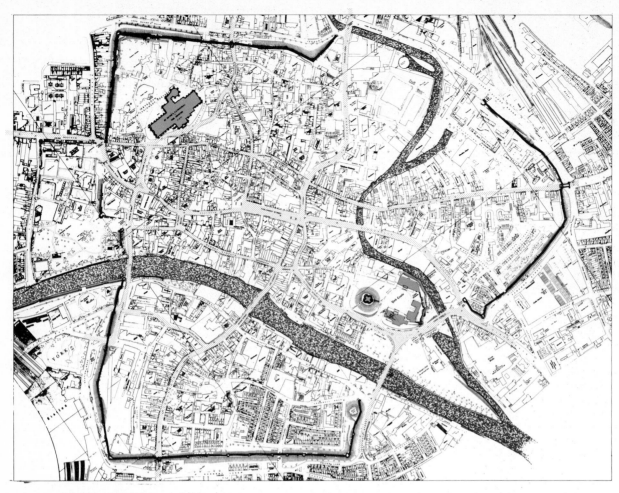

13 Main features of the walled City

14 Plan defining sectors

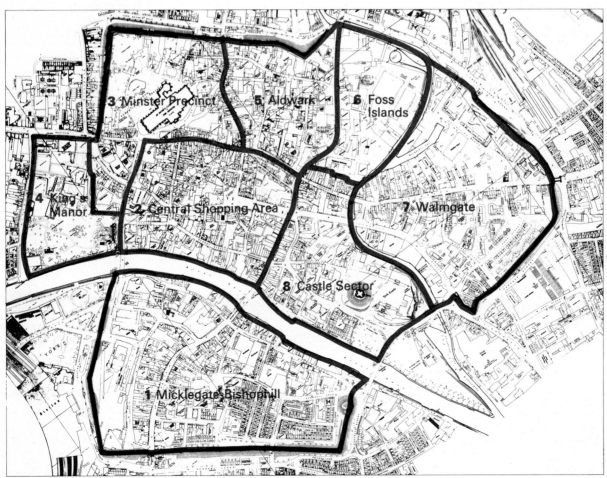

old components which makes rebuilding in much larger frontages so hard to handle successfully. The streets themselves are often no more than slits in the dense texture of buildings, or alleys running off under low openings to dwellings and workshops giving on to tiny yards.

The 8 Sectors

2.5   Within this general pattern the historic core is clearly differentiated into individual sectors, and we have identified eight of them, each with its own life and personality.

2.6   The most clearly defined is MICKLEGATE-BISHOPHILL: the old Roman *colonia* south-west of the river and bounded by walls on its other three sides. Micklegate Bar is the city's historic entry from the South, and still the best approach to its heart. The 'ceremonial' Victorian by-pass from the station to the Minster over Lendal Bridge, with its breaches in the walls, is more spectacular but lacks surprise. Micklegate-Bishophill has four kinds of townscape: Micklegate itself, the beautiful curving and falling village street with twin churches and fine collection of house-fronts; the railway headquarters sector to the west of it, where a scale of building has now established itself that is notably larger than elsewhere in York; the pleasant corner of Victorian terraces and chapels to the east of it, and finally the warehouses and workshops along the river. Characteristically, two tiny residential remnants, medieval at All Saints North Street, Georgian at Skeldergate, survive among the warehouses.

2.7   Cross Ouse Bridge and you plunge into the CENTRAL shopping sector, which extends up Stonegate as far as the Minster and up Pavement as far as Stonebow. It contains one of the prettiest luxury shopping streets in the world (Stonegate) and one of the least unpleasant streets of multiple stores in any British city of this size (Coney Street). It has so far baffled the big developers, and even assimilated one or two jumbo facades without incurable damage. It contains, at one end of the scale, the historic civic nucleus (Guildhall, Mansion House, Assembly Rooms) and at the other end a complex mosaic of tiny workshops, warehouses, offices and dwellings, which has been taken as the first of our detailed study areas.

2.8   Beyond the quadrilateral of the shopping centre, the MINSTER PRECINCT lies wide open to the town, its seclusion invaded by the Deangate short-cut. The sunlit flank of the great church is as public as St. Paul's, but its north side is silent, lapped by the trees of the Dean's Park, and to east and west are tiny cobbled lanes perfectly scaled to set off its size. The Precinct is defined by the angle of the Roman walls, terminating in Monk Bar to the east and Bootham Bar to the west, each reached by narrow streets largely medieval in character.

2.9   Emerging through Bootham Bar into noise and glare, we pass through a breach in its own wall-system into KING'S MANOR, tacked on to the western edge of the historic city. This now wears a prosperous municipal air, with the Art Gallery, City Library, Theatre Royal, and the Doric Yorkshire Museum in its romantic riverside park, created out of a wilderness by the Yorkshire Philosophical Society and recently donated to the City. In the midst, the 16th century King's Manor buildings now house an offshoot of the University. Over the whole sector the western towers of the Minster preside.

2.10   The corresponding quarter to the east of the Minster is ALDWARK, a total contrast: silent, deserted, its last Georgian houses falling into decay, its half-empty workshops and **warehouses**

15   'A scale of building has now established itself that is notably larger than elsewhere in York'

16   Victorian housing in the Bishophill sector

17   Mid eighteenth century merchants' houses in Micklegate

18   A Georgian town-house in Skeldergate

awaiting clearance. Here, secluded by the City Walls within a stone's throw of the Minster and the thriving central shops is the second of our detailed study areas.

2.11   Across Stonebow is another complete change of scene—the FOSS ISLANDS industrial sector—York's back-yard. Dominated by a fine cooling tower and by the great warehouse rising sheer out of the dark waters of the Foss, this sector makes a by no means unworthy contribution to the character and variety of the York scene. Fossgate, which defines its S.W. boundary leads straight over a humped and cobbled bridge into

2.12   The WALMGATE sector, Micklegate's opposite number, equally clearly defined by the loop of the Foss and the wide curve of the City Walls. Like Micklegate, it has its backbone village street with twin churches and its industrial hinterland, but unlike Bishophill it is low-lying and traditionally insalubrious, and it has a long history of congestion and squalor. Slum clearance and municipal housing have been in progress here for some time and await completion. To the West, Piccadilly has cut through the workshop hinterland with a swathe of garages and new office blocks forming the least attractive of all entries into the walled city.

2.13   Finally, across the Foss and occupying the sharp peninsula between it and the Ouse is the airy CASTLE sector, now traffic-ridden and car-park infested, but still full of character and potentiality, with the finest Gothic spire and several of the most handsome Georgian buildings in the city, as well as a gloomily romantic Victorian Street. At King's Staith the Castle sector looks across the river to the Skeldergate warehouses, and we have completed the circuit.

2.14   So far we have looked at the city as a kind of stage-set. Now it is time to bring on the actors.

19 The medieval core : Shambles from King's
Court
20 'One of the prettiest luxury shopping streets
in the world'
21 St. Helen's Square, the historic civic nucleus
22 Early morning in Coney Street

26 The Minster from the walls

27 St. William's College and the Great East Window

28 'Tiny cobbled lanes perfectly scaled to set off its size'

29 'Curves are free and non-geometrical with the sole and striking exception of St. Leonard's Place '

30 Aldwark : Aldwark Sector

31 Aldwark : Merchant Taylors' Hall from the Walls

32 Ruins of St. Mary's Abbey in the Museum Gardens

33 The Castle precinct : the Debtors Prison of 1701 and Carr's Assize Courts

34 Walmgate: Foss Bridge looking towards Wormald's Cut

35 The Castle sector from the Skeldergate warehouses

36 Industrial townscape of the Foss

37 St. Saviourgate

38 A restored terrace in the Walmgate sector

39 'A gloomily romantic Victorian street'

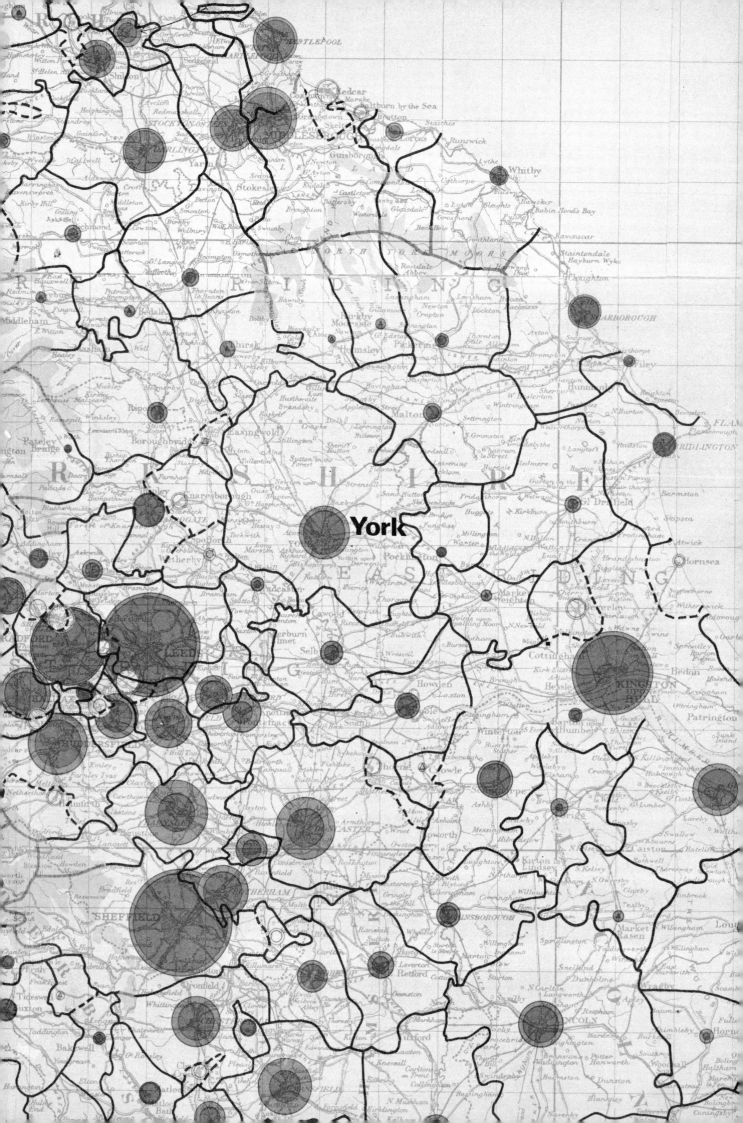

3 Activities I

40 Population density in the York region
Scale: 10 miles to the inch

3.1 A city is not a work of art. It is shaped by human activities, and in turn shapes them, and nobody has ever been able to analyse or order them precisely enough to achieve a fully controlled townscape. But we must do our best to understand them, because our plans will fail to work if we study a town as a mere arrangement of streets and buildings.

3.2 This chapter looks at the life that goes on in the heart of York in two parts. (Figs 42 and 43). The first, at Appendix C, is a sketch by a resident of a typical day in the life of the walled city. The second, with Appendix D, is an analysis of central York as a commercial and employment centre.

Seven Activities

3.3 We propose to systematise the impressions given in Appendix C by breaking down the activities of the central core, for practical purposes, into seven. They are:
    Residence (fig 46)
    Shopping (fig 44)
    Servicing
    Manufacture (fig 47)
    Office Work (fig 45)
    Education
    Visiting

3.4 *Residence*
At 3,576 in 1965 the population of the walled city had sunk to a third of its medieval numbers, though recent rehousing had lifted this figure fractionally over 1961's which at 3,498 is likely to prove the all-time low. This evacuation of the central core is a world-wide phenomenon, and its causes are too familiar for repetition here. The people who still hang on in the walled city are either people with a 'service' dwelling connected with churches, schools, nursing homes, hotels, etc., owner-occupiers or tenants of small Victorian terrace houses, mainly in Bishophill, tenants in buildings converted into flats, or council tenants on the new estates, mainly in Walmgate. There is evidence that few of those who live in the walled city want to move out and that there is an unsatisfied demand for small middle-income dwellings, provided a suitable environment can be carved out for them and safeguarded. The University's policy is that a third of the student population should live out, the more in the walled city (with its good communications) the better; but at present, of 900 students living out, only 31 live within the walls. It can be concluded that the depopulation of medieval York is no longer, if it ever was, what people want.

3.5 *Shopping*
This is of course the primary economic activity of central York in the

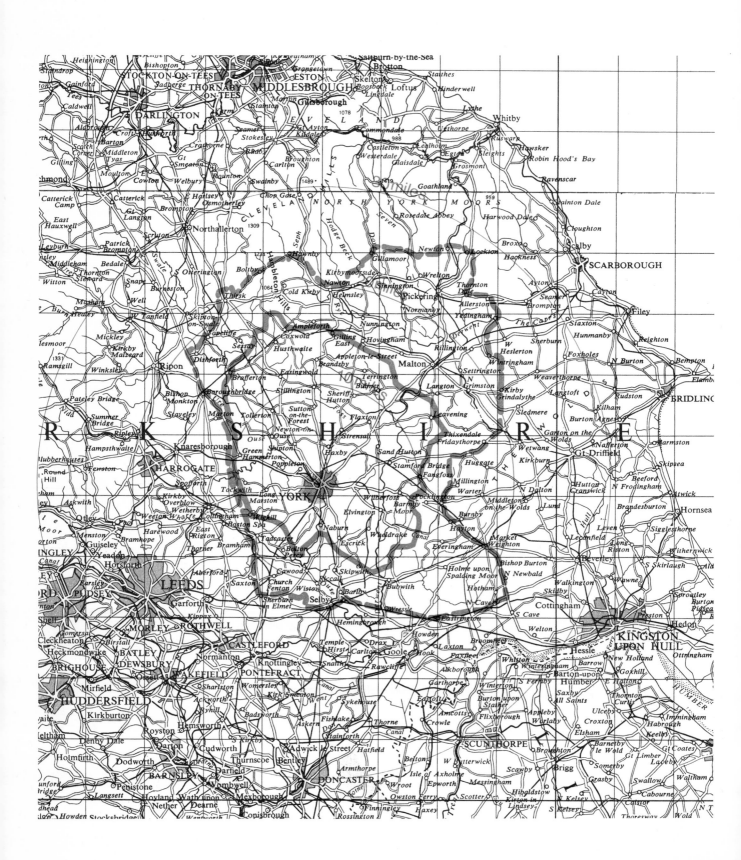

sense that its loss or even its eclipse would be more damaging than any other to the prospects of survival of the fabric of the city centre.

In their report printed as Appendix D Messrs. Gerald Eve and Partners estimate York's present 'close-support' shopping population at 175,000, with a growth to something over 200,000 by 1981 (fig 41). There are about 1,500,000 sq. ft. of shopping floor space already in use, with a further 57,000 sq. ft. building or sanctioned and an unsatisfied 1981 demand (on certain assumptions) of only 33,000 sq. ft. These are not figures which could conceivably justify a policy of decommercialisation. York, as the report points out, is one of the country's major shopping centres outside the conurbations, with a specific tourist as well as regional base, and one in which supply and demand are at present well-matched. Given continued or improved accessibility its survival as such seems assured.

3.6 *Servicing*

This is, and must remain, the main occupation in a city centre. It includes those (estimated at 3,500) who work in shops; municipal workers, both manual and white-collar; the 500 odd who work in hotels and restaurants within the walls, the 224 in the telephone exchange and the 90 (temporarily doubled) in the G.P.O. in Lendal. It includes the 250-odd who work in garages and the similar number who work in road haulage, the dentists, bankers, architects, lawyers and estate agents, the nurses, firemen, gardeners, and odd-job men, and (for lack of another place for them) the 45 Minster staff. For the planner, all these employments are necessary to the life of the centre; the problem is their journey to work and the motor traffic that brings them in.

3.7 *Manufacture*

At the time of our survey, there were nearly $2\frac{1}{2}$ million sq. ft. of industrial or similar floorspace within the walls, divided as follows:

Industry	800,892	sq. ft.
Garages	519,335	,, ,,
Warehouses	1,081,160	,, ,,
Statutory Undertakers	94,498	,, ,,
	2,495,885	

These are astonishing figures for the medieval core of a cathedral city which still conveys a first impression of ancient narrow streets containing large numbers of listed buildings, and they confirm statistically, as the plan (fig.90) does graphically, the extent to which backland, originally gardens and orchards, has been eaten up by industrial users of various kinds. There are, of course, two mitigating factors. One is that a proportion (rather less than a fifth) of this industry is properly sited within the Foss Islands industrial area. (But over a million sq. ft. of warehouses, for example, are outside, mainly S.W. of the Ouse.) The other is that the density of workers is low, with a total employed in manufacturing industry within the walls of 1,800 (1,340 males, 460 females)—a reflection of the large proportion of warehousing. In other words we have within the walls a large amount of low-density, low-investment industry, the removal of which would cause comparatively little dislocation.

3.8 *Office work*

There are at present about 7,500 office workers within the walls (as opposed to administrative staff in shops and industry). Of these the largest single employer is British Rail, with about 1,700 office workers in their present buildings in Tanner Row. With the amalgamation in 1967 of the Eastern and North Eastern Regions and the concentration of the combined regional staffs in York, this number will increase steadily in coming years and new buildings are planned in Toft Green to provide an eventual floor space of the order of 250,000 sq. ft. Other recent office buildings of some size are the Yorkshire Insurance

42 Generalised land uses within the city boundary

Scale : 1 mile to the inch

Residential

Civic, educational, recreational

Public open space

Shopping

Offices and business premises

Industry and warehousing

Building (about 1,400 staff), United House in Piccadilly (200) and Hilary House (150 civil servants). With its excellent communications and growing university population there seems every chance of York growing in importance as a centre for regional headquarters' staffs.

3.9 *Education*

About 700 children attend school within the walls, plus about 1,300 full-time and 2,000 part-time students. This of course excludes members of the University, which already exceed 1,000 and are planned to reach 3,000 by 1972.

It was widely regretted at the time that it was not found possible to site the new universities within their parent cities, with the consequence that the effect of the university as an agent of urban renewal, both in terms of buildings and in terms of new population, has been minimal. It is hard to believe that the nearest point of the University campus is only half a mile from Walmgate Bar, so little influence has this proximity had on the vitality of the Walmgate sector in particular or of the walled city as a whole. However, the University architects, in their Development Plan report (1962), state their belief that :

'The site of the University is potentially near enough (if not at present accessible enough) to the City for each to be able to enrich the life of the other without the identity of either being compromised, and not so far away as to make the life of the University excessively isolated.'

It must be the object of both parties to achieve this, continuing and increasing the University's admirable policy of investment in historic buildings within the city, by a dramatic increase in the number of students living within the walled city and by improving the physical links between the two areas.

3.10 *Visiting*

With the Castle Museum, the Yorkshire, Railway and Military Museums and the City Art Gallery, York is rich in indoor attractions, and spends more per head of population on its museums than any other British city. It is rewarded by an annual attendance at the unique Castle Museum of 657,600 (1966), comparing favourably, if one remembers the huge difference in scale, with the British Museum's estimated 980,000. Of these visitors in 1966, some 85 per cent came in the six summer months, over half from Yorkshire and only one in forty from abroad. Attendance at the Yorkshire and Railway museums, though much less spectacular than this, is still high by the standards of similar museums elsewhere. As to York's outdoor attractions, the photographs in Chapter 2 need no elaboration.

Yet the great majority of these are day visitors only and spend the minimum of time and money in the town. This is hardly surprising considering that only 92 hotel rooms out of 540 have private baths. Employment in hotels, etc., in York is comparable with Doncaster's and a third of Harrogate's where a single hotel had 10,000 Swedish overnight visitors in 1966. York has only half the hotel bedrooms of Bath and Chester, and a quarter of Harrogate's, despite its larger population.

In an attempt to explore the visitor's reaction to this state of affairs a sample survey, under the guidance of a York University statistician, was organised in August 1967. From the report printed as Appendix E it will be noted that of the sample about 1 in 5 were from abroad, 1 in 4 were staying at least one night and 2 in 3 had come by car. The figures show that visitors to the Minster (which are not officially counted) exceeded visitors to the Castle Museum by a third, which would if projected give an annual figure for the Minster of 880,000.

We claim no statistical value for this pilot survey, but it is a technique which needs to be employed on a massive scale, both locally and nationally, if this country is to invest soundly in tourism, as this report will recommend.

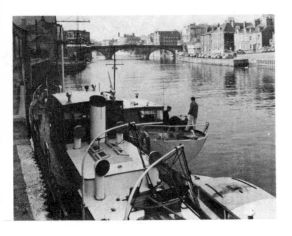

Studies in conservation

Classified guide to selected topics

	Bath	Chester	Chichester	York
Advertisement control				
Areas of special control		L.2.4.14	4.48ff	
			7.64	
			10.03	
Window stickers			7.115	
Agencies for Conservation				
(See also Civic Societies				
Economics & Finance, Ownership)				
Role of the local authority	112	4.3	8.31	6.3
	123	L.3.5.8	8.49	10.3ff
	136		Chapter 9	
	238			
	247			
Historic Buildings Council	112ff	L.4.1	7.139	6.4
Housing Societies		4.3.3		7.37
Land Commission		L.4	8.34	8.13
			Chapter 8	Appendix G
A National Agency ?	124-5	4.3.4		10.3
		4.3.5		
		L.3		
University Grants Committee	142			9.20–21
	Appendix B 1a			
Churches				
Condition & Use	62		2.09	6.6
			2.17	8.105
			4.43	8.123
			6.26	
			7.81	
Cathedral cities		3.3	3.03ff	
			3.27	
Civic Societies				
As agents in rehabilitation schemes	100	L.4.6.11	4.44	6.5
			7.138	
			9.08-09	
			9.12	
Conservation Areas				
Conservation section proposed				10.3
Criteria and check list for			Appendix II	
Designation of		4.2	5.01	6.18
Differing views about their proper size and function	35	L.2	5.01-02	10.5
			Chapter 9	10.9
				10.10
Development control in		L.2.4	7.102	10.7
			10.13	
Cost-Benefit Analysis		2.6	8.05-10	Appendix G 4.0
Densities				
Residential		2.7.1	4.02	7.18
			6.76	7.27
			7.33ff	8.12

	Bath	Chester	Chichester	York
Design of buildings				
Control by planning authorities	92ff	2.3		
New design in relation to old buildings	94-100	2.3.9	5.09ff	8.144
	243-5		6.40ff	10.17
			7.66	
			7.99-124	
			9.45ff	
			10.10	
			10.13	
Height of new buildings				8.138
Materials			5.11-12	
			6.40-43	
			7.94ff	
			9.40	
			10.03	
			10.11	
Economics and Finance				
Costs of conversion and renovation	143-4	2.6	Chapter 8	9.15ff
	149-152	4.3	9.49	Appendix G
	156-7	4.4		
	160			
	Appendix B			
Grants				
(a) By local authority	112ff	4.4	4.40	6.15ff
	133	L.4.3	7.139	
	136		Chapter 8	
	161		10.17	
(b) By Exchequer	121ff	4.3	Chapter 8	6.15ff
	239	L.3	10.17	
	241	L.4.1		
Historic Buildings Council and Town Schemes	112ff	L.4.1	7.139	6.4
Housing improvement grants	117ff	L.4.3		
Recoupment			Chapter 8	9.19ff
				Appendix G 5.0
Employment		1.4	3.29-31	3.6
			6.78	3.8
Industry				
Compatibility with historic area	70	2.7.1		3.7
Relocation of		2.7.1	4.02	4.7ff
			4.47	
Legal Aspects				
Present legislation considered adequate	101ff			
	246			
Changes in compulsory purchase and			Chapter 8	
compensation provisions suggested			10.18-19	
Possible conflicts with particular enactments	103ff	2.8.4	7.99	10.7
(e.g. Building Regulations, Housing Acts)	142ff			
General review of legislation		L.1-L.4		
Use Classes Order				8.144
Lists of buildings of special architectural or historic interest				
Assessment of the lists and	18ff	2.8.6	7.130-141	6.11-13
suggestions for revision		L.1	10.12	
Offices	68-69	2.7.4	6.49	3.8
		4.1.3	6.52-54	4.15
			7.65ff	
			7.85	
			10.06	

St. Clements Fosh & Cross Limited, 80/92 Mansell Street, London E1

48 An alley in the Castle sector: Lady Peckitt's Yard

Objectives

1 That the commercial heart of York should remain alive and able to compete on level terms with its neighbour cities, new or old.

2 That the environment should be so improved by the elimination of decay, congestion and noise that the centre will become highly attractive as a place to live in for families, for students and single persons, and for the retired.

3 That land uses which conflict with these purposes should be progressively removed from the walled city.

4 That the historic character of York should be so enhanced and the best of its buildings of all ages so secured that they become economically self-conserving.

5 That within the walled city the erection of new buildings of anything but the highest architectural standard should cease.

49 Freemen walking through the Shambles after annual service in All Saints' Pavement

4 Activities II

4.1   The general analysis of the walled city's history, physical character and activities that has occupied the first three chapters of this report will already have suggested certain basic lines of thought. They are formally stated in the five Objectives set out on page 41. It is implicit in these Objectives that of the activities described in the last chapter some need encouragement, some discouragement, some removal. In turning now from analysis to proposals, it is logical that these should be first in terms of activities and second in terms of the physical changes required to cater for these activities. This chapter deals with the first of these aspects.

4.2   It is conflict between activities that depreciates our environment, and the main zones of conflict are familiar. At the extreme, residence conflicts with industry because industry generates noise, danger, smells and visual intrusion. In a lesser degree, residence conflicts with commerce for similar reasons, though here the demands of both activities for road and parking space are the main difficulty. Education conflicts with all traffic-generating activities because of their noise. Tourism conflicts specifically with industry but also to a lesser extent with residence because of tourism's intrusion on privacy. More narrowly, servicing conflicts with shopping in old streets with no rear access, and through traffic conflicts with all city centre activities, except possibly the catering trade.

4.3   These conflicts can only be resolved by separating conflicting activities on a basis of agreed priorities, and these priorities must now be settled.

4.4   As a secular city, York was built for commerce, but unlike other fortified cities such as Edinburgh and Avignon it was not so constricted by its walls, or so prosperous, that it acquired in the 18th or 19th centuries a commercial New Town outside the medieval core. Now the economics of such a move, whatever its physical advantages might be, have made it impracticable even in cities where the planning case for it is much stronger than in York. We need not therefore consider the evacuation of commerce and must consequently face the environmental and traffic problems of retaining in the heart of medieval York a regional centre capable of holding its own with more modern competitors. These will be dealt with in the next chapter.

4.5   In terms of shopping floorspace, Appendix D makes it clear that while post-war rebuilding has virtually caught up with potential demand 'the scale of York's shopping activity is such that national multiple retailers not already established in the centre will seek representation in order to compete for a share of this very substantial trade. To compete successfully such traders will only consider locations within or immediately adjoining the existing peak shopping frontages . . . and large enough to accommodate a large shop or store unit of a size appropriate to their activities'.

Non-conforming land

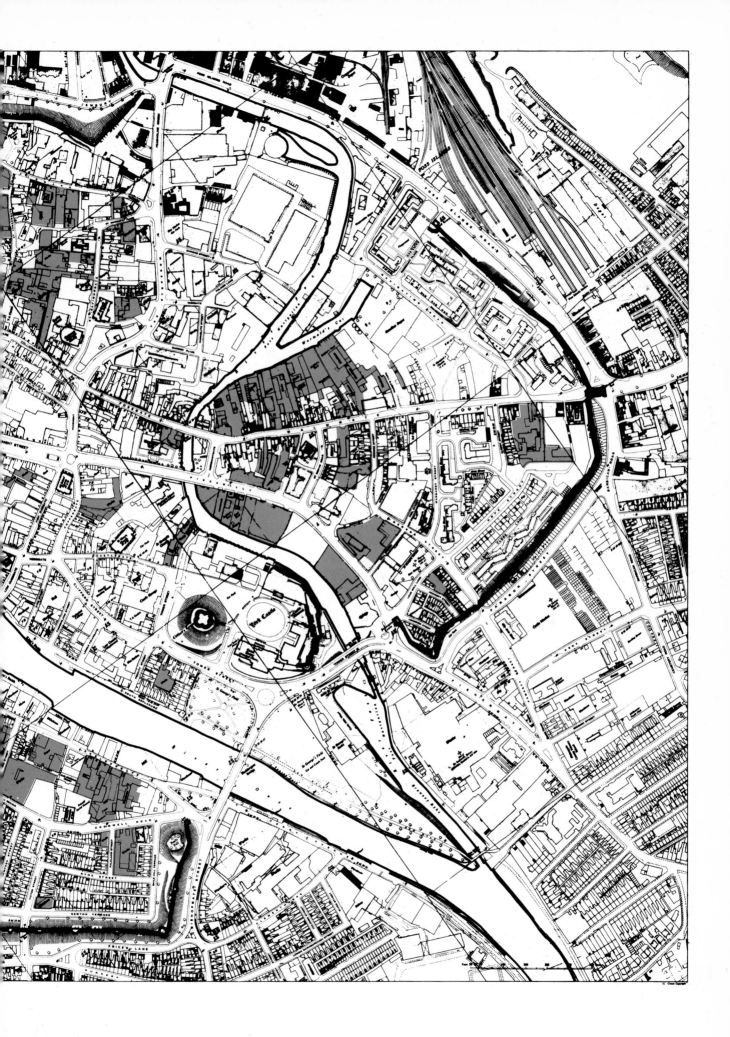

4.6 Such locations must be found, and the area of search is effectively confined to that which lies between Marks and Spencer's new store in Parliament Street and Rowntree's store in Coney Street. Recent development leaves only one major 'soft' frontage in this area, namely the south side of Parliament Street. Apart from two Banks of some architectural interest (both contemplating rebuilding in due course) the mainly rather shabby properties here date from the breaking through of Parliament Street in 1834, and while handsome in scale are not of great architectural importance. With the market for which it was designed removed, Parliament Street is now unnecessarily wide. By advancing the building line here the Corporation has an opportunity of providing sites of the required depth, of minimising the disappointing effect of new commercial architecture by reducing its visual impact, and perhaps of recouping the costs of improvements elsewhere. It is also fitting symbolically that one of York's first moves in this new era of urban design should be the narrowing rather than the widening of a carriageway.

4.7 For it is clear that the activities which must as far as possible be removed from the walled city are those which generate heavy traffic. Since *all* urban activity generates traffic, we must give preference to activities that need to be in the centre over those that could as well or better be conducted outside. We suggest that the following criteria could be used in deciding priorities for the removal of an industry or business from the historic core.

1 Its scale and size
2 Its need to expand
3 The traffic it generates
4 Its situation (e.g. on the backs of existing or potential residences)
5 Its noxious characteristics (noise, smell or smoke)
6 Obsolete location derived from river transportation that is no longer used
7 Agricultural or market activities no longer appropriate within the walls.

4.8 All seven criteria are obviously variable in degree, and the weight to be given to one or another can only be a matter of judgment in the individual case. But clearly a business which offends in several of these respects must have a high priority for removal. Fig. 50 shows these high priorities as proposed, and has been prepared after carefully weighing the criteria in individual cases. One qualification is necessary. Urban uses change continuously, and this plan, which was believed to be accurate when it was prepared, may already be incorrect in certain instances.

4.9 It should be emphasised that these proposals relate only to the environmental criteria here listed. There may be other reasons, for example the need of sites for public purposes of one sort or another, which reinforce these criteria or affect properties not otherwise objectionable. These appear elsewhere in this report.

4.10 As with other aspects of conservation, the problem of removing non-conforming users is primarily a financial one: what ought to be done is easier said than paid for. In the profit and loss equation, which will be more closely defined in later sections, easy re-location can make all the difference. Most of the businesses requiring re-location have a distributive function of some sort and are therefore best sited alongside a major distributor road. In proposing an alignment for the Fishergate Loop in the next Chapter an important factor has been the existence of the St. Nicholas tip area of 43 acres already in the Corporation's ownership. Against this, of a total of 57 acres in the walled city at present used for industry and warehousing, this report proposes the removal of 24. Some of these businesses have less space than they need, but some have more.

4.11   The problem is thus soluble in space terms, but we nevertheless recommend that the Corporation should adopt a long-term re-location budget geared to a programme of central area clearance, and that sites preferably adjacent to the outside of one of the major loop roads should be earmarked as far ahead as possible.

4.12   It will have been noted that this is by no means a wholesale clearance of workshops and warehouses. We saw in Chapter 2 that the medieval mix-up of small trades and workshops with shops and houses is one of the charms of the inner core of York, and the general approach in this section has been 'if in doubt, let it stay'. A central area with no workshops is just as dreary as a central area with no homes.

4.13   It should now go without saying that a main object of the exercise is to make the walled city livable again. Of its potentialities as a place to live in something has already been said and more will be said later. Here it must be emphasised that the essence of conservation is continuing economic use, and that the great majority of the best secular architecture of York was built for living in and is still eminently livable, given the right environment. The exodus from city centres which has been a feature of the last half-century has been due not to any love of commuting but to a revulsion from the dirt, noise and congestion that invaded them in the Victorian era, and that more than cancelled out the convenience of living in them. If the invaders could be ejected, the balance would at once swing the other way. The proposals made later in this report will in fact, if implemented, raise the residential population of the walled city from $3\frac{1}{2}$ to 6 thousand, with the prospect of further gains as urban renewal proceeds, particularly in the Walmgate sector.

4.14   The activities which conflict least with residence are education and office work. It has already been argued that everything possible should be done to bring University activities into the heart of York, and the same goes for postgraduate and adult education, of which the Institute of Advanced Architectural Studies (now a part of the University) has been an outstanding example. The activities of the Arts Centre committee should be given every encouragement, and we hope that the Centre may be the means of conserving by conversion either one of the redundant churches or another historic building of the first importance. Private schools, convents and nursing homes are other users of large town houses who we hope may be encouraged to stay on or move in by environmental improvement and a steadily increasing intra-mural population.

4.15   Officer workers may introduce conflicts because of the large scale of modern buildings they inhabit and the cars they like to come to work in, but provided these two are carefully controlled (as is proposed later in this report) it would be wrong to exclude this activity from the vicinity of the big shops and cafes that staffs like to visit at lunch-time. Both environmentally and in terms of regional communications York could have an unexploited potential here, but it is impossible to forecast it at long range. Sites are therefore suggested in the Piccadilly and Skeldergate areas which could be progressively re-developed with office buildings of moderate size as the demand arises, or with flats where it does not.

4.16   Last but perhaps most significant of the activities of the walled city is Tourism. We noted in the previous chapter the present size of the annual intake of visitors, despite hitherto totally inadequate facilities both in bed-spaces and car-spaces.

4.17   We have read with interest the Junior Chamber of Commerce's Report (1964) on Tourism. It is not within our terms of reference to enlarge on this subject, but we are bound to point out that its place in the economy of York is crucial, because it will be a primary source of financial return on environmental improvement. This aspect is dealt with in Professor Lichfield's report at Appendix G.

4.18   With its exceptionally good communications and its exciting new University, York could develop its new role as a conference centre in step with its old role as a historic city. It is also a museum centre of national importance, so that there is no lack of all-weather attractions. It should be the aim to encourage and provide for overnight stays rather than the few hours most people spend at present. Floodlighting, river spectacles, late opening of shops in summer, the creation of an enticing Information Centre (perhaps in St. Mary's, Castlegate) containing a large illuminated model of the walled city and the appointment of a full-time Director of Tourism—these are among the activities which others have suggested and we endorse. Most vital of all is accommodation, and the building, step by step with the provision of large-scale car parks, of attractive hotels in different price-ranges on the sites proposed for them later in this report. For it is clear to us that York has nowhere near reached its *present* potential as a tourist centre, let alone that which it will possess when it has been fully restored and renewed.

5 Traffic

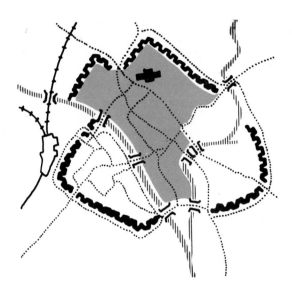

51 The inner enclave

5.1 By far the greatest single obstacle to the rehabilitation of the historic core of York is road traffic and its familiar accompaniment of noise, smell, congestion and visual intrusion. Money spent on buildings will be wasted unless the traffic problem is progressively solved at the same time.

Objectives

5.2 In most respects the problem in York is the familiar one, with the following main elements:

To define environmental areas

To exclude through traffic from these areas

To exclude local cross-town traffic from these areas

To provide a pedestrian network and pedestrian spaces where traffic intrusion is absent or minimised

To provide vehicular accessibility to premises which is adequate in the sense that it is no hindrance to their economic use and development

To substitute off-street for on-street car parking which is adequate in the same sense

To provide an attractive public transport network.

5.3 York is also a special case in the following senses:

1. Its medieval walls define an historic environmental area, but within it the industrial zone north of the Foss, the area between the Foss and the walls and the Micklegate sector apart from Micklegate itself, are obviously of an altogether lower order of importance. In other words, the walls, the Ouse, the Foss, Stonebow and Peaseholme Green define an inner enclave (fig. 51), not much larger than the Roman city, which needs special protection.

2. This inner enclave is not a typical city centre, not only because of its exceptional beauty and charm, but also because of the exceptionally small scale of its streets and spaces, its unsuitability for large scale office buildings and its potential suitability for residential development.

3. The inner enclave depends for its economic vitality on two interests, trade and tourism, which any traffic solutions must safeguard and encourage.

4. The damage to these interests and the physical damage to historic buildings caused by heavy traffic gives the problem an urgency and national importance that are not present elsewhere.

5.4 It is not within the terms of reference of this Report to put forward traffic proposals for the city as a whole, nor have we the data on which to do so. At the same time the effect of any such proposals on traffic within the historic core, and in particular on the Walls and Bars which are such a vital part of it, must be considered.

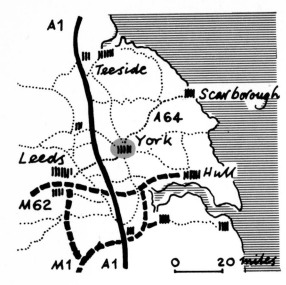

52 Regional road pattern

Problems of a ring road

5.5   A fortified city tends to create a ring road round the walls, and this has happened to some extent in the case of York. It would be natural to complete the circuit and upgrade it to handle projected cross-town traffic. But there are a number of difficulties which must be frankly faced.

1.   It is impossible to find a ground-level route for the section Queen Street—Lord Mayor's Walk which is not open to grave amenity objection.

2.   For reasons given later in this section, limited vehicular access through Micklegate Bar and Monk Bar is highly desirable; but a ring road adjacent to the Walls at these points can only provide such access by means of unattractive traffic lights and right turns which are themselves a disincentive to the use of the ring road.

3.   The scale of a 4-lane divided carriageway and particularly of the roundabouts and junctions associated with it would dwarf the City Walls and above all the Bars, whose impressiveness is dependent on the contrasting scale of small buildings in their vicinity.

4.   An inner ring road is unsuitable for *through* traffic because of the overloading of the radials which feed into it and the resulting noise and congestion brought close to the heart of the city. Consequently it must be supplemented at great cost by an outer ring or loop on the city circumference.

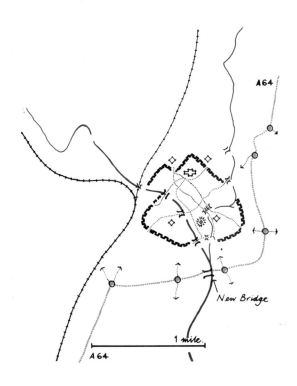

53 The Fishergate Loop

Through and cross-town traffic

5.6   These difficulties have made it necessary to look at the strategy for handling through and cross-town traffic in the city as a whole in the light of the Travers Morgan (1961) Report and other available information and to offer the following observations.

5.7   York will eventually lie in the angle between A1 and the Cross-Pennine Motorway (fig. 52), and will thus be by-passed by all long-distance traffic between major centres of population (e.g. Tees-side—Hull, Leeds—Hull). The only *through* traffic that will eventually traverse or approach York is Leeds—Scarborough.* As Travers Morgan has shown, a 'right hook' or loop passing east of Fishergate would effectively tap the great majority of through traffic (figs. 53, 59 and 62).

5.8   The vital question is whether the Fishergate loop, plus Clifton Bridge suitably linked to local distributors in Acomb and Clifton, could also handle *cross-town* traffic and prevent its penetrating the historic core or washing against its walls. There seems no question that a 6-lane loop linking Acomb Road with Malton Road need not be duplicated at an average distance of 500 yards by an inner ring on the line at present proposed. The western and northern sectors are the problem. Clifton Bridge, because it is corked up by poor connections at both ends, at present only carries half the load proposed by Travers Morgan. The first step in this sector must surely be to link it with York Road and Wigginton Road so that it effectively connects the western and northern suburbs, and in particular the 30,000 people who live in Acomb and the 8,500 people who work at Rowntrees. None of this movement should touch Lendal Bridge or Bootham (fig. 54).

5.9   It will still be necessary, as will be shown later, in order to secure the distribution of parking and servicing traffic in the city centre, to provide a local distributor road close in to the west of Lendal Bridge and St. Mary's Abbey. But it is important that the Acomb—Clifton loop should by then be in effective operation so as to ensure that such local distributors are not used by cross-town traffic for which they were not designed.

5.10   Within the walls these familiar problems of transferring traffic from one route to another, with their parameters of desire lines, surveys and projections, are absent. *It is a fundamental assumption of this plan that through and cross-town traffic are excluded from the walled city, either by the means discussed above or by a better if it can be found, and that the only vehicles to be catered for within the walls are those that live or have business or bring visitors there.*

5.11   In chapter 3 we looked at the complex web of human activity that is spun by even a small city centre, and in chapter 4 proposed some modifications in these activities that would lighten the traffic they generate. We must now analyse this residual traffic and decide what provision needs to be made for it.

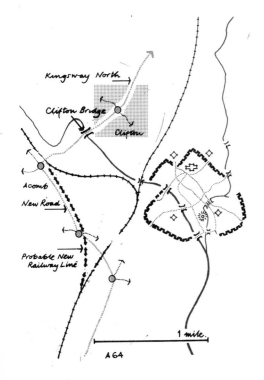

54   Clifton Bridge and its connections

*The existing through-traffic desire-line diagram will then be modified by the virtual elimination of the Tadcaster Road—Hull Road leg.

55   Nose to tail in High Petergate

56   Parking in the Swinegate study area

57   Foreground to Clifford's Tower

58   Parliament Street

62 Existing desire lines
Through traffic : blue
Local traffic : yellow

60 Erosion in College Street

61 Toft Green

63 'The Bars, whose impressiveness is dependent on the contrasting scale of small buildings in their vicinity' Monkgate

64 The servicing problem

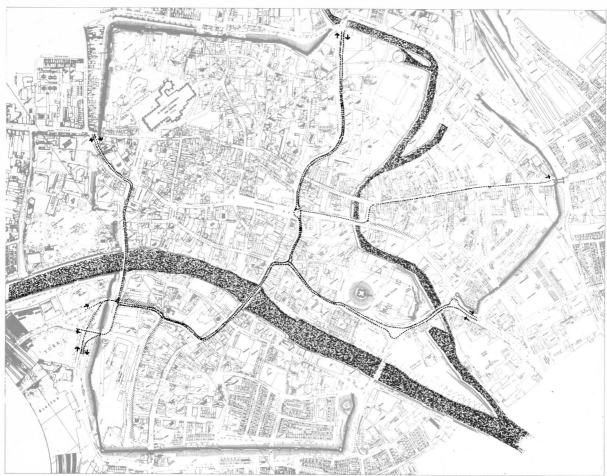

65 Existing bus routes

66 New bus routes

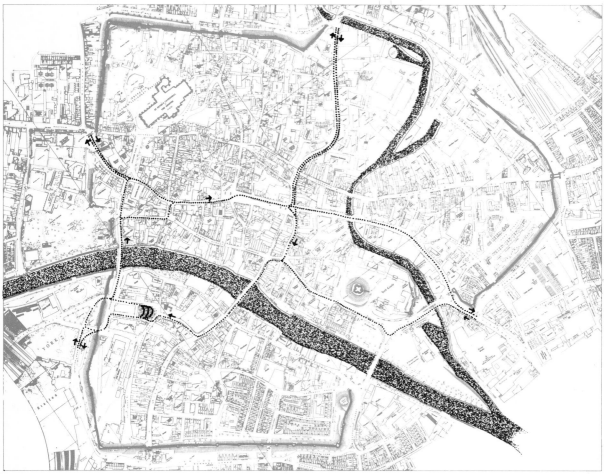

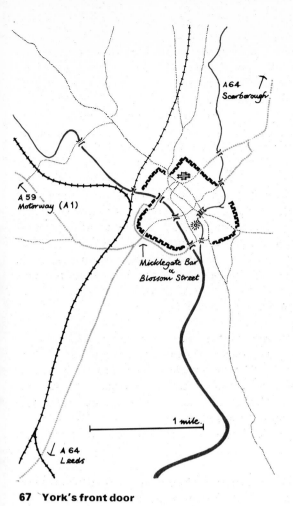

67 York's front door

Local traffic in the walled city

5.12   In order of importance, there are the people who live in the place, the people who work in it and the people who visit it. We take them in turn.

5.13   The **Residential** population, at present about 3,500, is planned in this report to increase by the end of the century to upwards of 6,000, representing about 2,500 resident cars. If their houses and flats, whether old or new, are to compete commercially with extra-mural housing it is vital that each should house one off-street car (but preferably not more), or be allowed a street parking space, and that these cars should have privileged freedom of movement within the centre—freedom, that is, to use all roads when not actually closed to vehicles. To secure this, there seems no alternative to the use of numbered locally-issued windscreen licences, renewable annually. Cars of doctors and certain officials would qualify for this licence. A system of visitors' labels for premises possessing off-street visitors' parking space would also be necessary.

5.14   **Workers** (apart from cyclists) enter the city by train, bus or car. Arrivals by train use the pedestrian network dealt with in a later section. The first group to be considered are therefore the users of the local bus services.

5.15   It is an accepted principle that to reduce private car traffic all possible encouragement should be given to public transport. On the other hand it has to be said that the present size of bus is out of scale with central York, and long single deckers will be equally so. It is unlikely that micro-buses will be economic in a city of this size. Fortunately, it is possible to serve the heart of York from streets where present and projected vehicles can be accepted physically and visually.

5.16   Fig. 65 shows the present routes and loadings, with the main interchange points. Fig. 66 shows a modified, gyratory system incorporating Parliament Street for eastbound services. But it would cause excessive noise and congestion to use Parliament Street as the main central bus interchange and crew control point. For this purpose Rougier Street seems well-placed and convenient to the Railway Station, and is capable of some development (see fig. 134). It may eventually be necessary to provide more spacious facilities by redevelopment either in Piccadilly or in Peaseholme Green.

5.17   The use of Exhibition Square and Toft Green for the marshalling of buses is unsuitable and should be discontinued when the new Rougier Street Bus Station is operational.

5.18   Finally, it is important that pedestrian routes into the shopping centre from the main setting-down points in Rougier Street, Piccadilly, Stonebow and St. Leonard's should be considered and improved as far as possible, and this is borne in mind in framing the pedestrian network proposals.

5.19   As to workers arriving by car, the tables in Appendix F show that over 39 per cent of non-through vehicles entering the city centre carry workers compared with only 4½ per cent carrying shoppers, and since the former (the great majority of which are private cars) remain all day, they are *at present* proportionally a far heavier burden. (This proportion will of course be drastically altered by the provision of adequate parking for shoppers.)

5.20 In a survey of central area offices conducted by the City Engineer in 1966 it was found that about 1,600 cars are brought into the centre daily by office workers alone. Since unrestricted off-street car parks within the walls can only hold 190, most of these cars must be tucked away in private yards or parked on unauthorised streets. The figures for shop workers are not available, but are probably about half this number. This form of parking must steadily diminish with the redevelopment of unused land and the enforcement (as is essential) of parking bans in all streets for other than residents' cars. While certain new offices in suitable locations will be required to house a minority of staff cars* it would be undesirable to enforce this as a general requirement in new commercial development because of its effect on streets of high amenity. Consequently in the summer tourist season, when the intra-mural car parks are full, the great majority of car-borne workers will have to park outside the walls and walk in. In other seasons when a walk of this length would be unacceptable, intra-mural car-parks could be opened to them. This flexibility could be enforced by restricting the use of the parks during the summer season to say a 5-hour period on weekdays.

5.21 Unquestionably this is the one department where some curtailment of existing freedoms in the general interest is inevitable, in York as elsewhere. Air photographs show the incredible ingenuity with which workers' cars will penetrate the interstices of the city fabric if given half a chance. The progressive removal of these infiltrators from the highway is necessary in order to restore small urban spaces for the pedestrian, and is something public opinion has come to accept.

5.22 **Shoppers and Visitors** are, of course, frequent though less skilful infiltrators, and we now look at their requirements. The first point is that while they vary in their incidence within both the week and the year, they are not visibly distinguishable. Consequently to provide for the one is to provide for the other. Together (see Appendix F) they at present constitute 55 per cent of persons coming daily into the centre. The problem is universally one of peak loads, i.e. the under-use outside working hours of facilities provided at public expense. In a city such as York with heavy and vital summer tourist traffic this is complicated by a seasonal peak. A balance has to be struck between seasonal needs and related to the environmental capacity of the centre, and an attempt has been made to do this in the proposals that follow.

Traffic and environment

5.23 We start with the environmental capacity of the walled city. It is often suggested that medieval York should be wholly pedestrianised. Apart from the problem of servicing, to which we turn later, wholesale pedestrianisation is neither practicable nor desirable. York lives by trade of one sort or another, and trade is strangled without accessibility. On the other hand the parking areas now being made available in some city centres, which are tending to become competitive and inflationary, are neither physically achievable nor environmentally appropriate in York. Here the environment, on which York's fortune finally depends, must have absolute priority, and the problem is to define this subjective quality and then quantify the motor cars it can absorb.

*See Chapter 8.

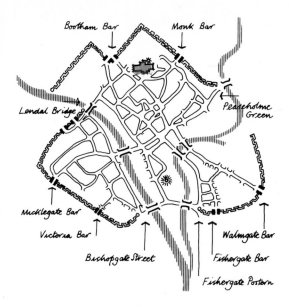

68 Entries to the walled city

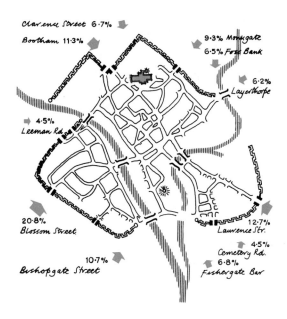

69 Percentages of traffic using each entry

Entrances

5.24 A feature common to York and Oxford is that most visitors approach these cities (which are of similar size) through one 'door'. Thus in the case of York :

Traffic from N.E. uses Malton Road, Hewarth Green and Monkgate
Traffic from S.E. uses Hull Road and Lawrence Street

Traffic from S.
Traffic from S.W.
Traffic from W. } uses Holgate Bridge, Tadcaster Road, the Mount and Blossom Street
Traffic from N.W.
Traffic from N.

Micklegate Bar at the head of Blossom Street, the traditional gateway from London, is thus in a real sense York's front door. But Monk Bar and Walmgate Bar are important side doors. Only Bootham Bar, the fourth point of the compass, faces a less-used radial and is in any case virtually inaccessible to traffic.

5.25 It would be a pity to pedestrianise the front door and the two side doors, particularly if the proposed inner ring road were to be constructed and traffic roared past them on the circuit. Micklegate in particular is too handsome a street and Walmgate too long a one for pedestrians only and people arriving in York from a distance should not be denied these attractive entries and be forced, as nowadays so often happens, into hideous back areas that were never meant to be seen. We therefore propose that Micklegate Bar should be open to private cars only and Micklegate itself be one-way downhill (reducing evening noise), and that Walmgate Bar and Monk Bar should be open both ways but to labelled residents' cars only.

5.26 There remain the following entries, which would be suitable for the needs stated :

Station Road } General vehicular traffic, but mainly public transport.
Exhibition Square

Peaseholme Green   Public transport, industrial and commercial

Navigation Road } Labelled private cars and servicing vehicles
Fishergate Bar

Fishergate Postern } General vehicular traffic
Tower Street

Skeldergate   Private cars and commercial
Victoria Bar   Labelled private cars.

These restrictions (see fig. 70) set certain limits to vehicular circulation in the walled city. We must now turn to the traffic needs and capacity of the different sectors. It was suggested in para 5.3 that the inner enclave, north of the Ouse and west of the industrial wedge and the Fosse, needed very special consideration, and this it must now receive.

5.27 While the five sectors within the inner enclave range in character from the Minster Precinct to the main shopping streets and from the quiet lawns of the King's Manor to the derelict warehouses and yards of Aldwark, they all need to be inhabited and therefore serviced and they all need to be protected from noise and from vehicles that have no business in them. There is consequently a prima facie case for *including* labelled private cars, taxis, servicing vehicles and pedal cycles and *excluding* coaches, industrial traffic and motor cycles. The problems in the inner enclave are twofold :

1 Accessibility for shoppers/visitors cars (which are not distinguishable).

2 Accessibility for servicing vehicles, particularly for shops and other commercial premises.

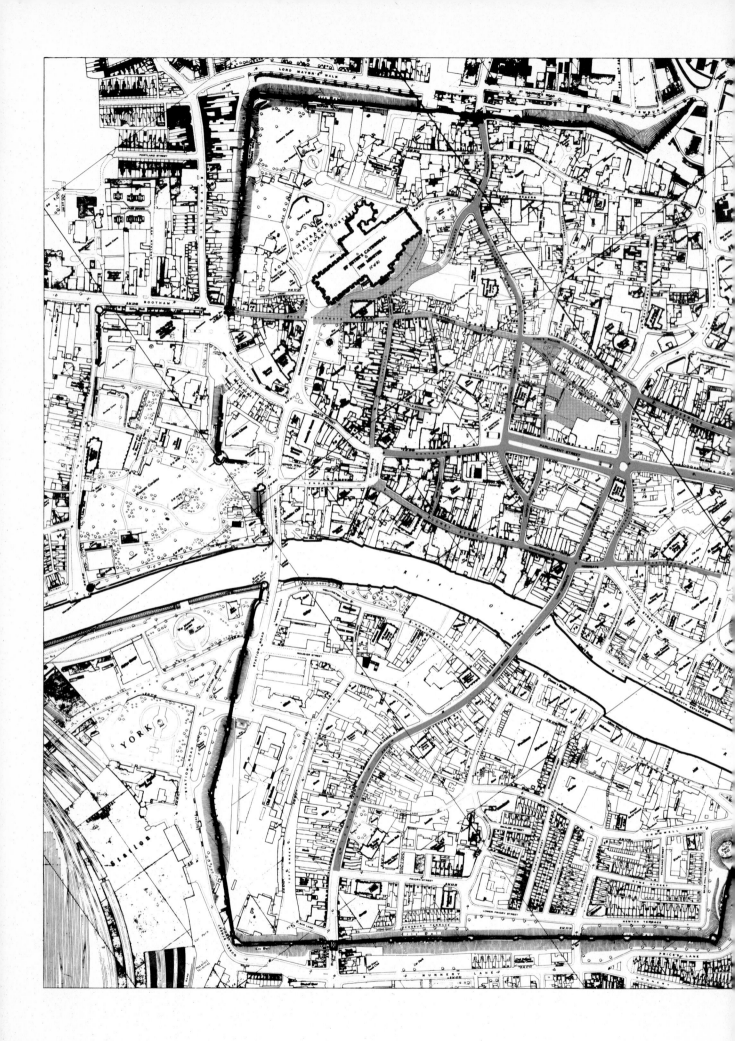

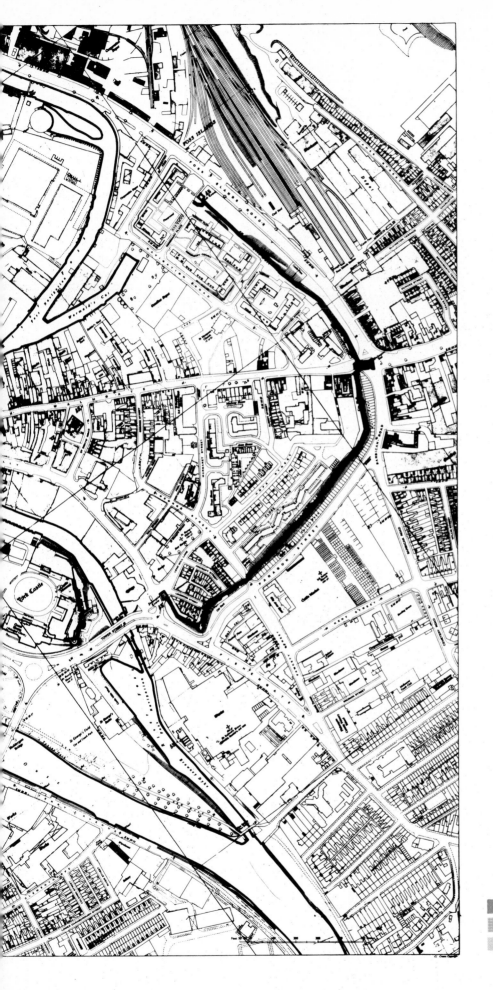

Restricted streets

Pedestrianised streets

Temporary turning heads

61

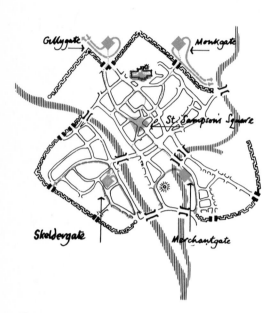

71 Car parks and connections

Accessibility for cars

5.28 Accessibility for cars is essentially a parking problem and within the enclave these two principles must be paramount:
1 On-street parking must be restricted to the locations indicated and to the use of locally licensed private cars.
2 Off-street parking, where provided in new buildings or surviving on waste land, must be restricted, in their own interests, to the use of residents and workers, and must not be used by shoppers/visitors.

5.29 The cars of shoppers/visitors can only be handled in adequate numbers by multi-storey parking garages and the provision of such buildings within the enclave would be totally inappropriate, not only because the traffic so generated would swamp the narrow streets of the inner enclave but also because the scale and use of such buildings would destroy the character and the residential values of every sector of the enclave. How then is accessibility, particularly of shoppers to shops, to be secured?

5.30 Fig. 71 shows sites for four multi-storey car parks each with an approximate capacity of upwards of 1,200 cars, giving a total of about 5,000 spaces. The medium-pace walking times from each of these sites to St. Sampson's Square, which we take to be the centre of gravity of the commercial centre, are at present as follows:

Skeldergate	$3\frac{3}{4}$ minutes
Merchantgate	$3\frac{1}{4}$ minutes
Gillygate	$5\frac{3}{4}$ minutes
Monkgate	$5\frac{1}{4}$ minutes

These times will be reduced when the walker does not have to wait for traffic to pass at intersections.

5.31 In the summer season the first two would no doubt be mainly used by shoppers, the second two by visitors. In other seasons (see para. 5.20) workers would take up the slack.

5.32 For those unable or unwilling to walk from car parks, a minibus or battery-driven minitaxi service could be included in the cost of the parking ticket, the type and frequency depending on demand. These services would be free to use all streets open to locally licenced cars.

5.33 The volume and design of these four buildings must be carefully related to their surroundings, but each is so sited and sized that the aesthetic problem is not insoluble.

5.34 The planning of the Gillygate multi-storey car-park gives an opportunity to reconsider the Council's proposals for the Gillygate-Bootham junction and an attempt has been made (fig. 72) to offer a solution which preserves the listed buildings which are such a vital element in the famous view of Bootham Bar, at the expense of buildings of less architectural distinction.

5.35 We must now turn to the problem of giving access to those car parks from the cross-town and main distributor routes described in paras. 5.8 and 5.9. The principle of doing so by means of loops which prevent short-cuts across the centre is now well established. It is also necessary to provide local distributor roads linking the car parks so that cars can try a second if a first is full. The system is shown in fig. 71 and provides access to the four car parks as follows:

72 A solution for Gillygate

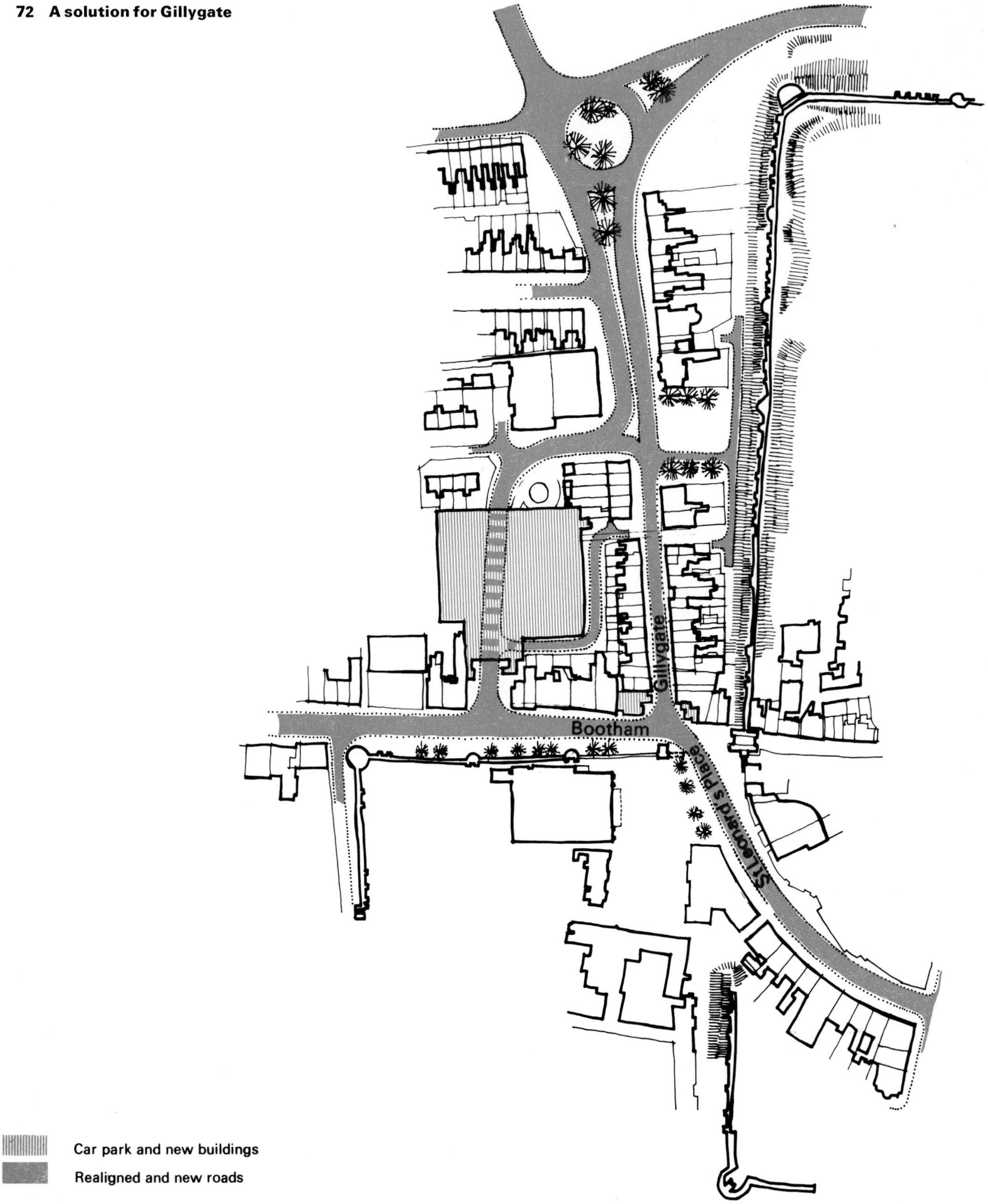
Gillygate
Bootham
St Leonard's Place
Car park and new buildings
Realigned and new roads

Skeldergate
enter the walled city off the loop by Micklegate Bar, turn right into Skeldergate (Ouse Bridge closed to unlabelled cars) and leave by Skeldergate or Cromwell Road. Alternatively enter by Cromwell Road.

Merchantgate
enter by Fishergate and Tower Street, turn right via a new bridge over the Foss and leave by Piccadilly.

Gillygate
enter by Bootham or Gillygate and leave ditto : no one-way system.

Monkgate
enter and leave by Monkgate.

This circulation system gives in every case an impressive approach signposted by a major landmark; the exit is psychologically less important and can be by an undistinguished route.

5.36　It must be emphasised that these routes are not merely routes by which cars can conveniently reach the car parks. They are the *only* roads ultimately open to unlabelled cars in the walled city.

5.37　Interchange between the four car parks is secured by the existing embryo ring road which needs no major improvement for this limited purpose. But it would be wrong to include the Station Road/Lendal Bridge/St. Leonard's Place leg in this circuit, since this would infringe the fundamental principle stated above (para 5.10) of not allowing extraneous traffic into the inner enclave. A connection from the Station to Bootham by means of a new 3-lane bridge, possibly restricted to light loads, is therefore necessary. Lendal Bridge should be closed to unlabelled cars.

5.38　It should be added that the demand for car spaces in city centres, at present insatiable, is unpredictable in the longer term. The four car parks here proposed could be supplemented by others outside the walls and may need to be.

Accessibility for servicing

5.39　Accessibility for **servicing vehicles** in a historic city where back access to commercial premises cannot be secured without unacceptable destruction is much less easy to rationalise. Yet no form of traffic does greater environmental damage in terms of congestion, noise and smell. Four measures are proposed which between them should reduce this damage to acceptable limits without impracticable restrictions on accessibility.

1.　Outside the inner enclave 24-hour servicing should be allowed except in Micklegate.
2.　In areas of substantial redevelopment back access should be provided where it can form part of a 24-hour servicing network.
3.　Within the enclave and in Micklegate servicing should be confined to limited hours (e.g. 5 a.m. to 10 a.m.) as soon as the general traffic situation permits.
4.　For businesses within the restricted area which must be serviced within the restricted hours, a municipal electric trolley delivering service could be operated from a central goods depot run on the locker system and a site (fig. 73) should be reserved for this depot in the Foss industrial sector.

5.40　The difficult and controversial item is No. 3 and some further comment is necessary. Continental experience has now established

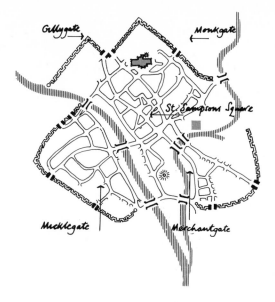

that the closing to vehicles of major shopping streets during shopping hours is not only practicable but is more beneficial to trade than unrestricted servicing. In some cities shopkeepers have offered to pay for the closing and paving of such streets. * The problem in York, as in other cities, is complicated by the fact that some of the main shopping streets are at present also classified roads subject to morning and evening (and to a lesser extent lunch-hour) traffic peaks. Congestion caused by servicing during peak hours led to the Corporation's draft Order of 1965, closing certain streets to servicing vehicles during these hours, which was the subject of a Public Enquiry in February 1967. These peak traffic hours are roughly those which would be used for servicing if one were endeavouring to prevent servicing during peak *shopping* hours.

5.41   It is of course one of the main purposes of this report to reduce traffic peaks in the historic core to negligible proportions by the provision of cross-town routes outside the walls and by the progressive removal of traffic-generating activities from the inner enclave. However until this has been achieved the congestion caused by servicing vehicles during traffic peaks is likely to increase and the Draft Order seems fully justified in principle as an interim measure.

5.42   But there is no need to leave it at that. The best of York's historic streets, and in particular Coney Street, New Street, Stonegate, Petergate and Shambles, do not have to be used by peak hour traffic and should forthwith be paved for pedestrians from wall to wall and closed to all vehicles between the hours of 10 a.m. and 5 a.m.

5.43   The short-term effect will be that the 'pedestrian' streets will be mainly serviced during the morning peak hours in the 'traffic' streets. Servicing vehicles having calls to make in both will tend to switch from one to the other at 10 a.m. Eventually the restrictions applied to the 'pedestrian' streets should be extended to cover the whole of the shopping sector, as will by then be normal practice in historic cities. The sole exceptions will then be two small all-day servicing loops, one off Museum Street via Blake Street and Lendal to serve the Mansion House, Guildhall and Post Office, the other off Tower Street via Clifford Street and Cumberland Street to serve the Law Courts and Fire Station.

*See 'Foot Streets in Four Cities' by A. A. Wood, City Planning Officer, Norwich. 'London Street Project' by A. A. Wood.

Minster label for cars
Yellow represents green

Minster labelled cars and
servicing vehicles only permitted.
Yellow represents green
Blue represents red

No right **turn except** for Minster
labelled cars and servicing vehicles.
Yellow represents green
Blue represents red

Pedestrianised streets sign:
servicing vehicles only allowed
past during permitted hours.
Yellow represents green
Blue represents red

Heavy transporters turn left only

Industrial traffic

5.44 Heavy vehicles connected with **industrial** rather than commercial premises will be progressively eliminated from the inner enclave and reduced in the rest of the walled city by the removal of non-conforming industrial premises. The rest must be confined to the lorry routes indicated on fig. 75.

5.45 In order to achieve one-way working in North Street and Skeldergate and thereby avoid conflict between lorries and private cars a right-turn off Station Road is necessary. This is achieved by an underpass close to the abutment of Lendal Bridge. This would involve the removal of the Boat House to a site in North Street where it could help to give character and enclosure to the public garden.

5.46 A bridge across the Foss to enable the industrial back land north of Walmgate to be reached from Stonebow is also necessary if the residential amenities of the Walmgate sector are to be protected.

5.47 A final category is MOTORCYCLES and MOPEDS. Noise is the curse of York and these are the main makers of it. They should be banned from the area N of the line Ousebridge/Peaseholme Green and from Micklegate and parking provision made for them in or adjacent to the four multi-storey car-parks.

The traffic plan

5.48 Figs. 70 and 75 summarise the traffic restrictions proposed for the walled city, in their immediate and ultimate form.

5.49 It is recognised that these rather complicated restrictions are open to two objections:
1. Signposting at all entries to the walled city and distinguishing marks in restricted streets will need considerable ingenuity if they are not to be confusing and/or visually objectionable. We indicate in fig. 74 a possible new statutory sign-posting system for use in historic city and town centres.
2. The Ministry of Transport's recent (1967) report 'Better Use of Town Roads' states 'In our view, the following measures would be either impracticable or ineffective in preventing or relieving traffic congestion in large towns:
(a) Limiting vehicle ownership, either by taxation or by regulation;
(b) Extensively banning the use of whole classes of vehicles in towns, with or without exemption by permit'.

5.50 But this report is concerned with *universally* applicable methods of reducing traffic in city centres. The essence of the system proposed for York is that it would be confined by Act of Parliament to a short list of historic cities of outstanding importance. Existing examples such as the banning of vehicles above a certain size from central Oxford and of commercial vehicles from the Royal Parks suggest that it can succeed.

5.51 It is the basic premise of this section that neither total pedestrianisation nor total freedom of movement subject only to parking arrangements can produce the right environment for the inner enclave of medieval York. It follows that the controlled access system proposed, or something like it, is inevitable.

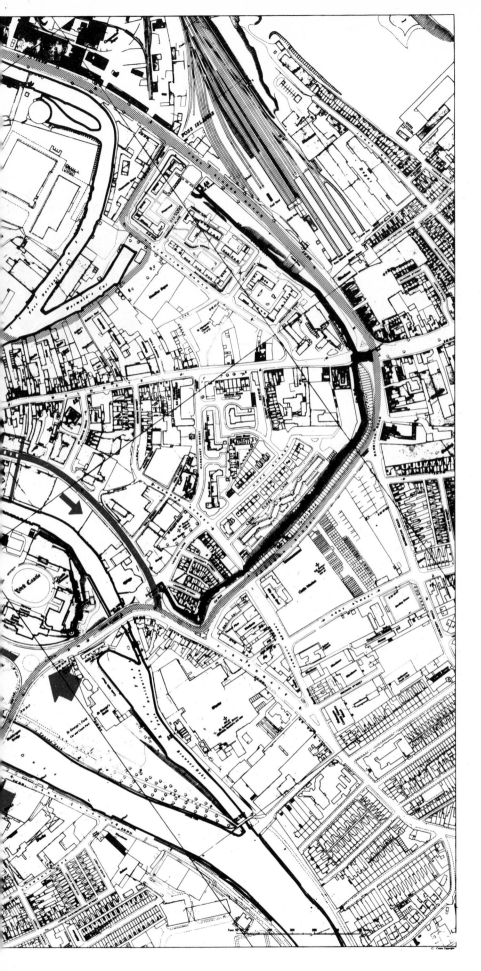

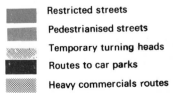

Restricted streets

Pedestrianised streets

Temporary turning heads

Routes to car parks

Heavy commercials routes

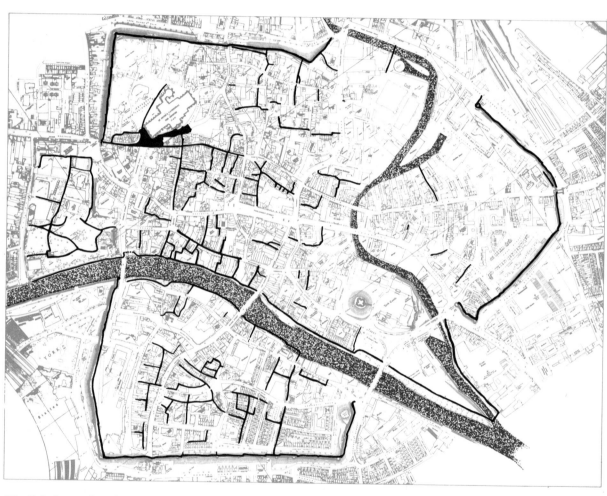

76 Existing pedestrian network

5.52 We come finally to the main purpose of this whole exercise, which is to make life in central York tolerable for the **pedestrian.** Like other medieval cities, York is exceptionally rich in narrow streets ideal for pedestrianisation, in secret alleys known only to the native or the inquisitive explorer, and in the elevated circuit of the Walls and Bars, which though incomplete could easily be made more accessible and more enjoyable than it is at present. Fig. 76 shows the network as it exists and brings out its disconnected nature. Fig. 77 shows the network as it will be on any weekday after 10 a.m. and at weekends, a network designed not merely for the tourist and shopper but as a functional system for those who live in York or come into it to work. The detail of these improvements as they affect the townscape will be dealt with in a later section.

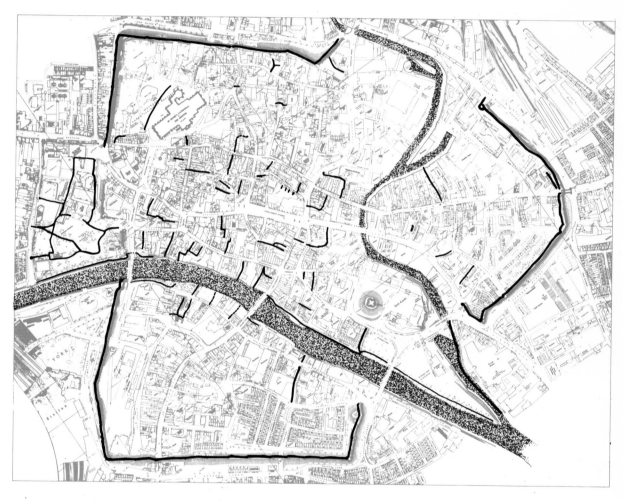

77 Proposed pedestrian network

6 General problems of conservation

78   Decayed upper stories in low Petergate

Conservation is the careful management of a limited or vulnerable resource so as to ensure efficiency of use, while at the same time taking such steps as are necessary to ensure continuity of supply.
Study Group No. 1 of the second 'Countryside in 1970' Conference.

6.   Of York's exceptional wealth of listed buildings 652 were within the area of this Study, divided as follows: (Map 81)

Statutory list

Grade I	Buildings of such importance that their destruction should in no case be allowed	98
Grade II	Buildings whose preservation is a matter of considerable interest and whose destruction or alteration should not be undertaken without compelling reasons	417

Supplementary list

Grade III	Buildings of architectural or historic interest which, though they do not rise to the degree properly qualified as 'special' to justify statutory listing, so contribute to the general effect or are otherwise of sufficient merit that a Local Planning Authority ought to try to preserve them	137

6.2   Since these lists were first issued by the Ministry of Housing and Local Government in 1954 much additional work, both voluntary and official, has been done on them. The York Georgian Society has prepared a large number of regradings and additions and Mr Antony Dale, Chief Investigator, Historic Buildings, MOHLG, has compiled a revised provisional list. But upgradings and additions have been more than offset by losses, which have been at a rate which, if it continued, would destroy nearly all York's historic buildings within a century. The following table shows the extent to which recent demolitions have impoverished the city:

	1954	*added*	*lost*	*1967 (August)*
Grade I	98	8	2	104
Grade II	417	21	30	408
Grade III	137	2	31	108
	652	31	63	620

A losing battle

6.3   The City Council can claim, with some justification, to have spent more money on the conservation and restoration of its heritage than any city of comparable resources in the United Kingdom. Since the war over £200,000 has been spent on such major projects as the restoration of the Walls and the four medieval Bars, the refurbishing of Burlington's Assembly Rooms, the reconstruction of the Shambles, and on minor improvements of which the Red House is a conspicuous example.

6.4   The Corporation's most recent activity in the sphere of conservation has been the 'Town Scheme', under which in consultation with the Historic Buildings Council, an annual sum of £15,000 for a trial period of 2 years (contributed to equally by the Central Government and The Corporation) is made available in approved cases to occupiers of over 400 properties in the most handsome of York's historic streets, of which 372 are within the Walls. Despite rather complicated and slow procedures involving two committees, the scheme seems to have been successful within its obvious limits: by June 1967 13 buildings had been awarded grants varying from £60 to £6,000. This is one of only 8 schemes at present operating in England and Wales.

6.5   In this concern and support for historic buildings the learned and voluntary societies have led the way, notably the Yorkshire Philosophical Society (1823), the Yorkshire Architectural and York Archaeological Society (1842) and the York Georgian Society (1939). Above all the Civic Trust which this year (1967) celebrated its 21st Birthday has been widely recognised as the outstanding body of its kind in the Country. Notable among its successes have been the restoration of St. John's Church Micklegate for the York Institute of Advanced Architectural Studies and the reconstruction of the 15th century Bowes Morell House in Walmgate. Mr J. B. Morell, whose distinguished place in the history of York it commemorates, himself founded the Ings Property Company, which has consistently set an example, too little followed, of enlightened restoration and management of historic buildings.

6.6   Latest in this fine record is the Report (1967) of the Archbishop's Commission on Redundant Churches under the chairmanship of Mr Marcus Worsley, M.P. With its recommendations, whose implementation of course depends entirely on finance, the writer of the present report wholeheartedly agrees.

6.7   Yet despite all this devoted work both by the Corporation and by private initiative the present state of the fabric of historic York, though from the street it looks cleaner and neater than it has done for over a century, is precarious and daily becoming more so, and the critical state of the Minster is representative of the state of medieval and Georgian York as a whole.

6.8   The historic process that has led to this crisis is clear. The ebbing away of fashionable life from York in the early 19th century left a vacuum both socially and physically which the small craftsmen and back-yard manufacturers alone could fill. Like those of other northern cities, the heart of York became less and less a place to live in and more and more a place to work in.

6.9   As Lewis Mumford has shown, the medieval city was essentially a city of gardens and orchards and only slowly degenerated into a city of yards and sheds. But once started the process was cumulative. Workshops jammed up against the backs of Georgian houses, as for example in Micklegate, St. Saviourgate and Castlegate, destroyed their own residential value and threatened their neighbours', accelerating the exodus. Too large for single families, it paid nobody to convert them into flats. So as the population of the city and its hinterland expanded, shopkeepers moved into ground floors, sometimes finding a use for the upper stories for storage.

6.10   What the backyard industries of the 19th century had begun the motor traffic of the 20th completed. Small traders might now move out, or be driven out by supermarket and multiple competition, but who would wish to move into such houses, gardenless, garageless and swamped in heavy commercial traffic? They became more valuable as sites than as buildings, with results that are plain for all to see. It must be recognised that all that has been done to rescue historic York in the past 20 years has been in the nature of first aid. The task now is to diagnose and prescribe for the disease.

Evaluation

6.11   The first stage must be the evaluation of what exists. The official tool for this purpose, the Ministry lists already referred to, invaluable though they are, were designed to convey information and not to imply action. They have weaknesses in the sphere of evaluation too, partly because they obsolesce rapidly in terms of taste and in terms of the condition of buildings. The cottages alongside All Saints North Street for example were unlisted until the Ings Property Co. did them up; now they are recommended for Grade II. Similar upgrading is now proposed for Victorian buildings and will soon be proposed for Edwardian. Moreover, as Mr George Pace has shown in writing of 'the York Aesthetic', buildings of no 'architectural' significance, even 'ugly' buildings and objects can have townscape value, a phenomenon which the official concept of 'group value' still fails to embrace.

6.12   It has therefore seemed necessary to take a fresh look at every building in the walled city with these criteria in mind, and the result is shown graphically on fig. 84. The classification is as follows:
- A.   Ancient monuments and buildings of national or major local importance.
- B.   Buildings of considerable architectural importance, but not quite in the first category.
- C.   Good buildings of major townscape value.
- D.   Buildings of some townscape value.

Buildings of the last half-century have been excluded from this analysis, as it is too soon and too individious to evaluate them.

6.13   Comparing this plan with the official map (fig. 81) it will be seen that the spread of buildings having some townscape value (classes C and D) is a good deal broader than the spread of the Supplementary List (III). Streets which come off noticeably better are Walmgate, St. Andrewgate, Coney Street, Clifford Street and Priory Street; and both banks of the Ouse between Ouse Bridge and Skeldergate Bridge are upgraded.

Priorities for preservation

6.14   It is now necessary to convert evaluation into recommendations for action. We welcome the increased powers conferred by Part V of the Town and County Planning Bill, now before Parliament, on local and central government to ensure that buildings in the statutory lists are preserved and not allowed to deteriorate. What remains to be done is to bring these powers and the existing grant structure into a clear relationship with the Conservation Areas whose designation is required by the Civic Amenities Act, so that these areas have a specific meaning in terms of action, which planning authorities can take into account in deciding where to draw their boundaries. Otherwise they will be defining nothing more than pious hopes.

6.15 Specifically we recommend that within a Conservation Area all Class A, B & C buildings will be preserved, and all Class D buildings should be preserved if possible. To extend absolute protection to Class D buildings would in our opinion stifle imaginative design and stop in its tracks the process of history which the streets of York so wonderfully illustrate.

6.16 We have deliberately adopted this new classification in order to encourage an entirely fresh look at the present statutory and supplementary lists, which we are convinced is necessary if the new legislation is to achieve its object in this field.

6.17 In terms of a grant structure for the conversion and/or repair of listed buildings, and using our own four grades as criteria, the effect would be to establish three forms of grant, which we call:

Mandatory
All Class A, B and C buildings in the Conservation Areas would be entitled to this grant. Freeholders would be required, whether they applied for grant or not, to keep these buildings in reasonable repair and to open them for half-yearly inspection.

Available
All Class D buildings in the Conservation Areas would be entitled to grant but freeholders not applying would be under no obligation to keep them in repair and could apply for planning approval to demolish and rebuild.

Discretionary
Any freeholder *outside* the Conservation Areas could apply as now for grant, but each case would be dealt with on its merits.

Conservation Areas

6.18 If the financial implications of this definition of Conservation Areas are borne in mind it will be realised that their boundaries cannot be too broadly drawn. There can be no question, for example, of designating the whole of the walled city on both banks of the Ouse. Even to designate (as its architectural homogeneity would suggest) the whole of the Inner Enclave defined in Chapter 5 would confer entitlement to conservation grants on many of the prosperous stores and banks in Coney Street and Parliament Street. Designation has therefore been closely drawn to include the following sectors or parts of sectors:
The Minster Precinct
The King's Manor
Aldwark
The Central and Castle Sectors excluding Parliament Street, Coney Street, Spurriergate, Clifford Street and their tributaries
A part of Walmgate
The surviving frontages of Micklegate
Small pockets in Skeldergate and North Street.

6.19 The jig-saw pattern that emerges is shown on fig. 87. It must be emphasized that this pattern has financial rather than visual significance. Visually the whole of the Inner Enclave and the whole of the Castle Sector are the indivisible heart of York, and the fact that a street like Coney Street is not within the Conservation Area does not imply that the protection of its character is of less importance than (for example) Blake Street's or Fossgate's. Chapter 8 will endeavour to put these matters in perspective.

6.20 Conversely, within the Conservation Areas large numbers of unworthy buildings exist, and others of minor townscape value or none. These must be progressively replaced by buildings appropriate to their setting.

External factors

6.21 But visual analysis, even in the light of sound scholarship, is the least of the problems of conservation, and we must now take a first look at the main factors which affect the viability of historic buildings and fine townscape. The paragraphs that follow should be read in conjunction with Professor Nathaniel Lichfield's report on the Economics of Conservation, printed as Appendix G.

6.22 The survival of buildings beyond their normal write-off period is primarily a matter of economics and only secondarily a matter of structural condition. Buildings will be kept in use, or even kept up unused, for as long as they are more valuable to somebody (with the financial power to maintain them) than the sites on which they stand. This value may be financial or sentimental or any combination of the two, but it will be undermined if the surroundings become inappropriate to the building's use. If industry encroaches, or view is spoilt, or neighbours are a nuisance, or the streets become dangerous, noisy and congested, then the maintenance costs and inconveniences of old buildings, which are nearly always greater than new, cease to be outweighed by the low cost of buying them or the satisfaction of looking after them. Their value drops still further, until they are worth less than the sites on which they stand, and only remain standing if their tenants present a rehousing problem.

6.23 Commerce is a tough market for old buildings. The demands of modern competitive retailing are exacting, and few old buildings meet them. Consequently the turnover of buildings in commercial and business centres is at its fastest and the chance of survival of old buildings at its lowest. 'The higher the site value, the greater is the need for the building on the site to be of maximum efficiency'.*

6.24 This generalisation of course conceals the wide differences in *scale* that mercifully still survive in retailing. While the big stores and offices are the main agents of destruction of old buildings, the 'quality' stores, boutiques and specialised shops are some of their most effective guardians, and are in a position to spend more money on them than most private owners. York has streets, notably Stonegate, which are among the best examples in Europe of this process, and the growth of the University has introduced a clientele which gives further support to it.

6.25 The normal market forces can thus be seen at work in their different ways in the historic centre of York. The picture is less complete than in other centres of comparable size because the free market has been inhibited by the exceptional quantity of listed buildings and the tenacity with which official and private resources have defended them. The big developers have stayed away, or taken a look and retreated, a state of affairs which we must in fairness regard as a mixed blessing.

6.26 But while *sites* in central York have for these reasons not reached their normal values, and old buildings have consequently

*'Economic Pressures and the Role of Planning'
Hadley Buck. Architects' Journal 18th January 1967

survived where in other cities they would have vanished, *buildings* outside a few favoured streets show all the symptoms of loss of appeal referred to in para. 6.22 above. The disease of urban blight can be seen in all its stages in the walled city. In Aldwark, and St. Andrewgate it has reached the advanced stage where only comprehensive redevelopment can meet the case; in Walmgate industrial encroachment at the back and traffic in front have for many years been inexorably exerting the same pressures, and in Micklegate one can see precisely the same disease at an earlier stage. Parallel to Castlegate and St. Saviourgate the 19th century and the 20th century have introduced relief roads which have removed one cause of blight, only to introduce a worse one in the form of unneighbourly new buildings. Of the 12 finest individual town houses in the walled city, only three have any sort of back garden, and the majority are hemmed in by industrial or other unsuitable structures. This encroachment onto back gardens is a feature of the aesthetically 'best' parts of the walled city. Fig. 90 shows graphically the brutal juxtaposition of attractive old houses with industry and warehousing.

6.27   The results in the form of empty buildings, empty upper floors and ramshackle conversions to unsuitable purposes are shown on figs. 95, 96, 115, 116. So widespread is this misuse of old buildings that it can be said that the great majority of the buildings shown as having townscape value on fig. 84 are in fact facades and nothing more.

Planning for conservation

6.28   It is obvious that if our ancestors had possessed our present planning controls they could have prevented a great deal of this dehumanisation and economic loss. We now know that it is useless to preserve old buildings unless we preserve with them (or restore to them) a setting which encourages their appropriate use. We are also learning that planning authorities can take positive as well as this negative action to guide economic forces in directions which will encourage conservation. Traffic management, the siting of car parks, the use of CDA procedures to encourage larger-scale commercial development in sectors of low architectural value, residential urban renewal on the American pattern designed to attract into conservation areas people with money to spend on conversion, and on the regional scale a proper adjustment of employment and population to the capacity of historic centres: these are all weapons the planner can use to encourage (or misuse to frustrate) investment in good old buildings.

6.29   At the best of times, when all this has been done, there will be a gap between what the market will bear and what the environment should be, and this gap can only be closed by public spending on a scale now normal in other European countries but still grossly inadequate here. But the object of the exercise must be to narrow the gap as much as possible by minimising costs (of which the greatest will be the relocation of industry) and by maximising profits (of which the greatest will be the opening up of new sites for commerce and business).

6.30   We have so far assessed the activities that ought to be encouraged or imported into the walled city, and those that ought to be discouraged or removed, and we have looked broadly at the physical implications in terms of land use and buildings. But to arrive at even an approximate balance sheet we need to get closer to the ground and this we do in the next chapter.

. . . and after

83 Fossgate

to showrooms and customers' car park

happiness
is egg-shaped!

NOW!
BARGAIN
TIME FOR

88   Lendal Bridge, the significance of good detail, iron and stone

89 Guildhall

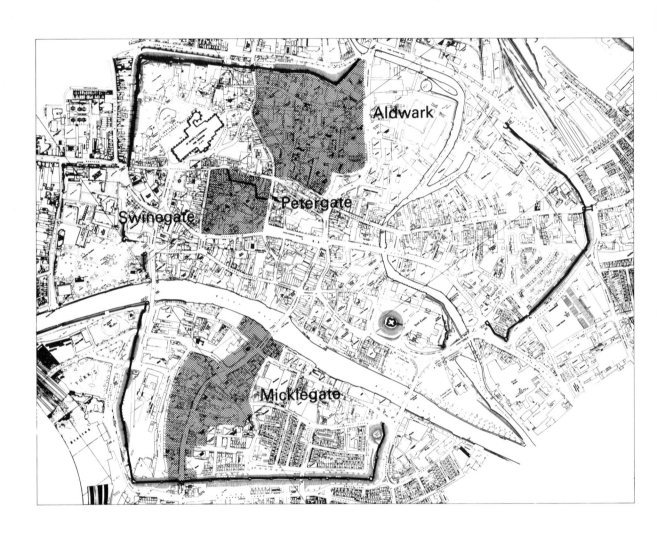

7 Conservation in detail

7.1   In this chapter and the next, within the context of the general proposals for the city centre, four Study Areas are analysed in considerable detail, in order to establish the action needed to conserve historic city cores and the economics of such action. They have been chosen to illustrate the range of conservation problems that occur in York (other than those of historic churches) and also, as far as can be foreseen, the size of the programme that the Government could be expected to underwrite in York.

7.2   The cases studied are as follows:
Aldwark
A derelict hinterland containing many historic buildings and in need of comprehensive redevelopment.
Swinegate
A congested central commercial area in need of selective piecemeal redevelopment.
Micklegate
An historic street suffering from blight due to backland encroachment; it is studied in the next chapter in its setting within the Micklegate/Bishophill sector.
Petergate
A typical group of beautiful York houses in need of conversion to ensure their preservation.

7.3   Fig. 91 shows these four Study Areas, and it will be noted that Aldwark is one of the 8 sectors defined in Chapter 2, that Swinegate is the core of the central shopping sector, that Micklegate is the central spine of the Micklegate/Bishophill sector, and that Petergate is the northern fringe of the Swinegate area.

7.4   When in the next chapter the remaining sectors are studied, it will be found that while outside the Study Areas a great many improvements are recommended, they are essentially improvements which could be achieved by the normal processes of local authority planning and of public and private urban renewal, if these processes are guided aright, and if the lessons afforded by the Study Areas are applied to them.

Y O R K - ACTION AREA SURVEY   AUTUMN   1966

Plot *P.13* . Address . *91-93 Low Petergate* . . . . Floors *3+ attic* .

Date . *2 November* . . Name of Premises/Business . *Peckitts* . . . .

Interview . . . *Peckitt* . . . . Signature . *DR Gamblin* . . . . . .

OWNER   W. *Peckitt* .

TENANT   GF   *Owner except 2 self-*   FIRST FLOOR (a) *flat* .
          SECOND   *contained flats.*   THIRD
          FOURTH   (a) *flat* .

SUB TENANT   GF   FIRST   (a) *flat* .
             SECOND ——— (a) *flat*   THIRD
             FOURTH

(INDICATE O FOR <u>OCCUPIER</u> ABOVE IF AND WHERE APPROPRIATE)

USES   GF   (a) *men's outfitters / storage*   (a) *flat*
        SECOND   (b) *shop / office*   FIRST   (c) *shop store*
        FOURTH   (c) *storage*   THIRD (attic) (a) *unused* .
                  (d) *storage*
                  (a) *self contained flat*
                  (c) *unused*

CONSTRUCTION   (a) *Mid Georgian brick*
                 2 shops at G.F. with entrance between to stone staircase to upper floors.
                 This passage leads straight through to yard at back and an opening
                 has been formed in that the wall that separated it from the shop on
                 the left to provide the shop with direct access to stairs and yard. This
                 opening is sealed off after business hours.
                 (b) roof light over this single storey section ..
                 (c) age uncertain probably c17 with c19 windows and roof. Access at
                 G.F. level through shop. 3 floors, ceiling hts greater than rest of bldg.
                 but connections through all at all levels via a couple of steps ..
                 2nd floor ceiling collapsed but roof appears to be in good condition.
                 (d) 2 floors C19.

Facade   *Mid Georgian brick painted white .*
                 2 shops at G.F level. One on right is C20.

AGE   (a) *Mostly Mid C18*
                 (b) *Probably c17*
                 (d) *c19.*

<u>ARCHITECTURAL QUALITY</u>

Townscape   *Fairly good.*

Intrinsic   *Fine curved stone staircase*
                 exterior fairly ordinary

<u>CONDITION</u> (V) GOOD (W) GOOD TO FAIR (X) FAIR (Y) POOR (Z) POOR
                 (W).

Fire Precautions

92   Proforma for study area surveys

NATURAL LIGHTING

Existing   Good.

Potential

ACCESS
Main Access   Petergate

Subsidiary Access   none

Potential Access   Passage at side within plot D 12
at present unused.

Vehicles   Petergate
(Yellow) Restricted waiting

CURTILEGE
Unbuilt Space   garden / yard
mostly unused.

Outbuildings   (e) neglected, 2 storey
G.F used as coal storage

ASPECT   Front N.E.
Back S. W.
PROSPECT   Front Fairly Good.

Back Fair.

POTENTIALITIES
For Residential Use   Upper floors of (a) already
residential

For other use

NOTES AND DIAGRAMS

Peckitt also owns D 31 leased to W. Simpson & Son Ltd.
and D 32   Barker & Deighton
D 33   Market gardener of unknown
identity,

K*

93 Georgian merchants' houses in St. Andrewgate

Aldwark

7.5 This sector of 21.25 acres (to centre lines of surrounding roads) has already been described (Chapter 2). Overlooked on the north by the city walls and on the other three sides by the backs of shops lining Goodramgate and Stonebow, its forlorn character is a surprise to every visitor who penetrates into it. This has been due partly to the destruction by 19th century backyard industry and 20th century office blocks of residential amenities, partly to 'planning blight' due to the long-standing proposal to widen St. Andrewgate to provide a new entry into the walled city as recommended in the 1948 plan.

7.6 The area nevertheless contains a great many good buildings, which are classified as follows in fig. 84:

A	19
B	15
C	64
D	23

These include the Merchant Taylors' and St. Anthony's Halls, the best early Georgian terraced houses in York (St. Saviourgate) and characteristic ranges of York street buildings in Goodramgate and Colliergate.

7.7 The pattern of land ownership in the sector is shown in fig. 99 and it will be noted that even along the historic street frontages, as well as predictably on the industrialised backland, properties are large by the standards of medieval cities, even though the frontages of individual old buildings, where they survive, are of course narrow. This in itself constitutes a significant threat to the survival of these frontages, to which some have conspicuously succumbed, and others have only stood up because of firm preservation policies either on the part of owners or of the Corporation.

7.8 The conventional *ground level land-use* map is in fig. 95, and shows shopping where expected and the large waste areas backing up to it. This plan is supplemented by fig. 102 which breaks down these conventional land uses into the multiplicity of businesses and other activities for which premises are at present used. Finally the *vertical land-use* sections in fig. 96 attempt to show in a new way the multiplicity of use within a single building which is characteristic of the historic streets of York. Unused upper stories feature notably in this diagram.

7.9 Fig. 98 shows the variegated pattern of buildings of different *periods,* with no preponderance in any one quarter, and the much greater area of ground space occupied by Victorian than by earlier buildings, and fig. 97 confirms, as the eye can see on the ground, the increasingly poor *condition* of buildings as one penetrates to the centre of the sector.

7.10 For reasons that need not be restated, it should be the object of policy in this area:

1 To assemble sites for residential redevelopment which would be attractive to private enterprise of high standard.

2 To remove from the area uses which conflict with this purpose for any one or more of the reasons given in Chapter 4.

3 To eliminate from the area heavy transport and traffic not having business in it.

4 To enhance the setting (and therefore the economic viability) of the area's historic buildings.

5 To provide reasonable extension space for the shops that fringe the area so that their prosperity is not handicapped.

94 15-18 Aldwark—recently presented to the Civic Trust

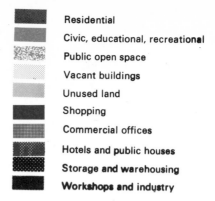

Residential

Civic, educational, recreational

Public open space

Vacant buildings

Unused land

Shopping

Commercial offices

Hotels and public houses

Storage and warehousing

Workshops and industry

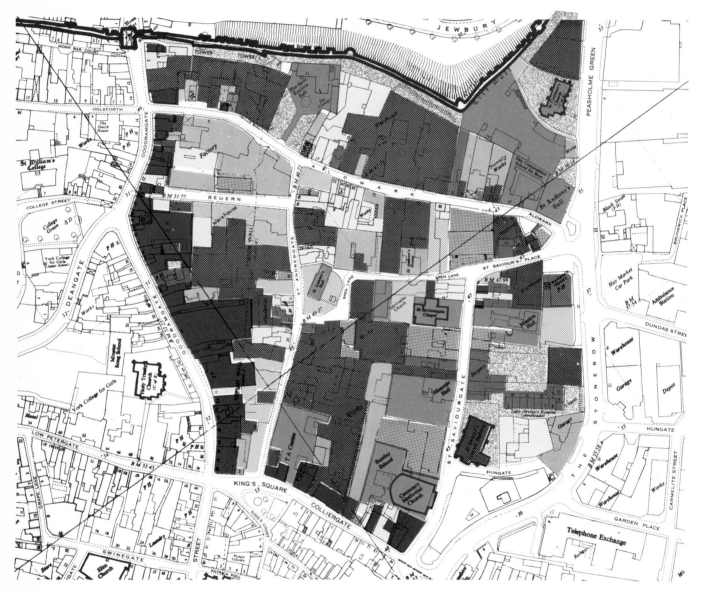

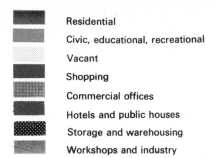

Residential

Civic, educational, recreational

Vacant

Shopping

Commercial offices

Hotels and public houses

Storage and warehousing

Workshops and industry

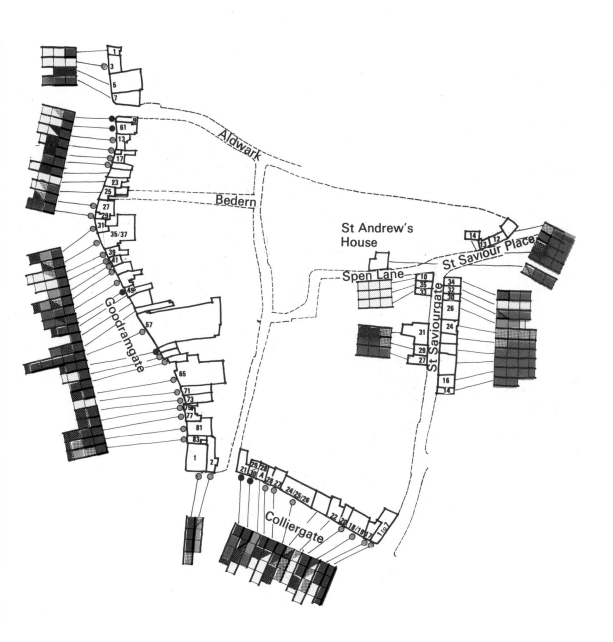

Access to upper floors

●   Existing separate access

◖   Separate access but needs improving

◉   Access through ground floor

○   Access through adjoining premises

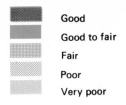

Good
Good to fair
Fair
Poor
Very poor

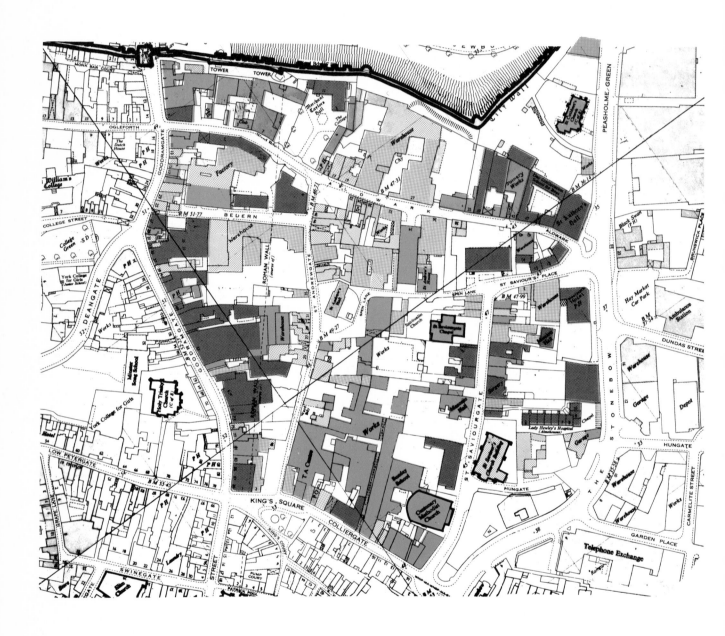

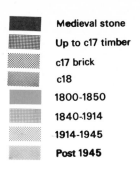

Medieval stone

Up to c17 timber

c17 brick

c18

1800-1850

1840-1914

1914-1945

Post 1945

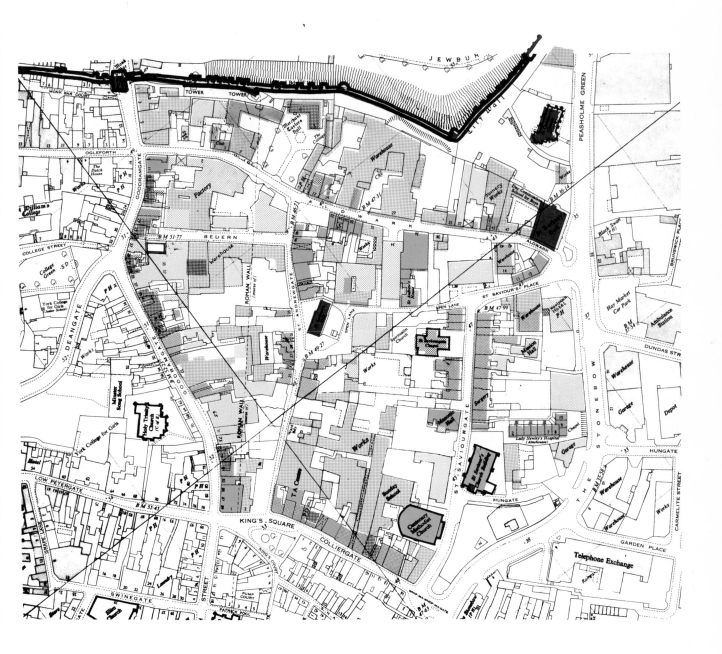

7.11 While rear service access to shops should be included where it can be done without prejudicing residential amenities, because it will lighten the servicing load on surrounding streets, there is no point in insisting on it since the far sides of both Goodramgate and Colliergate must in any event be serviced from these streets.

7.12 Businesses referred to in para. 7.10.2. above include Camerons Brewery, which has already made plans for removal and replacement by residential development, a meat pie manufacturer*, a large builders' yard, a manufacturing chemist and a furniture depository.

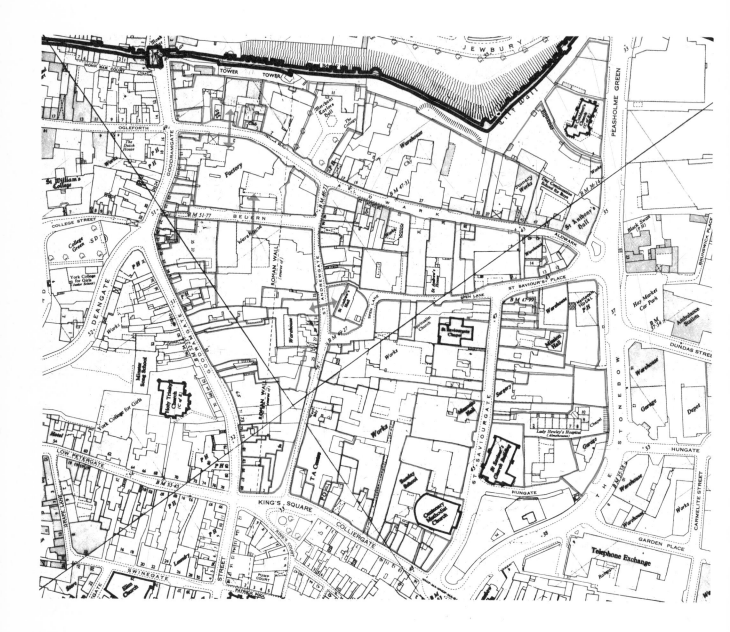

The total industrial area for clearance, including miscellaneous parking, amounts to 182,590 sq. ft., or about 4.25 acres. This, with other (mainly waste) land necessary for comprehensive development, will provide a total site for redevelopment of 6.5 acres.

*This business has since moved out of its own accord, thus illustrating a tendency which will affect the balance sheet in favour of the local authority.

7.13 The traffic control system proposed in Chapter 5 will affect this area as follows:

7.14 Monk Bar will be closed to all but labelled private cars. Goodramgate and Colliergate will be open for servicing during the early morning and at other times closed to all but labelled cars. To enable servicing vehicles to circulate in Goodramgate a turning circle is provided round existing buildings just inside Monk Bar. Stonebow and Peaseholme Green will be unrestricted and would be the baseline from which the Aldwark residential area would be serviced. All roads except these last two will be closed to heavy vehicles.

7.15 Within the sector, servicing and the circulation and parking of labelled cars would be unrestricted except that Hungate would be one-way eastwards and St. Andrewgate one-way northwards south of the junction with Spen Lane. It would of course be entirely contrary to the concept of Aldwark as a residential precinct for St. Andrewgate to be widened beyond the normal 18 ft. or to be broken through the Walls (as previously proposed) so as to bring traffic into King's Square. In order to restore the sense of enclosure and the pedestrian amenities of the Square, the buildings on its north side should now be rebuilt on their old frontages, with an archway entrance into St. Andrewgate and an unloading space for commercial vehicles 70 yards north of the archway.

7.16 As to the design of the new housing in the residential precinct, fig. 106 shows an indication of the kind of development which would, we believe, be attractive both visually and commercially and would re-interpret the York tradition in 20th century terms. The old street pattern has too many good buildings on it to be written off, so it is retained with new spurs opening up backland. Present building lines, with their subtle bends, are respected and retained as far as daylighting and highway regulations permit. In detail, if we enter the precinct from King's Square, the following points should be noted (fig. 106):
1 The arched entry hides from King's Square the new rear extension of the Goodramgate shops. The TA facade is retained if possible. Trees hide the backs of shops from new housing.
2 By constricting its three entries an apparently spacious square is formed at the centre of gravity of the precinct and planted with trees. A new pedestrian short-cut connects with 51 Goodramgate (with its fine black and white back) and on past Holy Trinity to burst upon the great flank view of the Minster. St. Andrew's hall should be restored.

100 The new Aldwark: Spen Lane looking North West

101 The new Aldwark: St. Andrewgate looking North East

3 Bedern survives but is wholly rebuilt, with the present break into Goodramgate closed to vehicles.

4 The present forecourt of Merchant Taylor's Hall is too large for this modest but vital building. It is suggested that the best view of it might be framed by a new 'lodge' low enough not to obscure the Minster Towers. Trees on the NW side complete the picture. A new footpath is proposed giving access to the Roman corner bastion and up on to the Walls. Opposite 17/19 Aldwark new houses are set back to improve sight lines and set off this fine facade.

5 The Cameron's site is shown redeveloped on the lines at present proposed by the owners, but with rather more emphasis on the old building-line. A footpath runs to and ascends the walls.

6 Trees on each side of Hilary House soften the vista up St. Saviourgate and continue the street line of Aldwark.

7 Peaseholme House is liberated, restored externally and converted to an appropriate institutional use.

8 From St. Saviourgate a new pedestrian route runs past Lady Hewley's Hospital down steps to the buses in Stonebow, and in the other direction through the new squares of houses into St. Andrewgate.

9 New cottages define a churchyard for St. Saviour's Church.

7.17   The housing itself (figs. 107 and 108) varies in height from two storeys to five, depending on the surrounding scale and on protected vistas. 'Town houses' with set-back built-in garages and private walled gardens are used wherever possible, with flats at internal and external angles. For dwellings without their own, 121 back-land garages with landscaped roofs are reached generally through arched openings in street frontages.

House types proposed are as follows:

	Area	No.	
Town Houses	1,350 sq. ft. average (including garage)	33	
Mews Houses	1,250 sq. ft. (including garage)	12	
Mews Houses without ground floor above common garage	1,000 sq. ft.	10	
Terrace Houses	1,200 sq. ft.	3	
		—	58
3 Bed Flats	1,000 sq. ft.	3	
2 Bed Flats	850 sq. ft.	92	
1 Bed Flats	700 sq. ft.	13	
		—	108
			166

7.18   The population on the 6.5 acres could amount to 555 giving a residential density of 82 p.p.a.

Key to specific uses

As shown in figs. 102, 103, 104 and
120, 121, 122.

Shopping

1 Department Store
2 Clothing
  M–Male, F–Female, T–Working Tailor,
  S–Secondhand, W–Wool and Knitwear
3 Furniture
  A–Antiques, C–Carpets only
4 Hardware
  C–China, G–General Domestic,
  Q–Ornamental Goods
5 Ironmongery and Metalwork
  Q–Ornamental Metalwork
6 Jewellery and Clocks
  J–Jewellery, C–Clocks and Watches,
  S–Silverware, Q–Ornamental Goods
7 Toys
8 Books
  R–Religious
9 Stationery
  N–Newsagent, T–Tourist Publications,
  C–Cards
10 Tobacco
11 Sweets
12 Grocery
  S–Supermarket, G–and General
13 Meat
14 Fish
  F–Fresh Fish, C–Fish and Chips
15 Restaurant
  R–Full Meals, T–Tea and Coffee
16 Cakes and Pastries
17 Pharmacy
18 Photography
19 Bicycles
20 Hairdressers (M, F)
21 Fruit and Vegetables
22 Flowers
23 Artists' Materials
  P–Paintings and works of art, B–Artists'
  materials
24 Leather Goods
25 Herbs and Health Foods
26 Dairy
27 General secondhand
  Q–Oxfam
28 Radio and TV
29 Equipment Services
  E–Electricity, G–Gas, H–Household
  Appliances, D–Paints and Decorations,

Q–Office Equipment, C–Cash Registers,
Y–'Do It Yourself'
30 Prams and Baby Equipment
31 Paints and Wallpapers
32 Guns
33 Post Office
34 Provender
35 Sports Goods
36 Music
37 Hand Made Goods
38 Poultry
39 Shoes
  V–Vacant

Offices

40 Office to firm *in situ* or adjoining
41 Bank
42 Insurance
43 Building Society
44 Estate Agent
45 Personal Services
  D–Dentist, Q–Optician, H–Hearing Aid
46 Betting Office
47 Government Offices
48 Local Government
  M–Mental Welfare Centre
49 Public Services
  G–Gas
50 General and Various
51 Architects
52 Solicitors
53 Photographers
54 Publishers
  M–Music
55 Piano Tuition
56 Business Equipment
57 Social Organisation
  F–Football Supporters' Club
58 Driving Tuition
59 Household Services
  T–Towels
  (For 60-64, see below)
70 Finance
71 Accountants

Civic, Educational & Recreational

60 Church
  A–Ancillary accommodation,
  S–synagogue
61 Educational
  S–School, C–Commercial School,
  F–Further Education, U–University
62 Social Halls
  F–Freemasons
63 Private Institution
64 Armed Services establishment
  D–Drill Hall, C–Club
65 Social Club

Storage

80 Ancillary to adjoining shop, office,
  factory, etc.
81 Furniture
82 Household Equipment
  M–Builders' Merchant, G–Gas
  Equipment, H–Household Electrical
  Equipment, R–Radio & TV, P–Paint,
  W–Wallpaper, F–Fireplaces
83 Clothing
84 Painters' and Decorators' Equipment
85 Fruit and Vegetables (including
  packaging)
86 Confectionery, Tobacco
87 Timber
  B–Builder's Yard
88 Pharmaceuticals
89 Scrap Materials
90 Newspapers and Stationery
91 Vehicles
  C–Commercial, P–Private
92 General Merchandise
93 Museum Exhibits
94 Meat
95 Business documents
96 Agricultural material and equipment
97 Funeral equipment
98 Beer
99 Hydraulic equipment

Workshops

100 Ancillary to adjoining shop, etc.
101 Woodwork
  S–Sculptor's workshop
102 Ironwork
  W–also Wires
103 Clothing and Fabrics
104 Public Service Equipment
  G–Gas
105 Plumber
106 Household Equipment
  H–Heating, E–Electrical,
  R–Radio and TV
107 Sign Painter
108 Electricity Substation
109 Timber Contractor
110 Shop Equipment
111 Broadcasting Equipment
112 Commercial Garage

Industry

121 Printing
122 Metalwork
  I–Iron, S–Silver
123 Pharmaceuticals
  S—Surgical
125 Bakery
126 Meat processing

102 Aldwark specific uses (1967)
Ground floor
Blue: shops and offices
Yellow: warehousing, storage and industrial

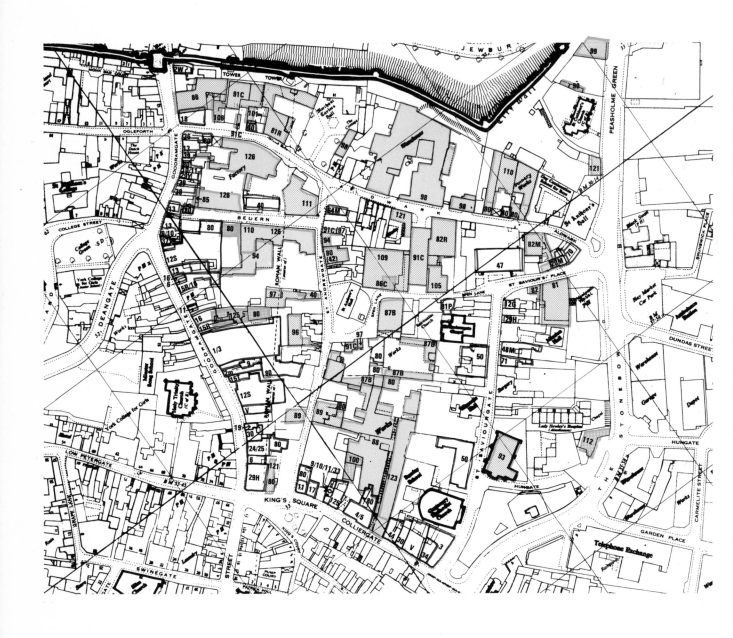

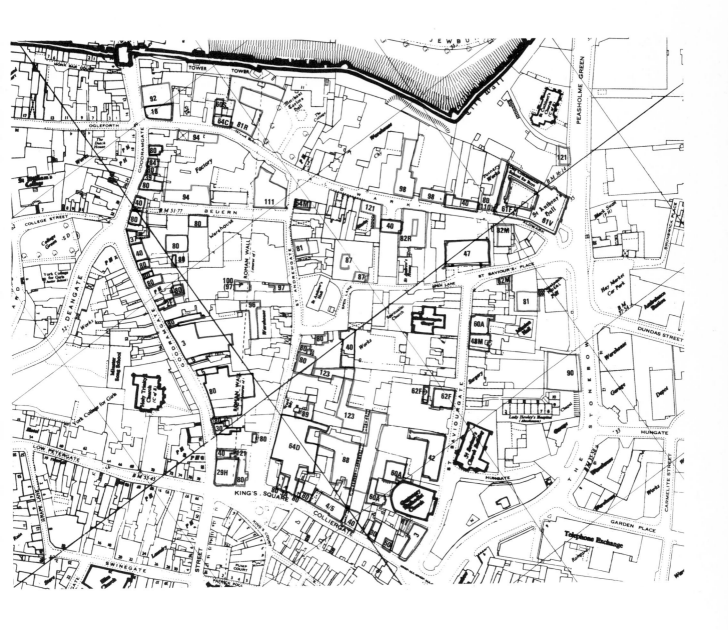

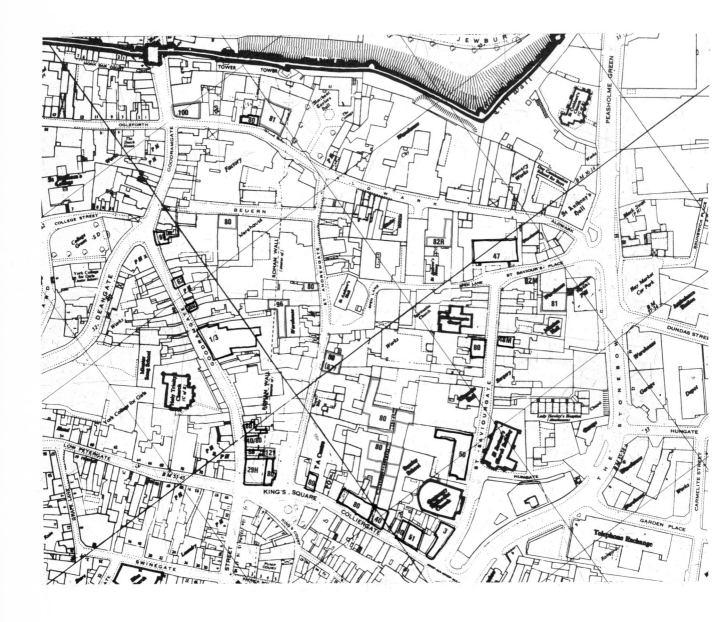

105 Aldwark sieve map
stippled areas indicate land assumed as
available in the new Aldwark (fig. 106)

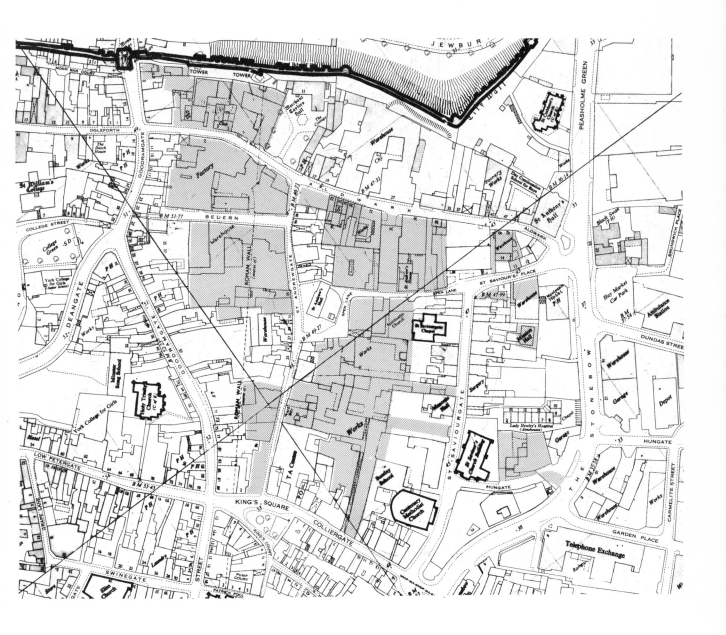

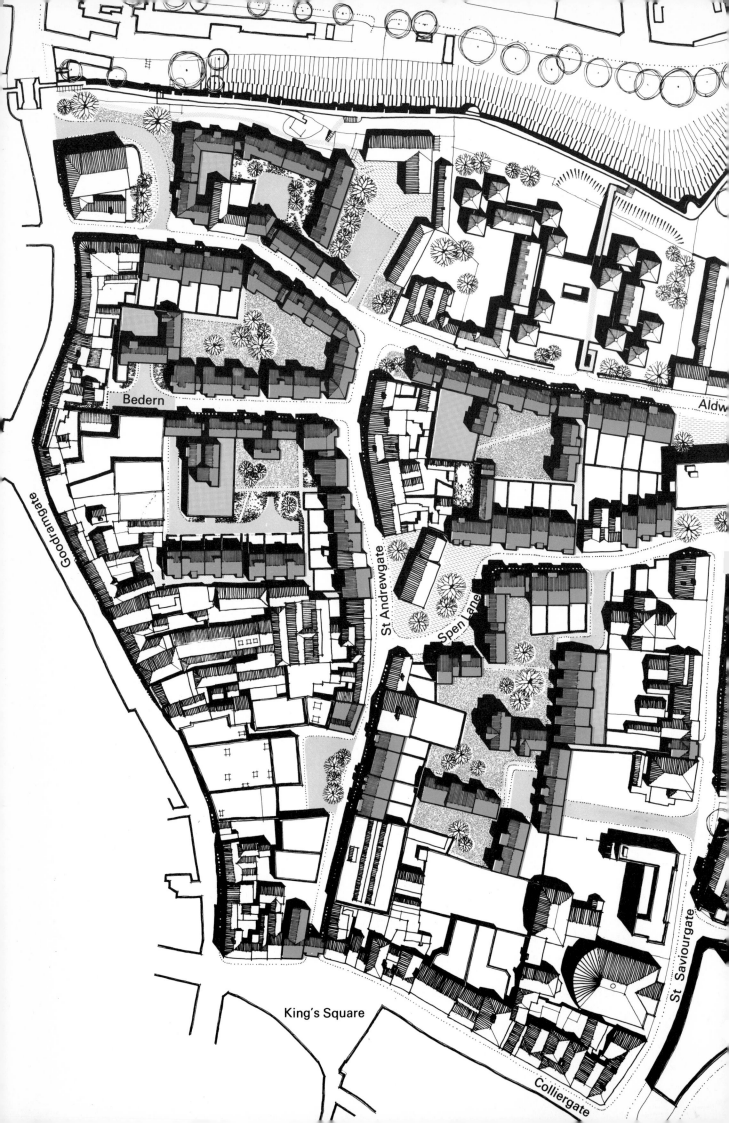

Goodramgate

Bedern

Aldw

St Andrewgate

Spen Lane

King's Square

St Saviourgate

Colliergate

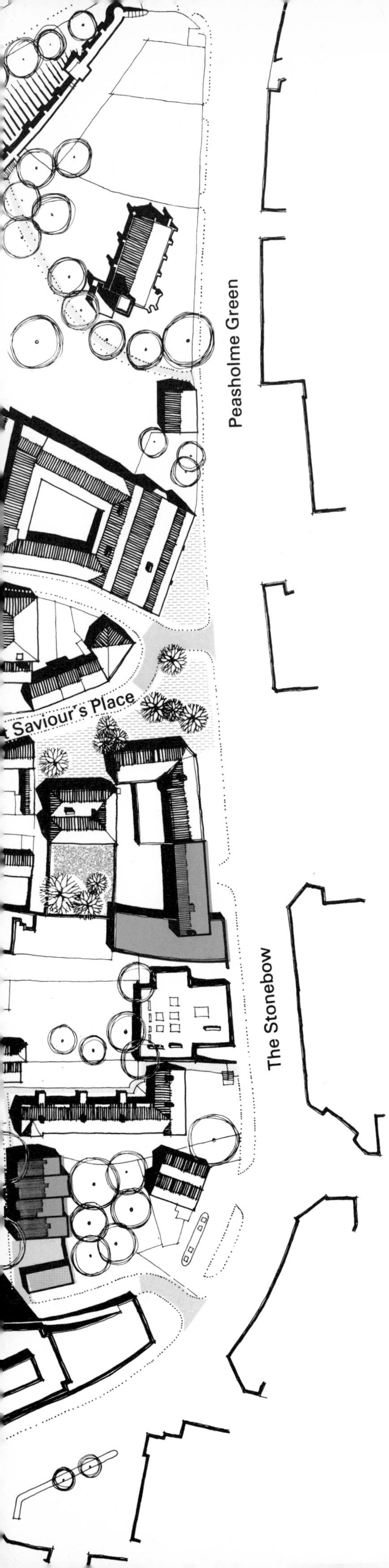
Peasholme Green
Saviour's Place
The Stonebow

106 The new Aldwark

New buildings
Garages
New roads
Paving
Grass/landscapes
Existing trees
New trees

107 Aldwark: section through Colliergate and Aldwark looking North West

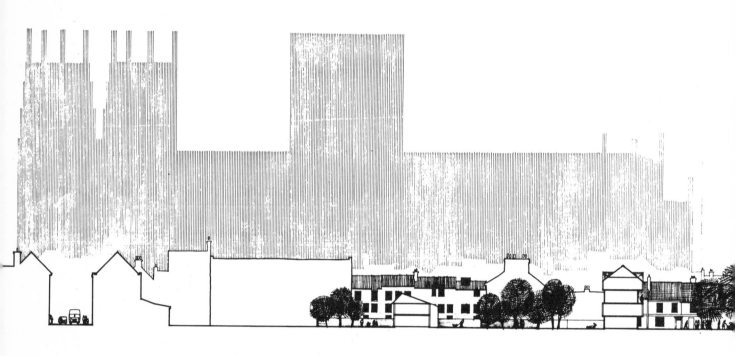

108 Aldwark: section through Goodramgate and St. Saviourgate looking North East

109 The Swinegate study area

110 Grape Lane, in the Swinegate study area   **111 The Swinegate study area**

Swinegate

7.19 Unlike Aldwark, this area of 7.75 acres is not a case of dereliction, but it is an area of great historic interest almost adjacent to the
south transept of the Minster (fig. 91), and it has been a mosaic of
complex activity and jumbled buildings ever since York has existed as
a city (being wholly within the Roman walls). It is chosen for detailed
study because of its typicality of the inner enclave, including as it does
some of York's best architecture and some of its worst.

7.20 The best is indicated by the fact that the area contains the
following numbers of buildings classified in the map on p. 83, fig. 84.

A 15
B 26
C 35
D 23

It includes one side of Stonegate and the most historically valuable
side of Low Petergate, which between them muster a collection of
street architecture perhaps unique in England for variety, antiquity and
charm.

7.21 The mosaic of *land use* is shown in the standard categories in
fig. 115 and as in the case of Aldwark it is seldom consistent over the
whole of a multi-storey building. This *vertical* multiplicity of uses
applies of course particularly to the taller buildings on the periphery of
the area, and is shown in vertical sectional form in fig. 116. This
brings out the number of unused upper stories, particularly in Low
Petergate, which forms the subject of the next study.

7.22 Also as in the case of Aldwark, fig. 120-2 shows the actual
businesses in occupation of each property in the area. *Ownerships,*
which are shown in fig. 119, are in noticeably smaller parcels than in
Aldwark, as would be expected in an area of higher land values and
much greater intensity of use. Finally survey figs. 117 and 118 show
that in regard to *age* the majority of historic buildings are on the
northern western and southern perimeter, and in regard to *condition,*
matters are predictably better on the fringes than in the hinterland.

7.23 It is, of course, the character and condition of this hinterland
that requires action more radical than the preservation (by conversion
if necessary) of historic buildings. The case for the removal of heavy
traffic—generating industry from this essentially pedestrian environment, with its world-famous narrow streets and its much-loved alleys
and short cuts, needs no elaboration. Users such as furniture deposi-
tories, garaging for commercial vehicles, waste paper storage and
paint and timber warehousing are obviously inappropriate. The area
occupied by users judged unsuitable under the criteria already given
occupy 59,263 sq. ft. There is 5,100 sq. ft. of vacant land and 1,250 sq.
ft. occupied by existing offices necessary to round off redevelopment.
The total including roads amounts to almost exactly two acres.

7.24 As in the Aldwark sector, existing services and attractive old
buildings, particularly on the W side of Grape Lane and the S side of
Swinegate, lead one to retain the present street pattern. On the other
hand it is vital to safeguard the pedestrian character of Stonegate and
Low Petergate and equally vital that the redevelopment of the key site
at the Petergate/Grape Lane junction should not be marred by sight-
line or set-back. The Stonegate/Little Stonegate and the Petergate/
Grape Lane junctions should therefore be bollarded so that the whole
of the redevelopment area is served from Church Street via Swinegate.
This pattern, while primarily intended to service the new development,
would also provide limited rear access to certain shops facing Stonegate and Petergate. Others could obtain rear access off Little Stone-

gate and Swinegate, though the planning must ensure that this does not prejudice residential amenities.

7.25   These restrictions on vehicular movement will safeguard the two main pedestrian short-cuts: one E-W from St. Sampson's Square via Finkle Street into the new central square with its trees, and thence by Coffee Lane into Stonegate; and the other N-S from Low Petergate via Grape Lane and thence via a new alley crossing Little Stonegate and emerging alongside St. Helen's Church. It is important that the redevelopment by the N.E. Gas Board in Davygate (if the demolition of these handsome buildings must indeed take place) should be designed to create an attractive entry at this point.

7.26   The clearance proposed in para. 7.23 above will still leave a variety of business in the area apart from retail trade, for example metalworkers, printers, sign writers, plumbers, and a piano tuner, and such should be encouraged.

7.27   But it is essential that cleared land should not be made available for business, as opposed to professional, use. One of our five Objectives was to restore to the walled city its traditional blend of living and working, and this small enclave in the very heart of ancient York is a test case for this policy. The redevelopment (fig. 124) is therefore strictly for residential or professional purposes, and is designed at a comparatively high density (130 persons per acre in the 2 acres of new development, and about 70 per acre including existing) so as to take full advantage of the unique convenience and amenities of this historic site, with its upper floor views of the full length of the Minster (figs. 126 and 127). The breakdown of house types is as follows:

Town Houses	3
2 Storey Houses	1
Maisonettes	16
2 Bed Flats	55
1 Bed Flats	14
	——
	89
	——
Garage spaces	131

7.28   It will be noted that there is an excess of car spaces over dwellings of 42, in order to provide off-street car storage to converted premises, particularly in Low Petergate (fig. 125).

112   The new Swinegate: Grape Lane looking towards Petergate

113   The new Swinegate: Grape Lane looking South West

114   Swinegate study area mapped proforma information

115   Swinegate: ground level land use

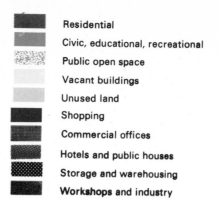

Residential
Civic, educational, recreational
Public open space
Vacant buildings
Unused land
Shopping
Commercial offices
Hotels and public houses
Storage and warehousing
Workshops and industry

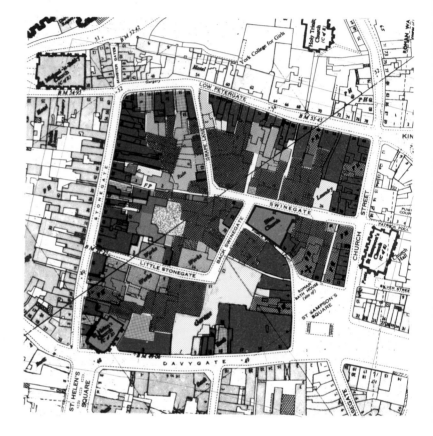

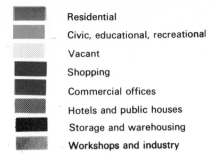

Residential

Civic, educational, recreational

Vacant

Shopping

Commercial offices

Hotels and public houses

Storage and warehousing

Workshops and industry

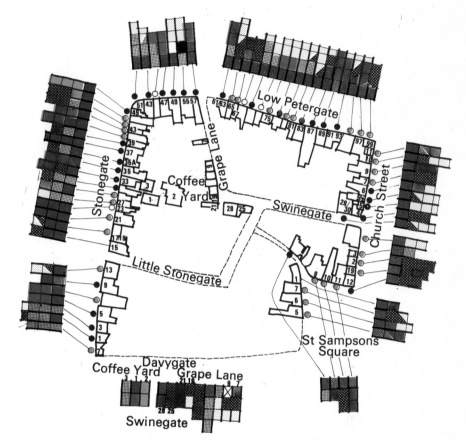

Access to upper floors

●   Existing separate access

◐   Separate access but needs improving

◓   Access through ground floor

○   Access through adjoining premises

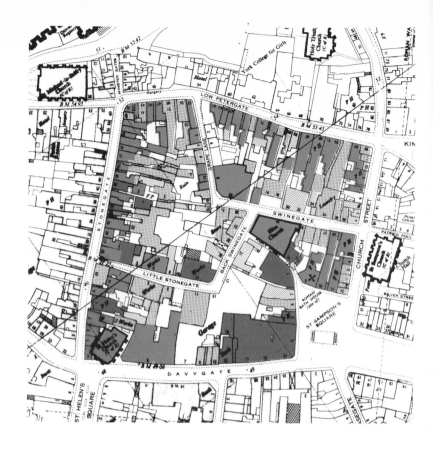

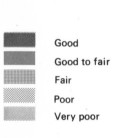

Good

Good to fair

Fair

Poor

Very poor

118   Swinegate: age of buildings

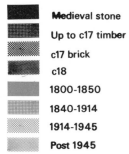

■	Medieval stone
■	Up to c17 timber
▒	c17 brick
■	c18
▒	1800-1850
▒	1840-1914
▒	1914-1945
▒	Post 1945

119   Swinegate: site ownership

120   Swinegate: specific uses (1967)
Ground floor
Blue : shops and offices
Yellow : warehousing, storage, and industrial

121   Swinegate: specific uses (1967)
First floor

122 Swinegate: specific uses (1967)
Second floor

123 Swinegate sieve map
Stippled areas indicate land assumed
as available in the new Swinegate (fig. 124)

New buildings
Garages
New roads
Paving
Grass/landscapes
Existing trees
New trees

Stonegate

Low Petergate

Church Street

Swinegate

Back Swinegate

Little Stonegate

St Sampson's Square

Davygate

Garages

Forecourt

Stonegate

Low Petergate

Church Street

Swinegate

Back Swinegate

Little Stonegate

St Sampson's Square

Davygate

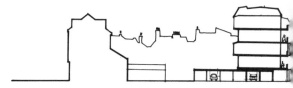

126 Swinegate : section through Davygate and low Petergate looking North West

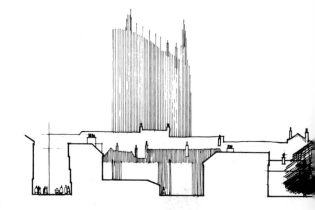

127 Swinegate : section through Stonegate and Church Street looking North East

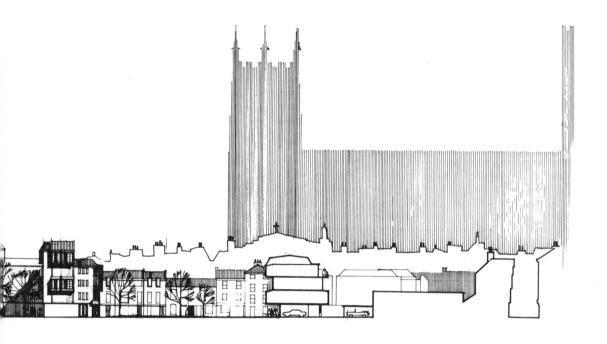

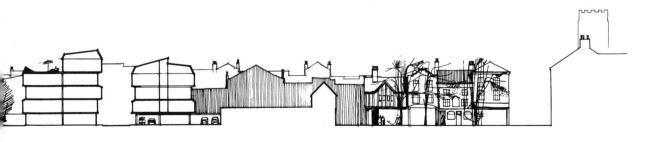

128 Low Petergate

Petergate

7.29   The object of this study was to see how easily the upper stories of a typical group of historic shop/houses could be brought back into residential use. The survey was carried out along one side of Low Petergate and Church Street, from Grape Lane to Swinegate, which contains 5 Grade A, 6 Grade B, 5 Grade C and 9 Grade D buildings. Fig. 129 shows to small scale the buildings surveyed, the street frontage to Low Petergate, and two upper floor plans.

7.30   It was found that in the upper floors investigated there were 144 rooms which either were in residential use already or could be made into habitable accommodation. This total excludes rooms which would be needed for bathrooms or which were incapable of conversion. Of this total nearly a quarter were used by the occupants of the ground floor shops or others for business purposes—as offices, showrooms or workshops. Those already in residential use fell just short of another quarter. There thus remained rather more than half the number of rooms which were used for storage or were vacant. These rooms would obviously be better maintained if lived in.

7.31   Living accommodation on upper floors requires separate access from the street or the rear, and all floors above the first must have separate means of escape in case of fire. The survey examined how these requirements can be satisfied without expensive alterations to the buildings.

7.32   Of the twenty-five separate addresses contained in the group, five have separate doors to the street giving access to the stairs serving the upper floors, three have stairs giving onto side passages which lead to the street. In the case of over half of the buildings, therefore, satisfactory independent access to the upper floors exists. In one more case the proprietors of the business on the ground floor themselves live on the upper floors and separate access is not at the moment necessary.

7.33   There remain eleven properties in which building works are necessary to provide separate access, or in which arrangements need to be made with adjoining owners, or both.

7.34   Points at which access exists or is suggested for future provision are shown on the plan in fig. 129. The plan also shows where passageways exist or might easily be formed from Petergate to Swinegate.

7.35   Nearly all the second and third floors lack alternative means of escape in case of fire. It is, of course, possible to provide the usual metal external fire escape stairs or ladders. It might often be cheaper and simpler, however, to arrange with an adjoining owner to form a fire escape through the party wall. This can be done by making an opening in the wall and blocking it up with bricks laid in sand. The bricks may be covered with a panel of plywood or plasterboard so as not to spoil the appearance of the room.

7.36   In some cases all that will be needed to make the property habitable will be redecoration. In others more extensive building work is necessary.

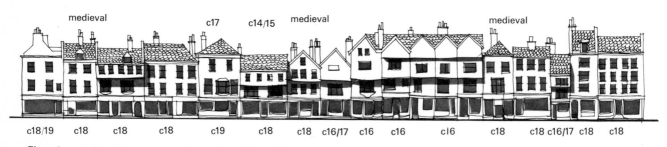

medieval   c17   c14/15 medieval   medieval

c18/19 c18 c18 c18 c19 c18 c18 c16/17 c16 c16 c16 c18 c18 c16/17 c18 c18

Elevations to Low Petergate   dates shown below refer to street fronts
dates shown above refer to fabric of building, where earlier

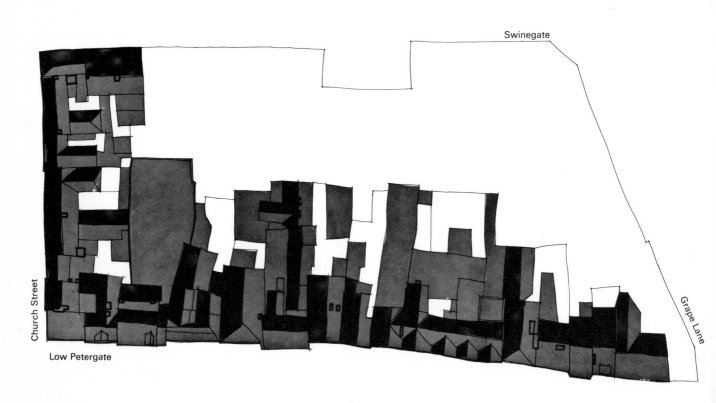

Swinegate

Church Street

Low Petergate

Grape Lane

Roof plan

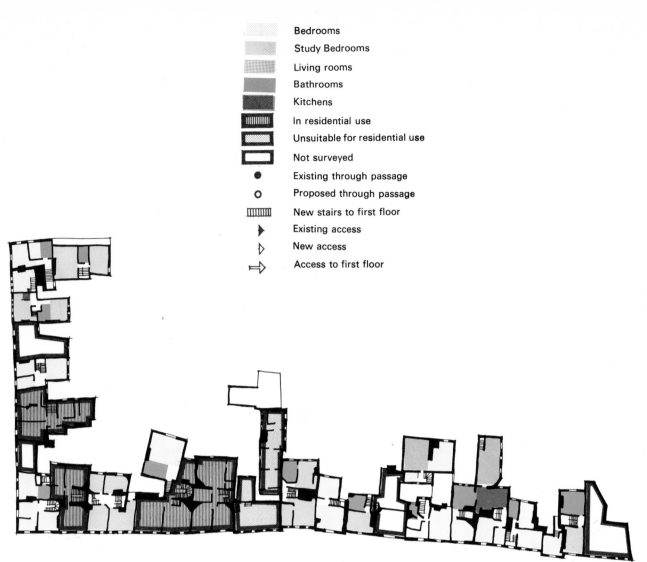

Bedrooms
Study Bedrooms
Living rooms
Bathrooms
Kitchens
In residential use
Unsuitable for residential use
Not surveyed
● Existing through passage
○ Proposed through passage
New stairs to first floor
▶ Existing access
▷ New access
⇨ Access to first floor

Second floor

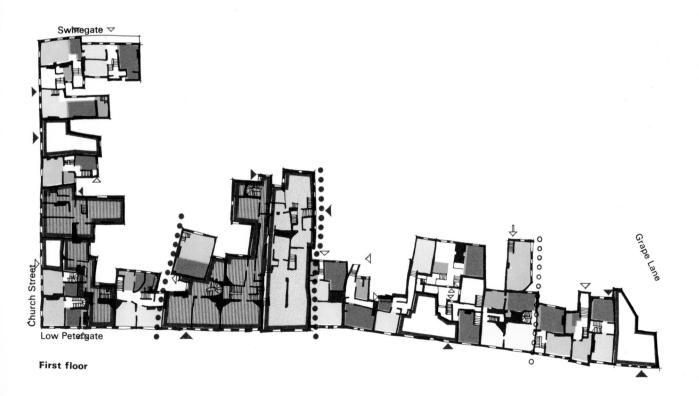

First floor

127

130 Micklegate example—second floor—before and after

131 Micklegate example—the kitchen—after

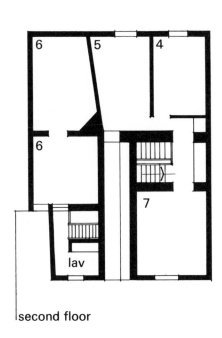

second floor

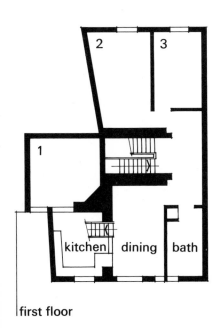

first floor

132   Micklegate example:
Floor plans showing conversion to
accommodate seven students

7.37   An illustration of what can be done with partly derelict property has recently been carried out in upper Micklegate and forms part of a programme of housing for students sponsored by a local housing association. The floor plans after conversion are shown in fig. 132. Figs. 130 and 131 show the appearance of two of the rooms before and after conversion.

7.38   The roof was sound, but some of the floors were decayed or weak. Two of the rooms in the roof had been closed off and forgotten. The heating, hot water and electrical installations were not adequate. The entrance from Micklegate was somewhat tortuous and cramped, and there was no separate means of escape in case of fire.

7.39   The building works cost £2,861, including architects' fees. A further £808 was spent on furniture, making a total capital expenditure of £3,669, for accommodation for one married couple and six single persons. Annual income from sub-tenancies is estimated at £955. Average weekly rents, allowing for seven weeks void in summer, are £3. Annual outgoings, including rent payable by the association as main tenant, rates, repairs and maintenance, part heating, water, electricity, telephone, and administration total £640. The balance of £315 represents a return of 8 per cent. on capital.

7.40   It is unlikely that many properties would require larger expenditure than that incurred on the example in Micklegate described above. Many would not require as much, and the return on capital in such cases would exceed 8 per cent.

7.41   With this background, the reluctance of owners to invest in improvements needs some explanation. It is to be found, in most cases, in one or more of the following :
1.   Complications of the grant structure, and slowness of procedure.
2.   Prejudice against potential tenants, particularly young people.
3.   Fear of protected tenancies.
4.   Fear of increased insurance rates.
Of the demand for flats in convenient converted houses, particularly from young workers in their first jobs, from students and from newly-married couples, there seems no question*. In these circumstances new procedures are obviously necessary and these are included in the recommendations in Chapter 10.

*An official of the Corporation is quoted in the Press as stating that for every flat on offer there are more than half a dozen applications.

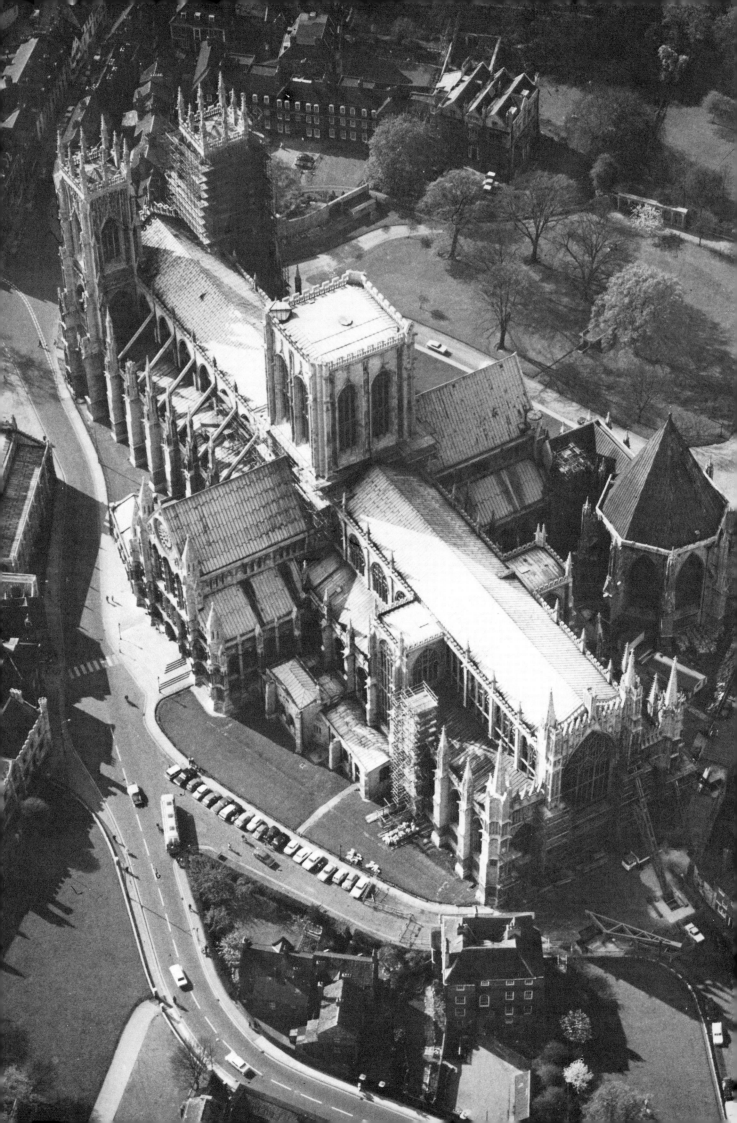

8 York renewed

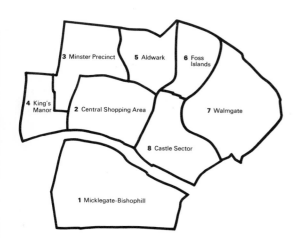

133 Plan defining sectors

8.1   In this chapter, sector by sector, proposals are made for the steady and progressive improvement of the city centre. Some of these proposals directly concern historic buildings. Others are civic improvements of all kinds whose effect on historic buildings and on the townscape of York may be indirect in varying degrees. Each will have some beneficial effect, and together their effect will be overwhelming and will restore to York the position it deserves among the cities of the world. In the order in which the sectors are defined in Chapter 2, we start with :

Micklegate-Bishophill (Sector 1)

8.2   The effect of the traffic proposals in Chapter 5 on this sector will be as follows :

1   Lendal Bridge (28 buses per hour at present) and Ouse Bridge (34 per hour) will remain major bus routes, with the present connection via Rougier Street and Railway Street and the new re-designed Rougier Street bus station. Circulation through the latter would be improved if land belonging to British Rail either N or S of the railway offices could be made available for one-way bus traffic only.

2   A 25 ft. one-way heavy transport route via Wellington Row, North Street and Skeldergate is proposed, requiring the following works :

a. The removal to the new building on Tanner's Moat of the electricity transformer and to a site adjoining the North Street public garden of the Boat House will enable a loop road off Station Road to pass under the abutment of Lendal Bridge with 14 ft. headroom.

b. Realignment of kerbs in the area of the riverside garden.

c. New building lines on the N.E. side of Skeldergate. It is important that the widening in this area should be wholly on the N.E. side so as to safeguard the important buildings on the S.W. side.

d. An improved junction with Bishopgate Street. Advantage could be taken of this improvement to re-align Cromwell Road so as to provide improved sites for redevelopment and open up a vista of Baille Hill from the W.

3   Micklegate Bar is closed to all traffic other than private cars and Micklegate itself is one-way northwards. Barker Lane is closed to vehicles and Trinity Lane bollarded at its junction with Micklegate, so as to prevent cars heading for the Skeldergate Car Park from entering the lane.

4   On the block bounded by Skeldergate, Buckingham Street Bishophill Senior and Fetter Lane a 5-storey split-level car park is proposed, with a capacity of 1,300 spaces. Pedestrians leaving the car park will cross an Ouse Bridge freed of heavy traffic other than buses and of all but labelled private cars. When the S side of Bridge Street is redeveloped advantage should be taken to create a high level footway above Skeldergate to the bridgehead.

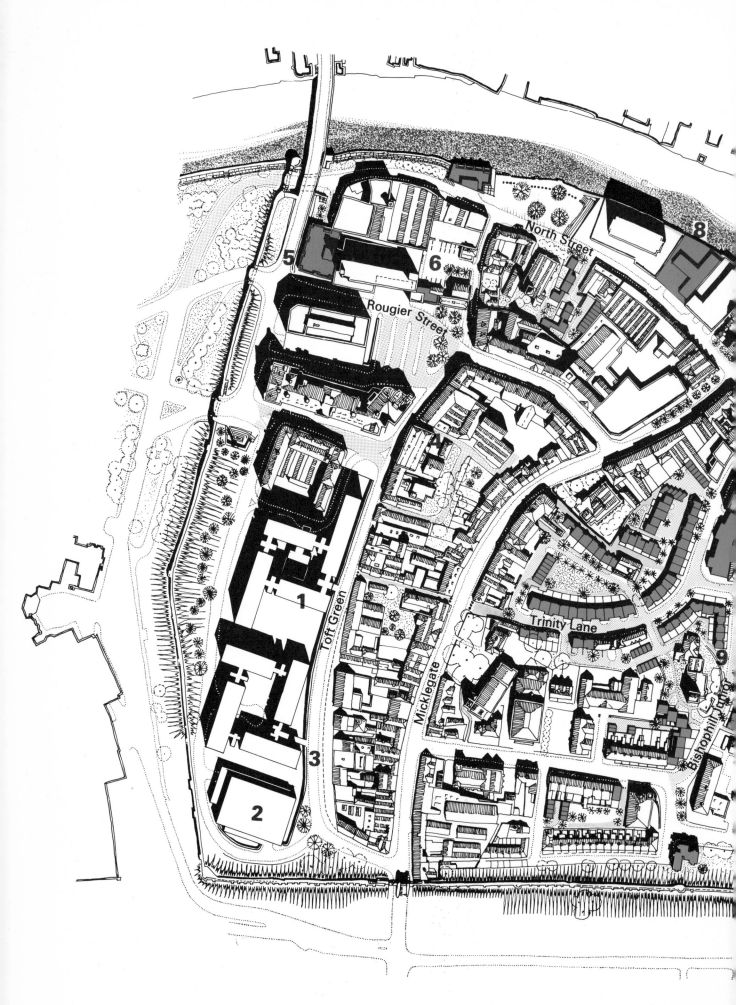

North Street

8

5

6

Rougier Street

4

Toft Green

1

Micklegate

Trinity Lane

9

3

Bishophill Junior

2

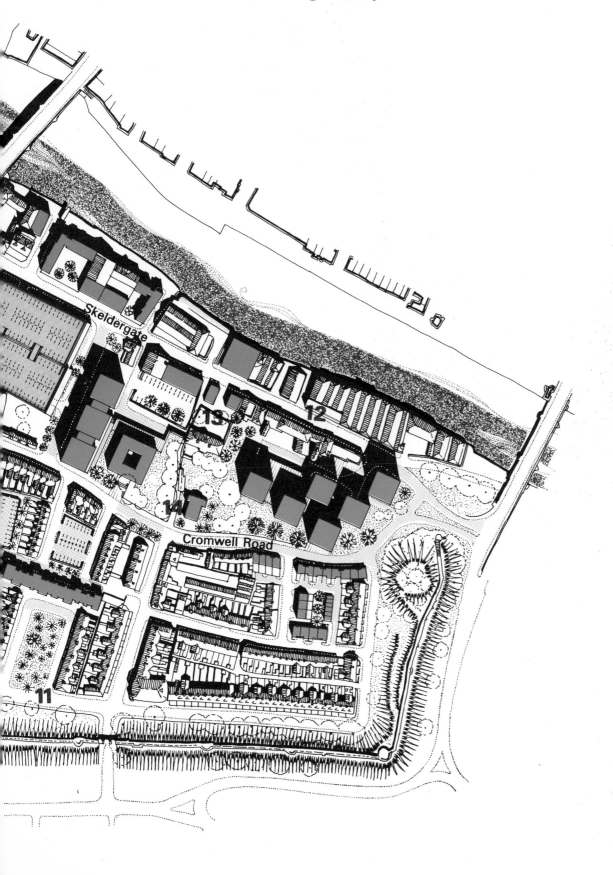

	New buildings
	New paving
	New roads
	New pedestrian areas
✳	New trees
◯	Existing trees

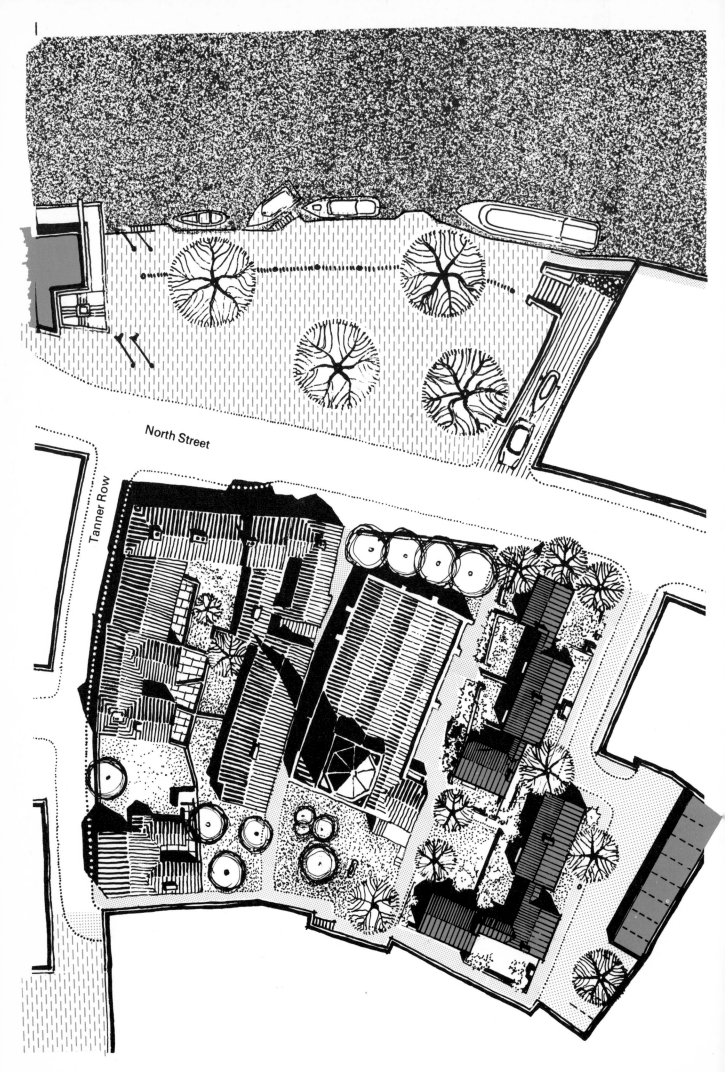

North Street

Tanner Row

135 A new setting for All Saints' Church, North Street

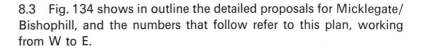

▓	New buildings
░	New paving
▒	New roads
	New pedestrian areas
✳	New trees
○	Existing trees

8.3   Fig. 134 shows in outline the detailed proposals for Micklegate/Bishophill, and the numbers that follow refer to this plan, working from W to E.

8.4   The new Railway Offices recently approved are shown in heavy outline and a suggestion is made in light outline (**1**) for their later extension in a manner which would allow of the survival and conversion of the Old Station of 1841 facing Toft Green and of the hotel building of 1853. It is suggested that car parking should be taken out of the courtyards of the new buildings and concentrated in a 4-deck car park at Bar Lane (**2**). This would accommodate 285 cars, required by BR on their present ratio to floor space, close to their point of entry to the walled city.

8.5   Toft Green (**3**) is unnecessarily wide for the uses to which it will be put and it is proposed that the warehouses, etc., facing it should be advanced, as and when rebuilt, to a new building line which will liberate the backs of the houses in Micklegate without loss of floor space : to encourage this process the carriageway could be narrowed at an early date.

8.6   An existing lane (**4**) is used to open up the backs of the Micklegate houses between Barker Lane and Railway Street so that excrescences can be removed and rear servicing and parking provided.

8.7   Tanner's Moat (**5**), being superseded by the new loop W of Station Road, is built over by a 3-storey office building providing 20,000 sq. ft. to help pay for the relocations referred to in para. 8.2.2 above. It does not infringe existing sight lines to the Minster and helps reduce the dominance of the tall buildings on each side of Rougier Street.

8.8   Tanner Street (**6**) off Tanner Row is opened up to give better rear servicing space and to enable the gap on Rougier Street to be filled.

8.9   A detailed study has been made of the environment of All Saints, North Street (**7**), perhaps the most beautiful of all York parish churches, so as to see how far the good example set by the Ings Property Co. cottages can be followed.. Fig. 135 shows all old buildings reconditioned for living in, and a group of new cottages on

136 All Saints', North Street

the vacant site at present proposed for a car park. The whole group, with its miniature scale, enhancing the view of the church from all angles, and with the good 17th century house to the W of it restored, could be further opened up to the river by a simplification of the design of the public garden which could be conveniently undertaken when North Street is realigned. It would also improve the amenities of the new hotel.

8.10   It is further suggested that the use of the vacant site E of the Viking Hotel as another public open space should if possible be reconsidered. The view from this point is less happy and the effect would be to isolate the regrettably tall block of the hotel on both sides. A restaurant or public house at the level of the riverside walk is indicated (**8**), with car parking below (displaced from alongside All Saints).

8.11   A similar but more extensive exercise has been undertaken to deal with the at present deplorable environment of St. Mary's, Bishophill (**9**), with its Saxon/Norman tower, and in so doing to enhance the amenities and viability of Micklegate itself. This whole quarter on the crest of the hill is of considerable interest and potentiality. There is the strongly marked Victorian character of Priory Street, which deserves to be protected by some improvements and the provision of garage space at the rear of the terraces, of which Dewsbury Terrace is the most attractive. There is the group of buildings dominated by the mid-Georgian No. 13 Bishophill Senior, which has a superb rococo ceiling and other good fittings (**10**)—all overshadowed by a large warehouse which must be removed. There are the good Georgian fronts in Trinity Lane, at present converted into a laundry. And there is the church itself, hemmed in between a large shed and a waste of car-parking.

8.12   It is proposed that the opportunity of the demolition of the warehouse on the corner of Bishophill Senior should be seized to realign Bishophill Junior so that it heads straight for No. 13 and gives space for a new setting for the church. Fig. 143 and fig. 144 show how it would form the centre piece of a 'village' of 75 3- and 2-storey terrace houses with garages, appropriate in scale and materials to the surroundings, with a further 12 flats in a small block at the entrance to Lower Priory Street, designed to recapture the sense of enclosure which recent housing has tended to weaken. The total of 87 dwellings on 4 acres gives a density of 80 p.p.a.

137   Micklegate : 'Virtually all the frontages of this handsome street have some townscape value'

138 Skeldergate: 'an important row of eighteenth century warehouses'

8.13 Bishophill Senior and the realigned Cromwell Road, which form the spine of the eastern part of the sector, are also the boundary between an at present acceptable residential area (**11**) of small terrace freeholds, some lately improved, and the more difficult block of mixed warehouses, obsolete housing and vacant land running down the slope to Skeldergate. As regards the residential area in the crook of the walls, a sketch layout is included to show how, by thinning out the more congested dwellings, the two needs of such areas—greenery and space for cars—can be introduced. In this case, for a net loss of only one-eighth of the dwellings (made good in para. 8.12 above), a large green square is gained, with children's play space, garages are provided for one-third of the houses and parking space for the remainder. Freeholders may wish to consider forming a local Housing Society with such or similar aims.

8.14 The area between Cromwell Road and Skeldergate contains an important row of 18th century warehouses (**12**) and Lady Middleton's Hospital (**13**), rebuilt in 1829. It is vital to the character of the area that these buildings should survive, and with them the steeply descending Carr's Lane (**14**), with its ancient flagstones and glimpses of north bank spires. With the clearance of all other buildings E of Buckingham Street a comprehensive development area of 2.75 acres will become available, exclusive of existing private open spaces and churchyards. Fig. 134 shows a possible redevelopment consisting wholly of offices in small blocks varying in height between 3-stories and 9, depending on their position on the slope, the overall height limit being below 117 O.D. (This limit is proposed elsewhere in this report to safeguard the silhouette of the Minster at long distance.) The use of discontinuous blocks rather than slabs is in deference to the fall of the ground, the need to preserve existing trees and make space for new, and above all the scale of York. The gross floor space is 235,000 sq. ft. and there is parking under the blocks, reached from the two ends of the site, for 235 cars, which is well within the capacity of adjacent streets. Office development on this scale is of course dependent on regional demand factors almost impossible to assess at this point of time. If the demand should not materialise, flats could replace offices over all or a part of the site.

8.15 We come finally to the Micklegate Study Area itself (fig. 143) the first conservation priority in this sector. Figs. 139, 141, 142 show the land use maps, building condition and building age maps for the study area. Virtually all (except 5) of the frontages to this handsome street have some townscape value, and some are outstanding, our grading being as follows:

A	12 units	C	52 units
B	13 ,,	D	29 ,,

Particularly important on the S side are the early 18th century range containing the Queen's Hotel, Nos. 53/55 (probably by Carr) and the 14th century timber-framed houses in front of Holy Trinity. Returning on the N side 118/20 is an outstanding facade of 1742-50, and further on are Micklegate House of 1753 and its 1727 neighbour, with a later top-storey added to match. As the street curves and descends towards Ouse Bridge granite sets replace tarmac and another great mid-18th century house (Nos. 52/54) dominates the outside of the bend. The new Co-op frontage then comes into view. (See Appendix B). Here it would be helpful if the recent widening of the carriageway, done to conform with a now obsolete improvement line, could be modified at least sufficiently to allow plane trees to be planted in the pavement.

8.16 Figs. 141 and 142 show, as far as possible where many units are of multiple date, the age and condition of the riparian buildings. As with other study areas, horizontal and vertical land-use diagrams (figs. 139 and 140) are given for both sides of the street and show a fairly consistent shopping use at pavement level and rather more residence upstairs than might have been expected. Vacant storeys figure less prominently than in Petergate.

8.17 We strongly support the Council's policy that both surviving frontages of Micklegate should be retained as they stand: the street is included for grants in the Town Scheme. It is equally important, if this result is to be secured, that residential or office use should predominate above shops. Of the two conspicuous non-conformers with this principle, the Co-op is too recent and Kennings Garage (which has a servicing value on a main motor car entry) too costly to remove. The vital task is therefore to protect the central stretch of the street between these intruders.

8.18 The closing of the street to all vehicles other than private cars travelling downhill and servicing vehicles for limited hours will alone increase its attraction. With the progressive removal of backland industry and redevelopment of backland dereliction planning will have done all within its power to enhance residential and business values.

8.19 We cross Ouse Bridge, relieved of the majority of its present traffic load, and (the noise reduction making it tolerable to do so) lean on the balustrades and look up and downstream at the four frontages of the river contained by Lendal Bridge on one side and Skeldergate Bridge on the other. This is a convenient point at which to give some consideration to this vital element in the York scene.

139 The Micklegate study area : existing ground floor land use

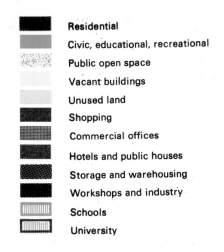

- ■ Residential
- ■ Civic, educational, recreational
- ▨ Public open space
- □ Vacant buildings
- □ Unused land
- ■ Shopping
- ▦ Commercial offices
- ■ Hotels and public houses
- ▨ Storage and warehousing
- ■ Workshops and industry
- ▥ Schools
- ▥ University

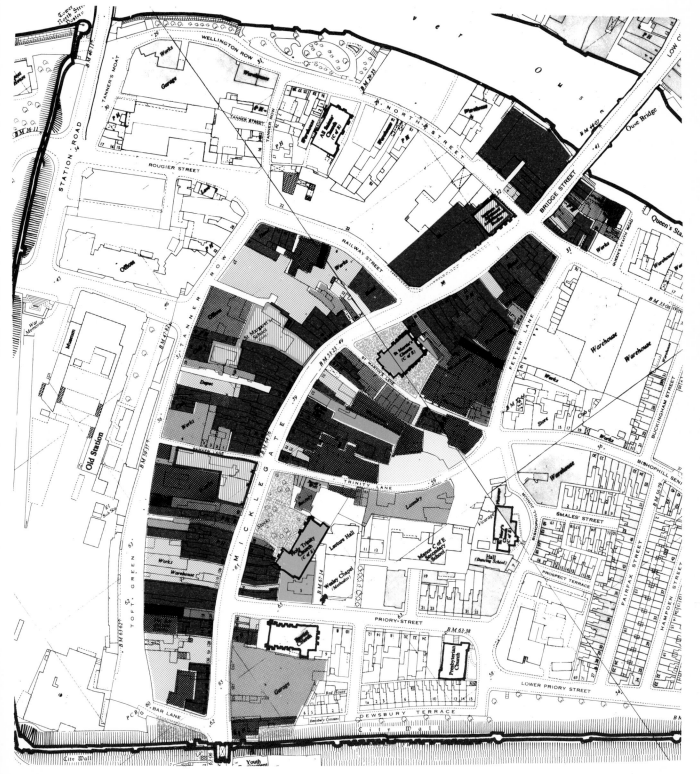

Northside of Micklegate

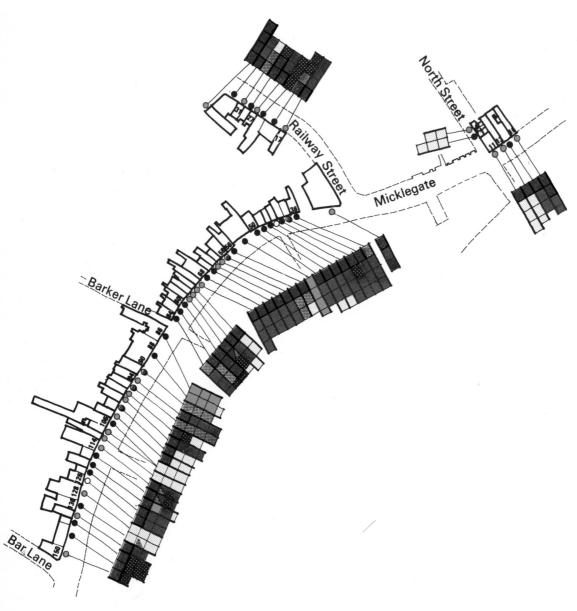

Residential

Civic, educational, recreational

Vacant

Shopping

Commercial offices

Hotels and public houses

Storage and warehousing

Workshops and industry

Access to upper floors

● Existing separate access

● Separate access but needs improving

◎ Access through ground floor

○ Access through adjoining premises

Southside of Micklegate

141 Micklegate study area : buildings condition map

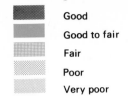

Good

Good to fair

Fair

Poor

Very poor

Micklegate study area : buildings age map

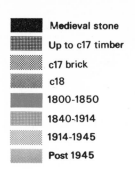

Medieval stone

Up to c17 timber

c17 brick

c18

1800-1850

1840-1914

1914-1945

Post 1945

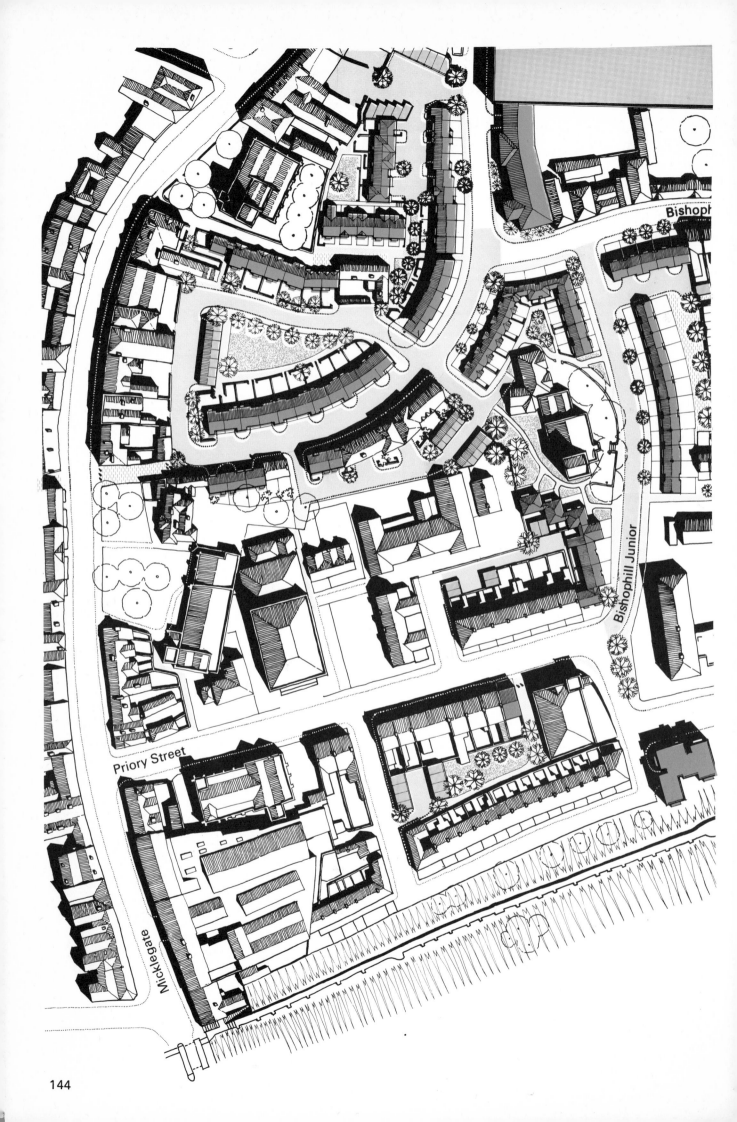

Bishoph

Bishophill Junior

Priory Street

Micklegate

144

143   Micklegate study area : proposal map

 New buildings

Garages

New roads

Paving

Grass/landscapes

Existing trees

New trees

144   A new setting for St. Mary's, Bishophill

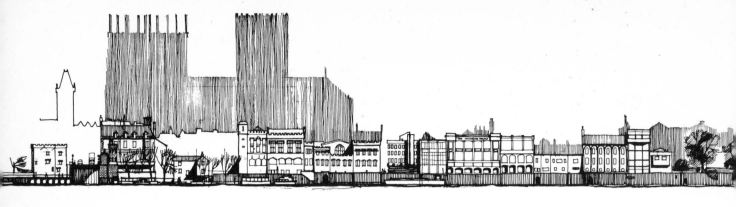

The River

8.20 'USE THE OUSE'. The fading slogan on the old warehouse on Queen's Staith symbolises the decline in river traffic which has persisted steadily for two centuries.

8.21 Vessels up to 230 tons can navigate the river up to York, and an average of two loaded craft a day now pass through Naburn locks. They may carry fuel-oil, coal, gum, straw-bond, wood pulp, paper, cocoa-beans, cocoa-butter, grain, soya beans, concentrated cordials, refined sugar or apricot pulp, but all are imports. Nothing comes out of York by river.

145   Left bank above Ouse Bridge : 'the middle distance is almost Venetian'

8.22 Of all the firms situated along both banks of the Ouse and the Foss within the walls, only eight use the river for goods transport. Above Ouse Bridge, Herald Printers bring in a barge a month carrying up to 50 tons of newsprint, and risk the floods which can bring the river up to 16 feet above summer level. Below the bridge on Queen's Staith, Rowntrees handle three or four barges a year through their bonded warehouse, the finest on the river, and an average of one a week through the tenants of the Corporation's modern warehouse upstream. Stewart Esplen and Greenhough bring in an average of a barge a day carrying dried fruit. Other warehouses on Queen's Staith prefer to use the road behind. On the Foss, Walkers operate a dredger which keeps the channel clear to Naburn and collects some 150 tons of builders' sand per week in the process. Three firms handle between them some 400 barge-loads a year, and three (including the Power Station) use the water for cooling.

8.23 Pleasure boats—launches and skiffs—are operated by two firms from below Lendal Bridge and from South Esplanade, and at present muster 8 large launches and 20 skiffs between them. The York Motor Boat Club has some 138 members; the Rowing Club, with its boathouse by Lendal Bridge (also used by the University) holds a regatta twice a year. For anglers, the most popular reach within the walls is the terrace of the Museum Gardens. The Foss (partly because of the 15s. lock charge) is little used for boating, though it has potentialities capable of exploitation and improvement.

146   Left bank below Ouse Bridge : urbane and civilised'

8.24 These mixed uses are reflected in the riverside buildings on both banks.

8.25 Looking downstream from Lendal, beyond the wooded landing stages, the middle distance is almost Venetian, with Gothic and neo-Gothic architecture rising straight out of the water. Beyond the Guildhall the left bank is frankly commercial, with the Evening Press and Yorkshire Herald printing works and the brutally ugly backs of some of the bigger shop premises on Coney Street; in between are waste spaces which are the former gardens of the once residential properties facing the street. Only two of the riverside buildings on this

147 Right bank above Ouse Bridge : 'a rugged rather than a sophisticated character'

148 Right bank below Ouse Bridge : 'The varied and picturesque warehouses of Queen's Staith'

stretch, apart from the Guildhall, are of individual merit; one with a solid round-arched Victorian facade, the other a quite handsome former brewery building close to Ouse Bridge. But the general effect all along, with buildings rising sheer from the water-side, interspersed with the vacant plots (on which a few trees grow) has a distinctive urban quality. The only public accesses to this stretch of riverside are an alley from Church Lane, close to the old brewery, and another adjoining Woolworths. They both lead to ancient landing stages. There were once others.

8.26 The right bank is wooded on both sides of Lendal Bridge, with a tall and glum warehouse rising behind. All Saints' spire and its tiny supporting cottages are seen beyond, soon to be overshadowed by the square mass of the Viking Hotel, made all the more dominant by the open space proposed on either side of it. There are no other buildings of interest above Ouse Bridge, but below it the right bank changes character again to a working quayside, with the varied and picturesque warehouses of Queen's Staith. These, except for an unworthy recent addition, increase in interest as one goes down-stream, the last before Skeldergate Bridge being outstandingly handsome.

8.27 The left bank below Ouse Bridge is different again, urbane and civilised, with cobbled quay, three riverside pubs and a consistent residential scale set off by the backcloth spires of the Law Courts and charmingly rounded off by the terraced cottages of Tower Place. Here the mid-city riverscape ends appropriately, as it began, in a mass of mature trees.

8.28 The three bridges are themselves all good of their kind, the monumental stone arches of Ouse Bridge (1820) delicately comple-mented by the Victorian cast iron of Lendal (1863) and Skeldergate (1881).

8.29 The strip elevations (which of course exaggerate the dominance of background features) show the riverside buildings as they exist, with proposals added. (Figs. 149 and 152.) These can be summarised as follows:

Left bank above Ouse Bridge
8.30 The Riverside Walk proposed by Professor Adshead in 1948 and recent criticism of it have been carefully considered. Whatever its merits as an idea and its likely popularity in use, it seems a pity now to draw back from a project to which recent buildings have been obliged to conform. It is all a matter of how it is done. Provided a continuous promenade or projected balcony are avoided and the route passes into and out of buildings, with frequent changes of character and links with Coney Street, it could liven up some of the drearier frontages without spoiling the good ones. Fig. 150 and fig. 151 show the Walk and its connections, new and old, with

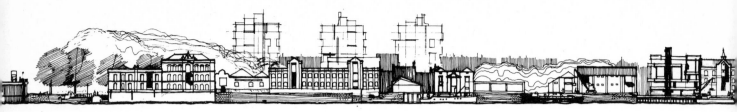

Coney Street, and show how it could thread through Camerons, improve the back of Woolworths (with help from paint), break out into a garden, be arcaded through Leak & Thorp, cantilever in front of the Yorkshire Herald, pass through the Guildhall and emerge at a lower level among the trees and boatyards below the Yorkshire Club.

Right bank above Ouse Bridge

8.31 The similar project on this bank gets less help from old buildings, and the flashy way it has been handled so far is not encouraging. It is important from now on to preserve or match the texture of the river wall and to aim at a rugged rather than a sophisticated character. The stretch NW of the new hotel is dealt with in the previous section.

Left bank below Ouse Bridge

8.32 King's Staith should no longer be used for casual car-parking. The setting is handsome, needing little to bring it into full pedestrian use as part of the N bank riverside walk. The view from Ouse bridge is excellent and only requires the incident of a middle-ground feature to throw the whole scene into strong perspective. For this, and to remedy the present lack of such facilities on the river, we suggest the building of a tea-room-restaurant, facing south and looking up and down river and across to the activities of Queen's Staith. This could be well sited above the junction of South Esplanade and King's Staith,

150 Riverside Walk

entered from the higher level road at the end of Low Friargate and spanning over the existing ramp. By siting the kitchens and service facilities on top and slinging the restaurant below over the water, the building would command unique views of the river.

Right bank below Ouse Bridge

8.33   It is to be hoped that river traffic will continue busy enough for Queen's Staith to retain the character of a working quayside, and for the best of its Victorian warehouses to survive. The Corporation's new warehouse is a sad come-down, and it is not proposed that warehouse use, with its heavy traffic generation, should be continued on the cleared sites adjacent to it. The drawing shows these sites redeveloped with blocks of flats and maisonettes (or a hotel) taking advantage of the beautiful view across the river; these should be powerfully modelled to accord with their neighbours. It also shows the crude jetty recently constructed brought up to the standard of the quays to the N of it.

8.34   The strip elevations show the disorderly way in which the right bank has developed, compared with the left. The new hotel contributes powerfully to this disorder. It should be the object in future to work towards a more unified picture and one more worthy of the heart of York.

151   The Riverside Walk from Ouse Bridge

153 Stonegate 'will be paved from wall to wall'

**154 St. Helen's Square, with the Yorkshire
Insurance building on the left**

The Central Shopping Area (Sector 2)

8.35 Considering the economic pressure upon it, the commercial and civic heart of York is still full of character and interest, but all is at present drowned in traffic. Consequently, the sense of liberation in this sector, and the economic gain, will be greater here than in any other part of the walled city.

8.36 This closely packed sector is bounded in the S by the river, on the E and W by important bus routes and on the N by the Aldwark renewal area. To the NE, where the Swinegate and Petergate areas have already been studied in detail, it forms part of the setting of the Minster, and beautiful glimpses of the Minster, which must be protected, are to be had from St. Helen's Square, King's Square and St. Sampson's Square.

8.37 The sector contains by far the largest number of our classified buildings of any in the city, and is outstanding among commercial centres in this respect. The numbers are:

A	42	C	103
B	100	D	124

8.38 The effect of the traffic proposals in this report will be to remove from this sector all but labelled private cars and taxis, all servicing vehicles except during the limited servicing hours proposed in chapter 5, all motor-cycles and mopeds, and all through traffic other than buses using the Parliament Street–Davygate–Lendal cross-route. Stonegate, Low Petergate, Coney Street and New Street will be paved from wall to wall and closed to all vehicles except during servicing hours, and paved spaces and trees will be substituted for tarmac elsewhere.

8.39 Fig. 156 (to which the following notes refer) shows the effect of these restrictions and the pedestrian network in its entirety, and it will be remembered that no point in the sector is more than five minutes walk from one of four car parks providing between them about 5,000 car spaces.

8.40 Coney Street (1) itself is likely to benefit most from these controls and the effect of the removal of the carriageway and of redundant street furniture is indicated by sketch 155. The riverside walk and the alleys leading down to it will enhance the interest of the street. But its charm, which derives from the contrast between buildings of many periods and sizes and a general verticality, could be lost (as has been demonstrated in Spurriergate) if its small units were to amalgamate into large frontages on redevelopment, and a firm planning policy will be necessary to control this. Additional provision for the big space users is made elsewhere.

8.41 The street vista is handsomely closed by the Yorkshire Insurance building, one of the two best buildings in St. Helen's Square (2). The paving of Coney Street, extended into the square and furnished with three plane trees to veil its one dull side, and the consequent narrowing of the carriageway, will enhance the dignity of the Mansion House and give a sorely needed sense of repose to this small but beautiful civic space (fig. 157). The pavement should also be widened to 10 feet on the W side.

155 Pedestrianised Coney Street

New buildings
New paving
New roads
New pedestrian areas
New trees
Existing trees

New building

 New paving

 Existing trees

 New trees

8.42   Continuing westwards, the important corner site at (**3**) should be rebuilt with four stories facing Museum Street and three facing and framing the forecourt of the Judges' Lodging. Returning to Blake Street the importance of the view back towards St. Leonard's is apparent, particularly in early morning sunlight. The portico of the Assembly Rooms has never commanded any vista or civic space, and the charm of the early 18th century range opposite precludes anything being done about it.

8.43   The S side of Davygate (**4**) demonstrates the inappropriateness in York of wholesale rebuilding to a unified design, and it is to be hoped that the Gas Board may yet reconsider their plans to do so on the N side.

8.44   With St. Sampson's Square (**5**) we break out of the medieval maze into the 'Thursday Market', which is still just intelligible as a market place despite the hole blown in its E side by Parliament Street and the solid mass of parked cars. Fig. 158 shows how the advanced building line on the S side of Parliament Street (for which the case is made in Chapter 4) gives the possibility of a terminal feature at the E end of Davygate and helps restore the sense of enclosure of the Square. The removal of the parked cars will enable most of the floor of the Square itself to be paved and cobbled, with access for servicing over the paved surface in restricted hours (fig. 159). The existing lavatories remain, with their superstructure redesigned. Plane trees complete the picture, so disposed that the vistas of the Minster from Feasegate and of St. Sampson's Church from the Square are not interrupted.

159 St. Sampson's Square

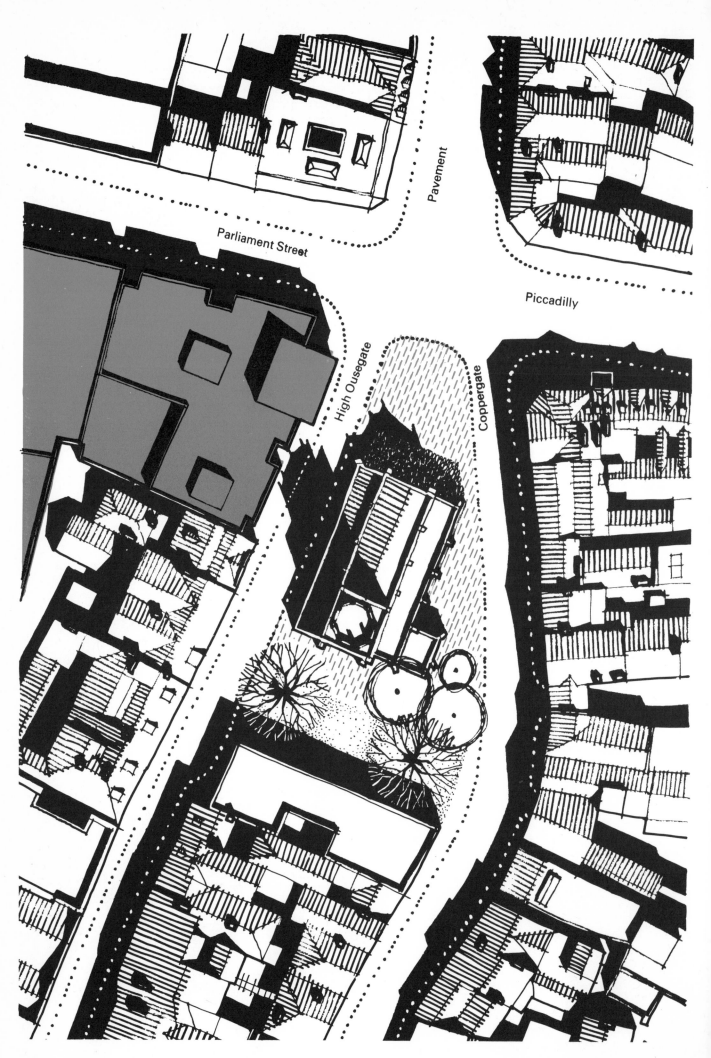

Pavement

Parliament Street

Piccadilly

High Ousegate

Coppergate

160 A new setting for All Saints' Pavement

 New building

 New paving

 Existing trees

New trees

161 A new setting for All Saints' Pavement

8.45 The narrowing of the carriageway of Parliament Street to 24 feet, which will allow of the rebuilding of its S side, can take place as soon as the Merchantgate car park is in use. It is proposed that the rebuilding (fig. 150) should leave the sensitively-converted Electricity showrooms untouched to form a small re-entrant, should allow of the extension northwards over a sight-line arcade of the Midland Bank, and should eventually allow Barclays Bank to extend similarly so as to restore to All Saints' Pavement its original setting in a re-entrant (**6**). (Fig. 160.) In the meantime the formidable visual competition it endures from Kirby's beefy Victorian facade could be softened by a projecting wing from the new frontage and some trees (**7**). (Fig. 161.)

8.46 The effect of the new market place (**8**), with its delightful backdrop of the restored backs of the Shambles, is totally ruined by the enormous backside of Marks & Spencer's, which has gone far to spoil a carefully handled and public-spirited enterprise. The goods entrance at the E end of Shambles is almost as damaging, and all in all there is no better example in York of the need to ensure that the big multiples are not let into sensitive medieval surroundings.

162 'There is no better example in York of . . .

163 . . . 'the need to ensure that the big multiples are not let into sensitive medieval surroundings

Goodramgate

Church Street

King's Square

Shambles

Patrick Pool

Market

Silver Street

new building

new paving

new trees

existing trees

8.47   In Shambles itself, recently so well restored, the existing paving is essential to its character and should be preserved.

8.48   King's Square (**9**), despite recent demolitions, is still potentially one of the pleasantest corners in York, but the din and muddle of traffic at present makes this hard to realise. A treatment similar to St. Sampson's Square is proposed for it (fig. 164), with all parking eliminated, the raised flower bed removed and the paved space at two levels extended right up to the buildings on the S and E, and furnished with seats and tubs. A lime tree or two near the kerb frame the beautiful view of the W towers of the Minster along Petergate.

8.49   We now head straight along this street (studied in Chapter 7) for the

165   King's Square—a potential oasis

166 Deangate: 'a main traffic distributor'

167 Minster Yard, the future Close

Minster Precinct (Sector 3)

8.50   This sector contains the following classified buildings, in which the Minster itself can only rate as a single unit:

A	21	C	55
B	74	D	20

8.51   The field of influence of the Minster, its precise boundaries as a precinct, are difficult to define. On the N and W they are the city walls, but to the S and E the changing pattern of the city has ebbed and flowed against its flank. The last ebb created Duncombe Place in 1860 and the traffic flow of Deangate from Petergate to Goodramgate in 1903 brought not only the precinct, but the fabric of the Minster itself into too close proximity with the daily movement of the city. The effect of traffic is not therefore only one of vibration and destruction but of acute environmental intrusion. This has cut pedestrian access down to bolt-hole proportions.

8.52   The present effects of through traffic alongside the Minster are too well known to need restatement here. The first principle of this sector plan is to restore to the Minster a precinctual sense of quiet and space worthy of the magnificence of the buildings. The Sector Plan (fig. 168) shows the strategy.

Approaches

8.53   The reproduction of part of Smith's City Map of 1822 (fig. 169) shows the roads introduced and the buildings demolished since that date. One can see from this plan how hemmed in the Minster was before Lob Lane was converted to Duncombe Place and when the Deanery faced across the Minster Yard with its garden running back to Holy Trinity. One can also see how College Street, built up on both sides, burst out immediately below the huge East End.

8.54   Now these spaces are all inter-connected but unrelated. Petergate–Duncombe Place is a traffic junction with car-parking. Minster Yard is a car park, Deangate a main traffic distributor, College Street a slip road which completes a circuit. Yet all these have the potential at foot scale of being connected, dramatic approach routes of variety giving onto a grassed and paved Close which echoes the Dean's Park on the N side. The difference would be that whereas the Park is a quiet area to which people have to go specially, the new Close would be busy with townspeople and tourists.

8.55   To achieve this Close the first necessity is to remove Deangate from the point where it no longer need service buildings, at the end of the Minster workshops. This would allow the workshops to serve the Minster without the hazard of heavy traffic. The West End would be approached by Duncombe Place, from which Precentors Court and the Purey Cust properties could be served.

8.56   Pedestrian approaches to the Minster would now be:

1   from Bootham Bar (via the new Exhibition Square, mentioned separately);

2   from Duncombe Place opened up around the War Memorial to allow movement across High Petergate and through the gap alongside St. Michael-le-Belfrey;

3   through Minster Gate from Stonegate, bursting into the new Close;

4   from Holy Trinity by way of Goodramgate as at present; and

5   from Low Petergate via Hornpot Lane (at present blocked).

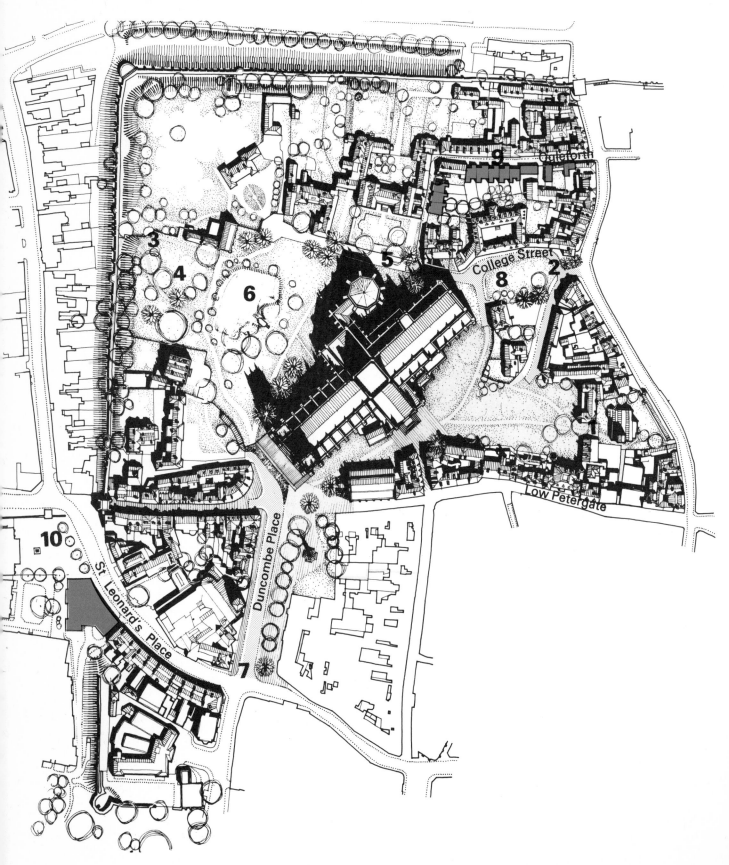

New buildings
New paving
New roads
New pedestrian areas
New trees
Existing trees

Road breakthroughs

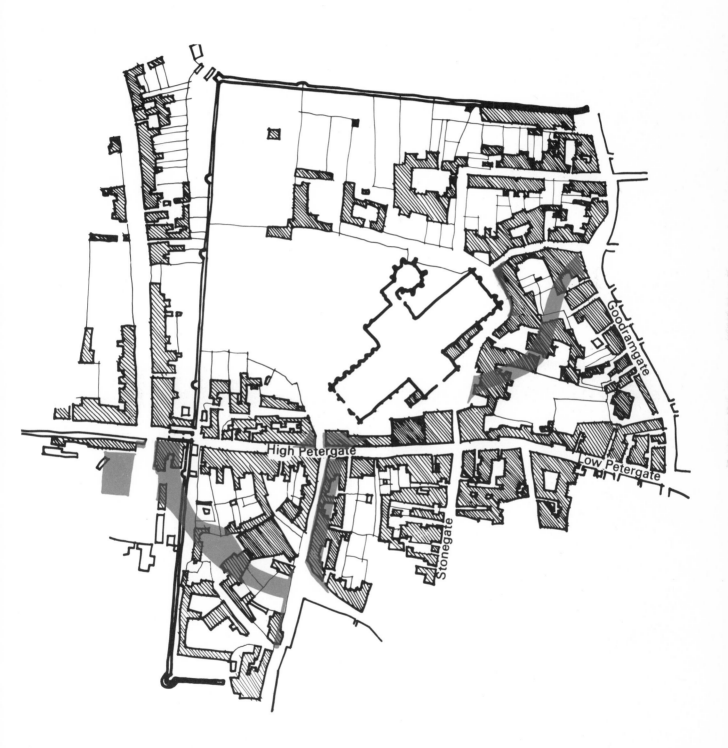

8.57 This last approach (**1**) would allow (almost in its entirety) the one flank view of the Minster which can be gained from the city side. To achieve it would mean opening up the grounds of the Minster Song School and acquiring part of the open space at the rear of the York College for Girls. It would also mean the demolition of the existing asbestos extension to this school, a building of no merit which ruins the glimpse of the Minster from Goodramgate. It would be possible to rebuild equivalent space on much the same site, but lifting the building to allow access under and reorientating it to provide a framework both to the Minster and to Holy Trinity.

8.58 This large space (fig. 170) created between the Minster on the W and Holy Trinity on the E would form the body of the new Close and from it pedestrians could approach both the South Transept of the Minster (the main entrance) and cross to the East End and round into College Street and Deangate.

8.59 At the junction of Goodramgate, Deangate and College Street (**2**) a simplification of the traffic and pedestrian routes would be necessary. The fragile gatehouse over the junction of the latter should be restricted to pedestrians. This means providing a short diversion across the end of College Green for vehicular traffic and forming a subsidiary junction onto Deangate. To do so both protects the Gatehouse and simplifies the Deangate/Goodramgate traffic junction.

170　The Close as it never was, but will be

8.60 Ogleforth and Chapter House Street would remain as the present delightful approach to the East End and Dean's Park, giving a splendid view of the Central Tower with the Chapter House towering over the walls of the Treasurer's House.

8.61 From the west a new access is proposed to allow pedestrians crossing from the car park in Gillygate to continue onto the city walls and by turning northwards for approximately 100 yards descend by new stairs into Dean's Park (**3**). This dog-leg is to deter short cuts —which intrude on the quietness of the Park—by making it much simpler for shoppers and workers to turn south and descend Bootham Bar.

8.62 The circle of pedestrian approaches is now complete. We turn to the consideration of the spaces themselves.

The Dean's Park
8.63 The north side is beautifully kept and a walk around the walls on this section reveals the Minster through trees and gardens maintained by the Dean and Chapter and enjoyed by all. It is the most exciting stretch of wall in the whole circuit; the Minster dominates and the park is a perfect foil. From the walls one's eye includes all the private areas behind and alongside Purey Cust Chambers, the Dean's Garden, Minster Court and Greys Court. It is only at ground level one realises how much smaller the park is.

8.64 It is suggested that as much as is compatible with privacy and security should be opened up to connect, physically as well as visually, the walls and Minster. The area available to achieve this is the land N of Purey Cust Chambers and S of the Dean's Garden (**4**). By re-siting the garden equipment store with the main body of the Minster workshops and by opening up the paddock behind Archbishop Roger's arcade (which would now form a landscape feature) virtually 100 per cent. more depth could be added to the park.

8.65 The main body of the existing park has paths which are too wide. When car parking can be provided in Monkgate the pressure for using the Park as reserve car space for St. William's College should be resisted and the present access converted back to lawn.

8.66 The road to the Deanery, Minster Court and the Treasurer's House (**5**) has to be kept open. It is unfortunate that for security reasons the Park is fenced off from this road, as it reduces the sense of space which should run into the forecourts of the buildings so that they and not railings define the precinct. Landscaping is needed which gives a larger sense of space around the Lady Chapel. The introduction of a few carefully placed trees would convey this, and these are shown on the plan. Similarly at the SW end of the Park against the flank of the Minster a group of trees of large scale but open texture such as planes would draw the Park down to the West End and give a visual connection with Duncombe Place.

8.67 The possibility of opening up the reservoir (**6**) and introducing water as a feature of the Park is being considered by the Dean and Chapter. It would form an attractive feature, giving reflections of the Minster and turning the present utilitarian and inaccessible area of underground tanks into an asset.

171 The Dean's Park

High Petergate

Duncombe Place

172   The new Duncombe Place

West Front

8.68   This needs more detailed attention and is shown in fig. 172.

8.69   The conversion of High and Low Petergate to pedestrian streets will open up Duncombe Place as a square, dominated by the West Front of the Minster. It must be the focal point of the whole Precinct. The present state of the area outside the West doors needs no comment. It has been impractical to attempt any proper setting whilst scaffolding obstructed the front. Now two objects must be achieved: a setting for normal day-to-day activity, and sufficient space and dignity for the great occasions when the West doors are used. (Fig. 173.)

8.70   The Plan shows a paved area the whole width of the West Front extending outwards approximately 50 feet from the central doors and descending by two steps to a cobbled and paved reception area. The area of tarmacadam has been greatly reduced and the carriageway remaining is sufficient only to serve adjacent properties and allow turning full circle. Turning in front of the West End will be possible over the cobbled apron on the removal of bollards.

173   The West Front repaved

174 The new Close

8.71 Duncombe Place (fig. 175) provides an excellent oblique approach to the West Front, framed asymmetrically on the W side by buildings and the E by limes and a few sycamores. The line of trees needs to be added to on a soft curve to continue the eye round St. Michael-le-Belfrey into Minster Close. Around the War Memorial the space demands a more sympathetic treatment than sterile dwarf walls. Urbanity could be introduced by more paving and opening up the lawns. The plan also suggests a pedestrian route through to Stonegate passing alongside the remains of the Norman house now buried in the Stonegate backland.

8.72 The junction with Blake Street (7) is shown simplified; the slip road removed and the area of paving and lawn, with a tree added, extending southwards to reduce the present road width and give a firm corner, as originally intended.

South Flank

8.73 From St. Michael-le-Belfrey to the South Transept the ground should be given over entirely to lawn and footpath (fig. 174). Minster Gate, which will still constitute the main approach to the South Transept, is shown with a wide area of paving and one tree in the angle of the building to the east. The large space from here to Holy Trinity extending up to the East End is proposed as an area of lawn and footpaths with some planting where necessary to screen backs of property or emphasise the view.

8.74 College Green (8), at present railed off, is shown opened up as a natural extension of the Close around the East End. A footpath is provided to take pedestrians to the old Gatehouse, and trees planted where they effectively screen the rear of the York College for Girls and frame the view of the Minster from Goodramgate.

8.75 Finally, two areas which are within the Minster Precinct sector but not within the immediate ambience of the Minster are dealt with separately.

175 The new Duncombe Place

176 College Green: 'a natural extension of the Close'

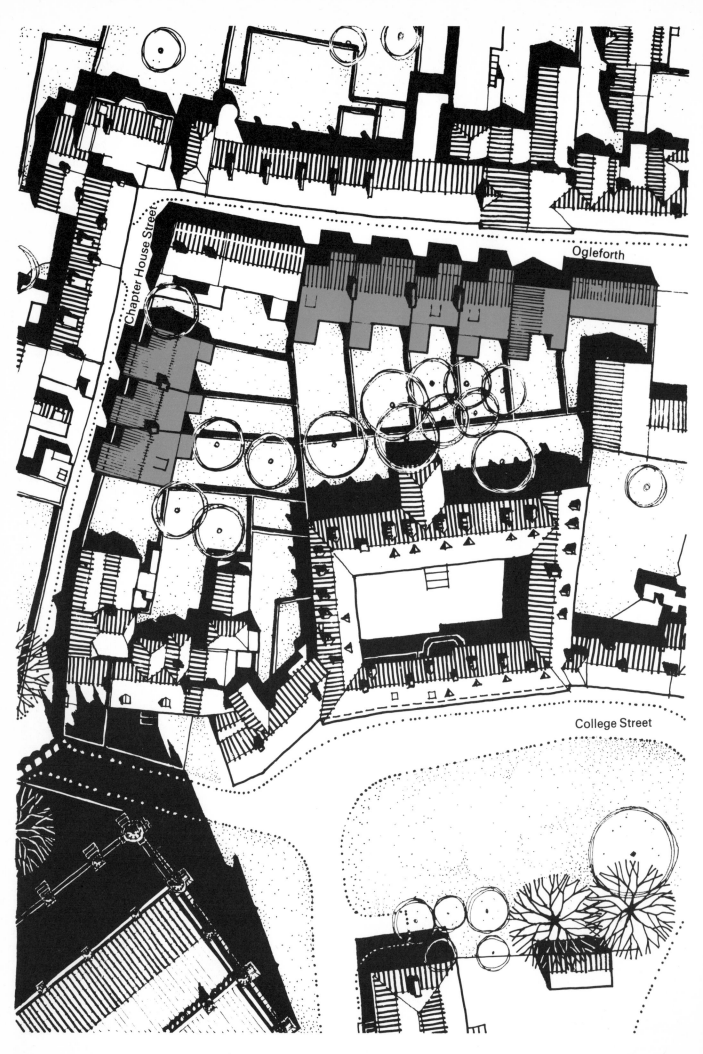

Chapter House Street

Ogleforth

College Street

New building

 Existing trees

 New trees

Ogleforth

8.76   This small street (**9**) parallel to the City Wall from Monk Bar and Goodramgate is shown (fig. 177) restored to intense residential use. The warehouses on the S side which devalue the street and are in close proximity to St. William's College are removed or drastically reduced in size. Housing is introduced on the sites acquired, extending over the cleared land already available. The rear of St. William's College which has a group of maples is incorporated in a courtyard group giving a view over the rooftops to the Minster. The Dutch House is shown incorporated in a small terrace of three town houses.

8.77   Access is provided to the one remaining 19th century brick warehouse which is capable of being converted to residential and studio use.

8.78   In Chapter House Street three small town houses are shown built over the wall on the E side utilising the rear of the large garden of No. 4 College Street.

178 Ogleforth: 'Intensive residential use'

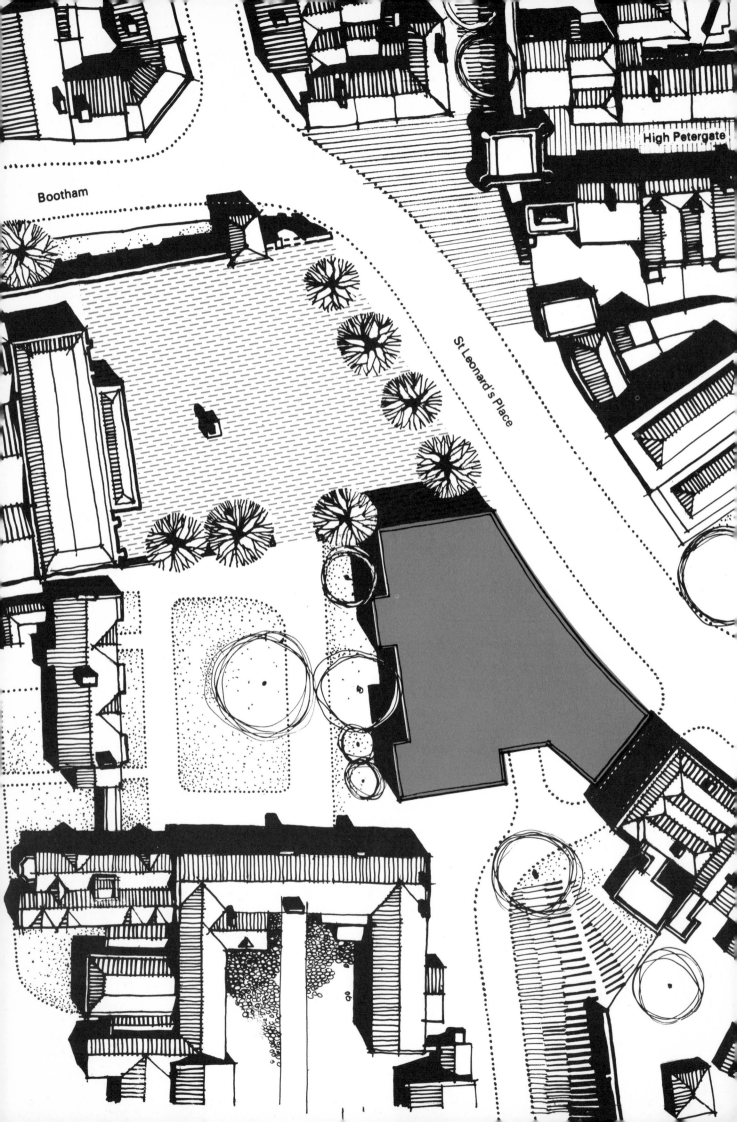

Bootham

High Petergate

St Leonard's Place

new building

---- new paving

☀ new trees

◯ existing trees

St. Leonard's Place

8.79   The conservation of St. Leonard's Crescent is no problem whilst the buildings are occupied by the Corporation and Municipal Offices. However, the space available is inadequate for future municipal needs and the long-term proposal is to provide new civic buildings in the Castle area. Meanwhile, if provision were made for the foreseeable future by extending the Crescent, great improvements to Exhibition Square would be possible and the pressure to move from St. Leonard's eased.

8.80   Our proposals (fig. 179) show the line of St. Leonard's extended to create a new square (**10**) to the front of the Art Gallery and from the third side of a new courtyard to King's Manor. This simple device gives form to an area which though attractive is at present shapeless. It removes the one eyesore, the municipal car park, to backland, strengthens the curve of the Crescent, appropriately frames the King's Manor and gives meaning to Exhibition Square itself —cleared of cars, paved and with lime trees framing the superb view of the Minster West Front. (Fig. 180.) The area made available for civic offices would be approximately 42,500 sq. ft., allowing for a major portion of the ground floor being left open to retain the remains of the city wall and incorporating the wall to St. Mary's Abbey in the building. Car access is provided adjacent to the existing building. The present buildings in St. Leonard's provide approximately 52,500 sq. ft. not including attics. The total available for civic use could therefore be about 95,000 sq. ft. This extension would bring the buildings into good relationship with the De-Grey rooms which could then be used in conjunction with the civic offices.

8.81   Car parking proposals and traffic for this area are dealt with separately, and Gillygate proposals which particularly affect the area are discussed in para. 5.34.

180 Exhibition Square

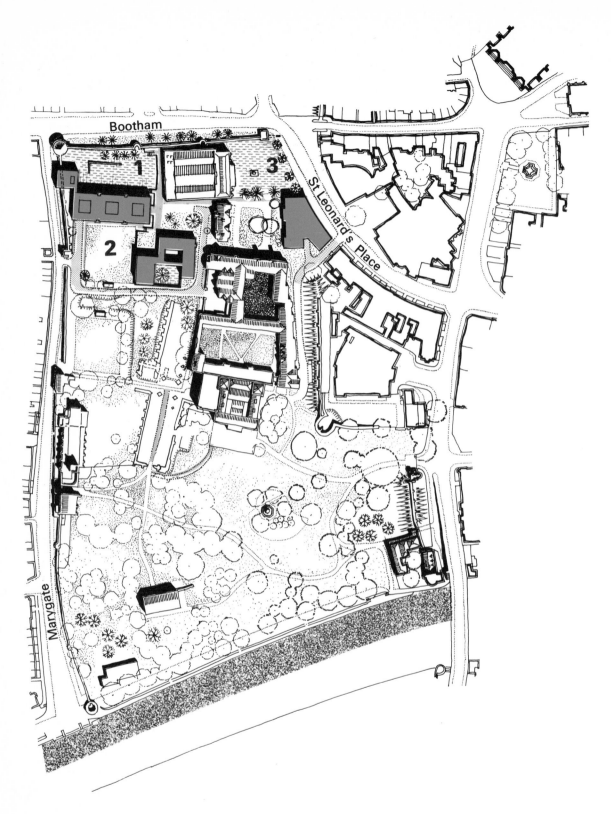

Bootham

1

3

2

St Leonard's Place

Marygate

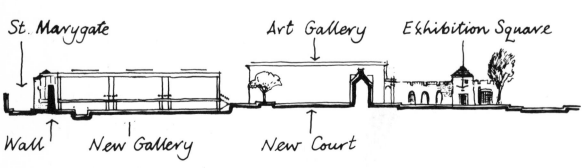

St. Marygate

Art Gallery

Exhibition Square

Wall

New Gallery

New Court

Section : East — West.

King's Manor (Sector 4)

New buildings
New paving
New roads
New pedestrian areas
New trees
Existing trees

8.82   This area, containing the City Art Gallery, the King's Manor, the Museum Gardens with the ruins of St. Mary's Abbey and the Museum of the Yorkshire Philosophical Society, forms an extension to the walled city, but is contained by its own walls and the river. It is the largest public open space within the historic core.

8.83   The sector has the following classified buildings (the King's Manor being one unit).

A 8	C 4
B 3	D 1

The City Art Gallery
8.84   The building dates from the 1870's and until the war had a large Main Hall on the site at present occupied by the Marygate Adult Education centre. This collection of single storey buildings in no way exploits the potential of the setting and our proposals (fig. 181) show a new courtyard (**1**) formed behind the present gallery framed with new civic buildings containing an extension to the gallery, an open sculpture court under the extension, and below ground a car park for 40 cars. This extension, with a small administrative block shown projecting through the gap in the walls of St. Mary's Abbey, could accommodate the School of Art, at present occupying a large part of the space in the existing gallery. Also shown is an additional University building (**2**) (which could be used for Further Education), thus establishing a complex of activities all of which are complementary (fig. 182).

Exhibition Square
8.85   To the front of the gallery the Square (**3**) is shown in its new setting, freed from traffic, paved to St. Leonard's and with a line of lime trees continuing the soft curve of the crescent (fig. 180).

8.86   Service and car access is removed to Marygate with the exception of the light traffic to the rear of the municipal offices, which is given access between the end of the old crescent and the new building which creates the Square. This latter proposal will entail the removal of the brick wall which runs parallel to the King's Manor and will enable the pedestrian walk into the Museum Gardens to be opened up, giving a view of the city wall.

8.87   The complex of courtyards, which give much of the character to the area, will by these proposals be extended and the whole area freed for pedestrian use.

8.88   The separate proposals for Gillygate (fig. 72) indicate how the exterior of the walls on the Bootham side are exposed and enhanced and show how pedestrian access is provided.

182   Extension to the Art Gallery

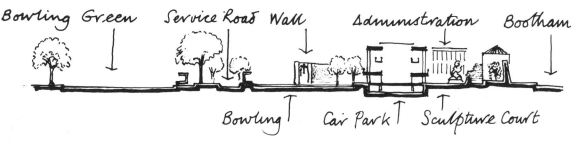

Bowling Green   Service Road Wall   Administration   Bootham

Bowling   Car Park   Sculpture Court

Section : North — South.

183 Entrance court of the King's Manor

King's Manor
8.89 This has been splendidly conserved and its recent additions show how strong but sensitive handling of new buildings in an old setting can be successful. The new service arrangements proposed will free the courtyards now formed on the N side from vehicular traffic (by the building shown continuing the curve of St. Leonard's).

St. Mary's Abbey
8.90 When first obtained by the Yorkshire Philosophical Society in 1828, the Manor Shore was an unsightly wilderness. The ruins of St. Mary's Abbey were rapidly disappearing : they were not only used as a stone quarry, but a row of kilns were converting the stone into lime. But for the protection then and the care since, there might not have been anything of this beautiful ruin standing. As well as preserving the Abbey, the Society also converted the site of the remainder into a Botanical Garden, which now shows all the results of good husbandry in its splendid trees and well kept lawns, and built the Yorkshire Museum abutting the King's Manor and facing the river down the sloping ground.

The Yorkshire Museum
8.91 The original Greek Doric building by Wilkins & Sharp has a 1913 addition of similar form (The Tempest Anderson Hall) designed by Brierley, boldly detailed in reinforced concrete and spanning over the vestibule to the Chapter House. The whole area was conveyed to the Corporation of York under covenant in 1961. Little is necessary in consolidating the established character of the gardens. Accretions, such as have accumulated at the back of the waterworks and obsolete buildings such as the old Baths are shown on our proposals removed and the areas made into open space in keeping with the rest of the Museum Gardens. Public lavatories are better built into the fabric of a larger building than made into free-standing objects disguised with shrubbery. The tarmacadam paths would be improved by gravel and the path which at present passes through the west end of the Abbey ruin is shown resited to the south. The Bowling Greens to the NW of the Abbey are retained, with the new service road to the King's Manor and the Art Gallery extension sited on the raised ground between.

8.92 The river frontage has recently been greatly improved by the work carried out by the Corporation and paid for by the Civic Trust. Excellent paving and cobbled areas have made this river frontage into a worthy termination of the Gardens. It is unfortunate that no provision for direct access from the gardens to the river was made and our proposals show two points allowing this.

Aldwark (Sector 5)

8.93 This sector is dealt with in detail as a study area in Chapter 7.

New building

New pedestrian way

New road

Existing trees

New trees

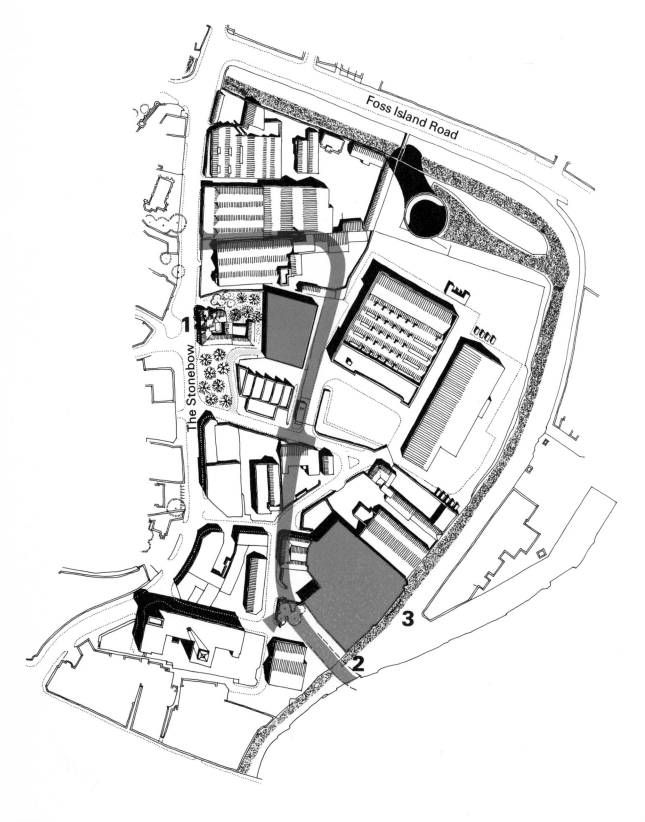

Foss Islands (Sector 6)

8.94 This low-lying area, originally known as the Marsh, developed late in the history of York, as a result of 19th century industrialisation. To the east, the area properly known as the Foss Islands was re-covered from what had originally been the Fishpond of the Foss. The whole area gradually became urban as the Foss developed as a navigable waterway after 1793. Foss Islands Road was constructed after the islands and marsh had been bought by the Corporation in 1853 and the land drained. The Foss Islands generating works were opened in 1900 and part of the undertaking constructed on the S Bank of the Foss including the timber cooling towers replaced in 1940 with the present concrete structure.

8.95 The area (fig. 184) is defined on its west side by the post-war construction of the Stonebow. There survived only one building of historic interest, the Black Swan public house (1), here classified Grade A, mainly because of its excellent interior. Nothing else in the area is of any architectural value, though the cooling tower is a land-mark—particularly from the Minster west end. The post-war develop-ments alongside the Stonebow are well-intentioned but mediocre, and to the rear the land remains under-exploited or contains miscel-laneous industrial uses. Alongside Peaseholme Green is a Victorian industrial group and adjacent to it a laundry. Behind the Black Swan is a forlorn row of Victorian houses.

8.96 It is proposed (fig. 185) that industrial traffic should eventually be siphoned off Peaseholme Green before it reaches the Black Swan, pass directly to the heart of the area and leave by way of the new bridge shown over the Foss (2) and so to Foss Islands Road. This will remove pressure from Stonebow, and the Garden Place junction could then be eliminated. This in turn would compensate the tele-phone exchange on its main frontage for the land acquired at its rear to provide servicing to the N side of Fossgate.

8.97 The housing is shown removed and new industrial activity replacing it allowing for the proposed road alignment. The laundry and works would not be disturbed or the proposal put into effect until normal redevelopment allowed. In the meantime traffic entering the section would continue to use Hungate.

8.98 Peaseholme Green as such has disappeared with the construc-tion of Stonebow, leaving a very poor relationship between the excellent group of buildings made up of the Borthwick Institute (St. Anthony's Hall), Carr's Peaseholme House (when it is restored) and the Black Swan, all of which once framed Peaseholme Green with its adjacent Hay Market.

8.99 With trees, the Black Swan could have the isolation of its set-ting reduced, and by careful planting (instead of the present municipal flower-bed), and a realignment of the footpaths, the flank and front of St. Anthony's could be shown to advantage, whilst the change would permit the Woolpack Hotel to be softened by trees in its forecourt, bringing the whole group together.

8.100 These proposals are partially shown on figs. 106 and 184 and the complete scheme is shown on the Master Plan.

8.101 Alongside the Foss, no change of use is proposed, but the derelict land is shown with buildings (3) of appropriate form (sited on the banks) to maintain the strong relationship of buildings and water reflected opposite in Leathams Mill.

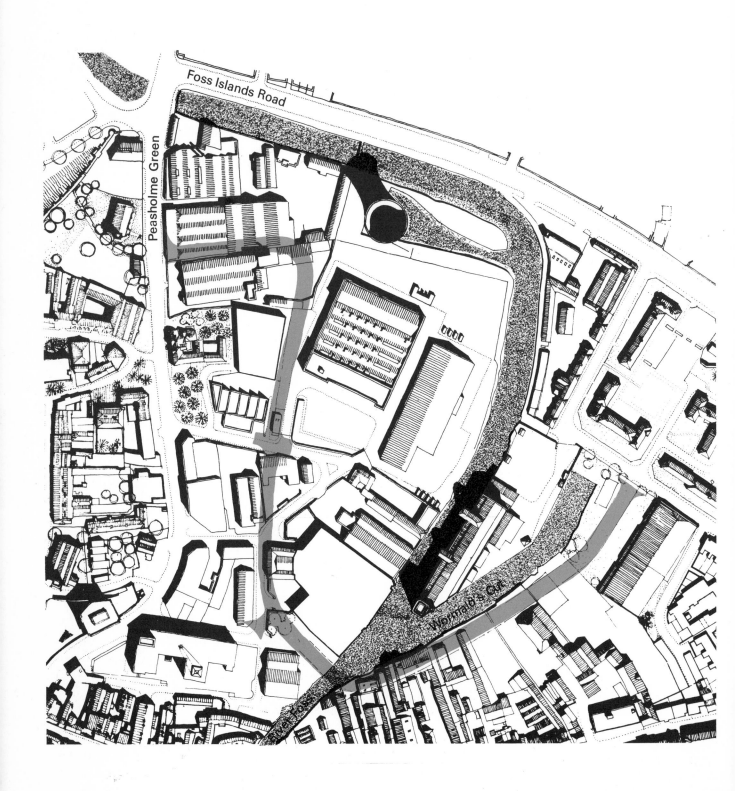

Foss Islands Road

Peasholme Green

Wormald's Cut

River Foss

186 Leatham's Mill. The great warehouse of the Foss

New buildings
New paving
New roads
New pedestrian areas
New trees
Existing trees

Walmgate (Sector 7)

8.102   The essence of the Walmgate sector is that it can hardly be claimed to have the status (as we believe all the others except the industrial wedge should have) of a Conservation Area within the meaning of the Civic Amenities Act. It has an average share of listed or attractive buildings but is neither better nor worse environmentally than a hundred similar obsolescent districts in the smaller cities of Britain. Its renewal is consequently not a case for special powers, but a normal local government activity. The following notes, which refer as before to the fig. 187, are offered as a contribution to the policies that will guide this activity.

8.103   While the Corporation's intervention as planning and housing authority will continue, the Walmgate sector, because of its proximity to the University, provides an ideal field of operations for conversions designed to house students on the lines already pioneered by the York Housing Association.

8.104   The sector contains the following classified buildings:

A	3	C	28
B	4	D	38

8.105   Most of these face or adjoin the western half of Walmgate itself, the principal exceptions being the magnificent Leathams Mill and the good early 19th century terrace in George Street. Of the groups in Walmgate, those in or adjacent to Merchantgate and those facing St. Denys's Church are alone worthy of inclusion in the Conservation Area. The two medieval churches, both with Norman porches (one moved from elsewhere) are listed as redundant by the Commission, but their preservation and conversion to appropriate use are regarded as essential, and the planning proposals that follow assume this. It may be that the population growth proposed for this sector will make it possible for one of them to be brought back into parochial use.

8.106   The sector can conveniently be considered in 5 parts:
1   Walmgate and its frontages
2   The industrial hinterland facing Wormald's Cut
3   The municipal housing belt
4   George Street
5   Piccadilly

188   Walmgate: 'decayed but well-scaled Victorian cottages'

189 New houses beside Walmgate Bar

190 A new setting for St. Margaret's, Walmgate

191 Walmgate: houses for conservation near
St. Denys's Church

Walmgate

8.107 Its general character is described in Appendix B and the restriction of its traffic load to labelled cars and servicing vehicles should make it possible for the present building lines and uses to be maintained. Economic factors will probably lead to a gradual concentration of shops into two groups, one based on Medway House (1) and the other just E of Merchantgate (2), which will tend to be upgraded by the new multi-storey car park. Elsewhere in the street terraced housing, new or converted, should replace redundant small traders.

8.108 The green oasis formed by St. Margaret's Churchyard, with the new trees planted opposite, gives a badly-needed break in the monotony of the street; but it needs a new setting, which is indicated (3) (fig. 190). It consists of small terraces of mainly two storey houses grouped round the church, scaled to its diminutive size and built on and over the existing wall surrounding the churchyard. The existing trees are brought forward by new planting into the Walmgate picture. The density is 60 p.p.a.

8.109 Beyond, apart from some decayed but well-scaled Victorian cottages next to the Bar, we enter the housing zone and the plan assumes the use for housing of the municipal scrapyard and shows (4) a possible layout which respects the urban scale of the existing flats on the one hand and the medieval scale of the Bar on the other. The density is 80 p.p.a. including full car provision.

Waterside industry

8.110 Obsolescent but expensive to buy, this strip behind the N frontages of Walmgate depreciates its residential value and attracts heavy transport through narrow and dangerous holes in the street facade. Wholesale purchase and use for housing is assumed to be uneconomic in the foreseeable future, but the plan indicates an industrial service road (5) which links the strip with the main industrial wedge by a bridge across the Foss. It would involve the removal of the less interesting of the two classified warehouses in the area. Leathams Mill itself, at present well maintained by Rowntrees, must unquestionably be preserved.

The Housing Belt

8.111 To criticise the Navigation Road and Hope Street housing projects for their manifest dreariness would now be superfluous as a higher standard has recently been set by the Huby Court flats. The good points here are the more interesting grouping and the use of 'hard' landscaping rather than tired grass; but the orientation runs against the grain of the surrounding buildings and the concentration on flats runs against popular taste. A similar density could be obtained with terrace houses and small walled gardens which would be more in sympathy with the traditional character of central York (fig. 189). A sketch scheme (6) is shown for the Lead Mill Lane slum clearance area which attempts to meet this need; part of the lane is built over to fully exploit the Rest Garden (site of St. George's Church) and the splendid Fishergate Tower and fine seed merchants warehouse are given a more worthy setting (fig. 192) by a paved and treed square. It would be necessary to reorganise the internal planning of the adjacent garage to make this proposal viable. The density is 60 p.p.a.

192 Fishergate Tower and the seed warehouse

193 The Merchantgate car park spanning
Piccadilly

194 Good lettering in Merchantgate

195 The Merchantgate car park looking towards Walmgate

George Street

8.112   This street, which threads the hinterland between Walmgate and Piccadilly, is now a tragic example of piecemeal redevelopment without a planning context. Cost must preclude the removal of industrial premises at this stage, and vacant land reserved for school extensions must be accepted. The long-term policy should be residential redevelopment, for which Nos. 9-31 set an admirable precedent.

Piccadilly

8.113   The same strictures, but on a larger scale, must be passed on this notorious example of 20th century non-architecture, and the same limitations must be accepted in our powers to do anything dramatic about it. The street contains seven large garages, and designates itself inevitably as a main motor route. The fronts to Piccadilly are bad enough; the backs on to the Foss are worse, and their glum influence spreads across the water to the Castle itself. One vacant site remains, and it is proposed that this should be used for a group of offices of good quality designed to reduce the isolation of United House, to break up the skyline into smaller elements, and above all to set a new standard in the strip between Piccadilly and the Foss which in the fullness of time may be emulated on the sites on either side.

8.114   But the main change proposed in the character of Piccadilly will be the multi-storey garage for 1,160 cars, carried boldly across the street so as to reduce its monotony and close the dull view out of Parliament Street (fig. 193 and 195). The design is broken into small units to reduce the scale along the waterside and stepped down in sympathy with the small old buildings in Merchantgate and Walmgate. At its W end it terminates in a bold drum, echoing the form of Clifford's Tower across the water, and containing a spiral ramp up which cars climb to the different levels, having been carried across the Foss by a bridge from Tower Street. Downstream from it pedestrians can re-cross the water by footbridge and so enter the heart of . . .

New buildings
New paving
New roads
New pedestrian areas
✳ New trees
◯ Existing trees

The Castle Sector (Sector 8)

8.115   This extends from the Ouse in the S to the N side of Fossgate and from Ousegate in the W to St. George's field in the E. It thus extends over a larger environmental area than that of the Castle site itself, and includes fringes of the central shopping area and the rivers. (Fig. 196).

8.116   The classified buildings in the sector are as follows :

Grade A	15	Grade C	48
Grade B	15	Grade D	55

8.117   *Fossgate*, because the present flow of traffic is eastwards only and because its connection with the main body of the town centre has been to some extent severed by the construction of the Stonebow, has lost its earlier importance as the main route inwards from Walmgate. There has been a distinct fall-off from primary to secondary shopping use and this may to some extent be aggravated by the difficulties of servicing. A new service road(**1**) on the N side will give some relief, and will give shop premises fronting the street, as well as the small service industries at the rear, a convenient access route from Peaseholme Green and the Industrial area.

8.118   On the S side, limited service access is already available from Lady Peckitts Yard, though this has spoiled the climax of the excellent pedestrian approach from Pavement. It does however allow the newly established Tesco's fronting on to Piccadilly to have off-street servicing.

8.119   The superb Merchant Taylors Hall (previously Trinity Hospital), which is entered by a tunnel from Fossgate, has had its S front partially obscured by the construction of the second part of Piccadilly (1913) on an embankment. We show the setting(**2**) improved by the removal of the brick wall and substitution of railing to the garden and by the introduction of more mature town trees. The garden of the Hall could also be greatly improved by cleaning up the banks of the Foss.

8.120   Adjacent to Foss Bridge the present under-utilised site is shown redeveloped to four storeys(**3**). This will screen the access yard and focus attention on the bridge and the new view from it to the spiral ramp of the car park in Piccadilly with Cliffords Tower in the background.

8.121   Plan 160 shows *All Saints Pavement* in an improved setting. The single-storey shop at its West End is removed and the grounds restored to grass and trees which will frame the view of the church from Pavement. The proposals show the new alignment for Parliament Street and the roundabout at its junction with Piccadilly removed. This allows an extensive area of paving and cobbling to be laid out in front of the church, which with its Victorian boundary walls removed will dominate an urban space worthy of itself.

8.122   In *Piccadilly* the site between the cinema and shops is shown(**4**) developed to four storeys, replacing the present advertising hoarding. Access for servicing is provided from Coppergate, in which the at present disused confectionery works are changed to shop and office use and the rear portion reduced to provide service circulation.

Coppergate

Nessgate

Clifford Street

new buildings

8.123 The existing embryo footpaths alongside the cinema are extended to communicate through to *St. Mary's Castlegate*, which in its suggested new role as a City Information Centre, would attract a substantial amount of foot traffic. It is therefore also shown (**5**) in a less cramped setting, with all the obsolete outbuildings removed and a properly paved and treed urban space. The spire which is an important feature of the town centre must remain the dominant landmark of any views down Castlegate and with this in mind, a new office block with shops at ground level is shown framing the new space, concealing the bulky flank of the St. George's Cinema, but keeping the view of the church intact.

8.124 The site of *Castlegate School* (**6**), which has a short lease to run as part of the Technical College, is shown redeveloped to take advantage of the proximity of the car-park in Piccadilly and echoing the developing large shop uses opposite, with a possible department store, or shops with offices above. The rear portion of the school site could be used as a garden extension to St. George's Hall if it were to be used, as has been suggested to us, as an Arts Centre.

8.125 *Tower Street* is shown extended as a road and bridge to give access to and from the new Piccadilly car-park (**7**). In doing so service access can be provided to the basement level of the Castlegate School site. To achieve this road several non-conforming industrial uses are removed on the E of St. George's Cinema, but its flank will be concealed by new development. The proximity of the car-park is likely to expedite the redevelopment of this area and facilitate the evening use of the proposed Arts Centre.

8.126 The junction of *Castlegate* with its present one-way system and the multiple junction of Clifford Street, Nessgate, King Street and Coppergate is unsatisfactory both in traffic and visual terms. A rationalisation of the traffic flow suggests the deflection of Castlegate (which carries only local service traffic) bringing it out into Clifford Street by way of an improved Friargate, thus simplifying flows on the three major routes. King Street is at the moment a one-way street away from the junction and should so remain.

8.127 The eventual removal of the oppressive Victorian building at the junction of Castlegate and Clifford Street and the building up of the vacant plot behind to face Nessgate would create a square out of this multiple junction, allowing improved sight lines from Coppergate and providing a paved apron with trees from which pedestrians from the Castle Museum and St. Mary's can disperse into the central area.

8.128 *Friargate* is shown widened on its E side, exposing the core of the Friends Meeting House, with a new frontage allowing the present entry in Clifford Street and the adjacent vacant plot to be developed to its full width, up to the Friargate junction. Fig. 197 shows these proposals.

8.129 The group of residential buildings in and around *Tower Place*, Tower Street, Peckitt Street and the S Esplanade are all worthy of conservation. Tower Place itself, situated so quietly behind the city wall, is a particularly charming row of small town houses. In the centre of this square of houses we show the present manufacturing industry removed (**8**), and the existing access from Tower Street utilised for a garage court containing 20 cars and with a short pedestrian way cut through for the benefit of the residents of Peckitt Street. Access from the other three blocks exists and only requires opening up. The advertising hoardings on the flank of No. 14 Tower Street should be removed.

198 Modillion cornices in Castlegate, with the great spire of St. Mary's

8.130 Tower Street cuts a swathe between St. George's Field and the Castle precint. By widening the approach islands a few trees could be introduced into the central reservation and a group of trees on the island itself would effectively fill the gap on the long view from Clifford Street and bring the greenery of St. George's Field over and into the Castle Precinct (**9**). The perimeter of the Precinct likewise would be immensely improved by trees to replace the screen once provided by the Castle Wall. The effect of heavy planting would then be brought into the heart of the area, at present particularly bald and open.

8.131 *The Castle Precinct* lacks all the stature and sense of care that one expects from such an historic and architecturally impressive site. Clifford's Tower stands forlornly trapped between the traffic of Tower Street and the parked cars and vacant sites flanking the Foss. In 1596 Robert Redhead the Gaoler began to pull down Clifford's Tower, intending to burn most of the masonry for lime. The Corporation petitioned the Lord Treasurer and the Chancellor of the Exchequer for its preservation. They represented it as 'an especial ornament for the beautifying of this City'—and were so far successful that spoliation was stayed. Their efforts must represent one of the earliest

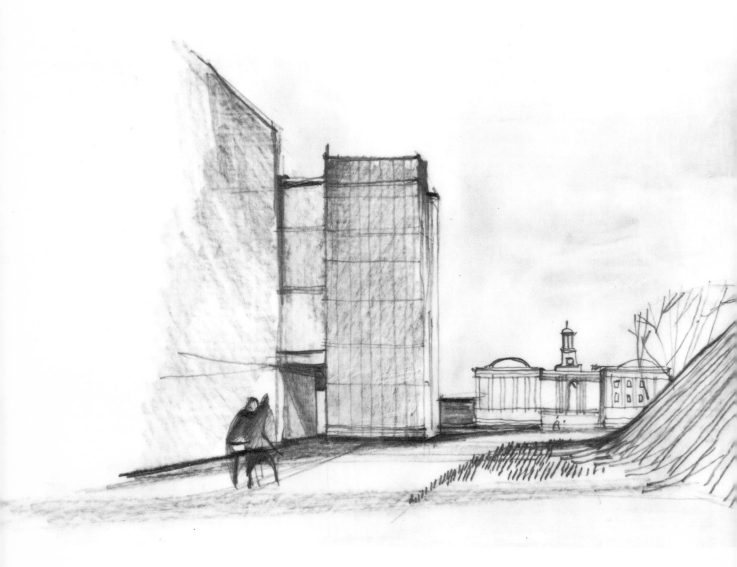

199 The Eye of Yorkshire: 'the whole area breathes the atmosphere of planning blight and dereliction'

attempts in English history to preserve an ancient monument as an amenity. *

8.132   The group of beautiful 18th century buildings which house the Castle Museum and Assize Courts stand round three sides of the exposed Eye of Yorkshire, but the whole area of the Castle Precinct breathes the atmosphere of planning blight and indecision. It comes to life only in summer months when full of tourists and crocodiles of excited schoolchildren.

8.133   Unfortunately there is no specific brief for the planning of the vacant areas between Clifford's Tower and the bank of the Foss. But in the context of what exists architecturally, some simple planning objectives present themselves. These are :
1   To wall in the precinct on the N side, shutting out the wide, shabby and shapeless landscape which permeates from across the Foss.
2   To give to the Castle Museum area just sufficient enclosure to make the group of buildings dominate the space about which they stand. (The view of this group from Castlegate is too far distant for them to stand up with any grandeur).
3   To create focal points seen from which the spaces inter-relate but contain themselves and the significant buildings.
Plan 196 seeks to establish these objectives as a starting-point for the future regeneration of this potentially beautiful group of buildings.

8.134   In the Castle forecourt the axis of the old Debtors' Prison (which travellers of the 18th century looked upon as the finest gaol in Britain, if not Europe) needs to be established in relationship to both Carr's Assize Courts and the Kirk Museum. To do this it is suggested that the Eye of Yorkshire—the green of its centre—should have placed in it the obelisk from the Tower Street roundabout, and that vehicles be restricted to the front of the Assize Court and the W side of the Court-yard. The remainder should be paved so as to allow essential vehicles only to have access to the museums. To create a sense of enclosure we propose that the new buildings should break forward, while still allowing the whole of the old buildings to be seen from the entrance to Clifford's Tower (fig. 200).

8.135   Trees at the base of the Tower will assist in defining the rest of the courtyard but will not obstruct any view from the top of the 'motte'. It will be noticed that a gap has been left in this planting to both give a view out from the mound towards the river, and allow a glimpse of the Tower from the street below, and that the view back towards Castlegate from the obelisk has been similarly preserved, keeping the spire of St. Mary's as the focal point.

8.136   The assumption has been made that a large Meeting Hall will be part of the future development and this is shown occupying the central part of the new development flanked on the E by three storeys (in sympathy with the Castle Precinct), but extending to four storeys on the W where the buildings take the alignment of old Castlegate. Behind the Main Hall a terrace is shown to the Foss, from which springs the foot-bridge by which visitors enter the Castle Precinct from the Merchantgate Car Park. Returning across it, we have completed the circuit of the renewed city.

8.137   The pocket drawing shows all eight sector plans put together to form a master plan for the walled city as a whole, and this chapter ends with some general suggestions affecting the whole city centre.

200   The Old Debtors' Prison in a new setting

*Victoria History.

193

Height of buildings

8.138   Because of the flatness of the plain of York, distant views of the Minster are hard to come by, but they do exist, particularly from the high ground round Heslington Hill and from Wigginton Road, and of course from the distant ridges of the Howardian Hills and the Wolds. An absolute height limit for new buildings within a mile of the Minster is therefore necessary, and it is suggested that this should be 117 O.D., which is the level of the top of the aisle roofs or the bottom of the clerestory. This absolute limit is not, of course, for indiscriminate use, and all proposals exceeding four stories will need most careful consideration in relation to the existing townscape and in particular to the parish churches with their miniature scale. Minimum heights (generally three stories) must also continue to be prescribed in the historic streets, and enforced.

Trees

8.139   A complete survey has been made of the species, size and condition of all trees within the walled city and the results tabulated and deposited with the Corporation. The many fine mature trees listed should be protected from crude lopping, if necessary by Tree Preservation Orders in appropriate cases. At present, trees are concentrated along the northern and western fringes and become progressively sparser as one moves east. Proposals have been made for individual planting in Exhibition Square, St. Helen's Square, King's Square and St. Sampson's Square, and these are all positions where semimature trees would justify their cost. The Castle perimeter needs more extensive tree planting for which a scheme should be prepared by a landscape architect, and much could be done in the course of redevelopment to soften the Walmgate sector and the banks of the Foss by forest trees. The densely urban character of the heart of York needs a wooded setting, and the walls are the clue to it.

Municipal gardening

8.140   The Corporation deserves credit not only for its charming floral decorations in St. Helen's Square, but for *not* attempting elaborate displays in the calmly romantic surroundings of Museum Gardens. The Esplanade west of Lendal Bridge is also a model of urban landscaping. These examples should provide the key to the future: paving and cobbles rather than rockeries; grass rather than shrubs; native forest trees rather than exotic ornamental species. Such extra funds as can be made available are better spent on a general tidying up of waste plots and disused street furniture than on a few floral showpieces.

Pavings

8.141   It has often been pointed out that the floor of an urban space is as important visually as its walls, and this applies particularly where the walls are old buildings or good ones: medieval buildings standing on a base of tarmac with yellow stripes look absurd. A survey has been made and deposited of existing floorscape, particularly of York stone paving and cobbles and setts, and this shows how patchy the pattern is, with odd lengths of concrete pavement interspersed with stone even in Micklegate, Goodramgate and High Petergate. Decades of hand-to-mouth repairs cannot be sorted out in a day, but a floorscape policy is now essential for the historic streets, so that old paving stones taken up elsewhere, and new stone paving (which costs 5 times as much as concrete) are concentrated in them. The candidates for

preferential treatment are Petergate, Stonegate, Goodramgate, St. Saviourgate and Micklegate, and particular attention should be paid to the preservation and careful repair of the cobbles in the Staithes, the granite paviours in the Shambles, and the setts on Micklegate and Foss Bridge (for which Tanner Row could be a source of supply). There are a number of minor open spaces, too small for grass, where new cobbles are required, particularly on both banks of the Ouse and in the forecourts of churches and chapels, and these are shown in sector plans. All the civic squares including the Castle Precinct should be paved with natural materials.

Street furniture

8.142 This includes lighting, signs, seats, fences, bollards, bins, etc., and a similar policy should be pursued as for pavings. With one familiar exception at the head of Stonegate, historic York is creditably free of obtrusive lamp standards and wirescape, and this successful resistance should be consolidated. As roads are de-classified their lighting should be redesigned appropriately for their major use. Narrow streets should be lit as now from walls only and to pedestrian rather than vehicular standards. It should be the aim to eliminate from the inner enclave all but tungsten lighting. It should also be the aim to remove all concrete posts, tubular fencing and chain-link from the walled city and replace it by cast-iron or welded steel painted black.

Floodlighting

8.143 This is generally considered an expensive luxury but need not be so, except in the case of the Minster when the time returns to do it. The lighting of the Mansion House and of All Saints (Pavement) belfry are examples of the effects obtainable by simple means: a single spotlight can often be effective. Features where special lighting should be considered include the whole of Stonegate, the King's Manor facade, the three facades facing the Castle forecourt, the spires of St. Mary's Castlegate and All Saints, North Street and the portico of the Assembly Rooms.

Development control

8.144 The Corporation's excellent *Guide for Developers* was no doubt prompted by some deplorable recent buildings and its recommendations are endorsed. The fundamental problem is not however to improve 'design'; it is to prevent the redevelopment of historic streets in parcels markedly larger than the traditional ones, because once this happens no amount of architectural ingenuity can produce anything better than a fake. It is therefore essential to historic cities that the Use Classes Order should be amended to distinguish between large multiple stores and supermarkets on the one hand and traditional shop units with normal wall-to-wall spans on the other, and that the former should be excluded from Petergate, Colliergate, Fossgate, Goodramgate, Stonegate, Blake Street and Micklegate. The area between Coney Street and Parliament Street (inclusive) must be reserved for the big stores and it is in Coney Street and the Ousegates that special ingenuity will be required to see that surviving old buildings on narrow plots are not squeezed into insignificance by corpulent new arrivals.

8.145 Development control in the heart of York will always be an exceptionally difficult exercise, requiring a rare mixture of firmness and sensitivity, and it can only succeed if architects of the very highest calibre are employed both to design buildings and to advise the planning authority.

203 Repairs and conversions within the study areas

9 Costs and returns

9.1 Our terms of reference require us to estimate 'the total cost of Conservation'. It is extremely doubtful whether this is meaningful. We noted in Chapter 6 that Conservation is a continuing activity and not a once-for-all operation, and that a great part of this activity consists in creating, through the normal process of planning, a healthy climate for old buildings so that their economic life is prolonged. The more that is done for them indirectly by planning, the less will have to be done directly by repair grants.

9.2 It is clear that these 'normal processes of planning', which benefit historic buildings as much as they benefit human health and safety, can no more be regarded as a charge on Conservation than they can be regarded as a charge on the Health Service. Road works, traffic management, multi-storey car-parks, slum-clearance and rehousing, the rehabilitation of late Victorian terrace houses, the planting of trees, the re-paving and re-lighting of streets—all these have indirect conservation value, yet all would go on over the years even if York possessed no old buildings of any importance.

9.3 On the other hand there are certain conservation measures which, in the present and short-run economic climate, would almost certainly *not* be undertaken. These come in 4 main categories:
1   The acquisition and relocation of non-conforming users in order to improve the environment of historic buildings, and the sale or leasing of cleared sites for residential redevelopment at less than an economic return.
2   The acquisition, conversion and re-sale of properties in need of upgrading, where the need arises.
3   Repair grants to classified buildings on the scale proposed.
4   Street works designed to improve the setting of historic buildings.

9.4 To these direct costs should be added the fact that it will certainly be necessary to give parts of the road programme abnormal priorities if the fabric of historic York is not to be lost before the roads arrive to relieve it. This acceleration will cost extra money, which has not been taken into account because it lies largely outside the area of our terms of reference.

9.5 There is a further difficulty, in proposing any programme for renewal and environmental improvement, of where to draw the line. For example it would produce an immense improvement in the atmosphere of the walled city if the garages etc. along the S side of Piccadilly could be replaced by tiered terraces of flats rising out of the Foss and looking across the water to the Castle and the sun; if the twilight area between Skeldergate and Cromwell Road could be comprehensively rebuilt with offices and/or tower flats; if the bye-law housing in the Fairfax Street—Hampden Street area could be opened up and revived in the manner indicated on fig. 134. We have not regarded any of these improvements, desirable though they are and inevitable in the course of time, as necessary to conservation, and

Micklegate Bar   Micklegate   Micklegate House

have consequently left them out of account, both in proposing the Conservation Areas shown on fig. 87 and in preparing the cost estimates.

9.3   Also omitted from our calculations are Ancient Monuments, parish churches, municipal buildings and buildings erected in the last 50 years.

9.7   In order to cost the 4 categories in para 9.3, it was desirable, if possible, to choose for investigation areas within the walls where these problems are largely concentrated and the 'normal 'expenditure described in para 9.2 largely absent. The Study Areas dealt with in detail in Chapter 7 were in fact selected for this purpose. There is an element of give-and-take in this selection. It could be argued for example that the whole of the Aldwark redevelopment should be

205   Costed proposals outside the study areas

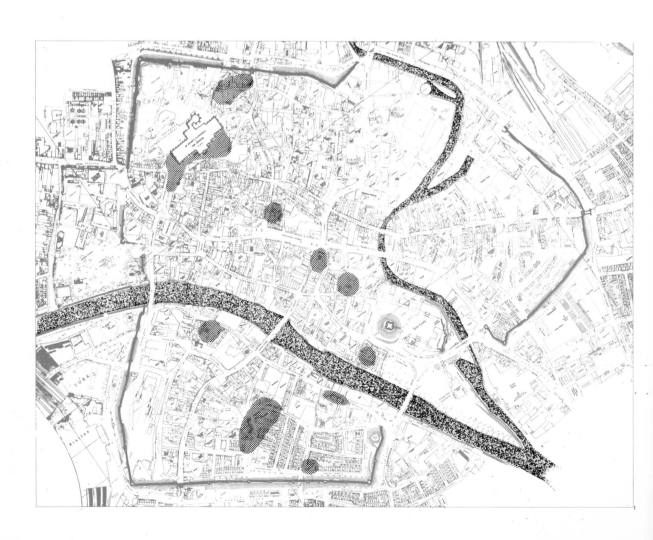

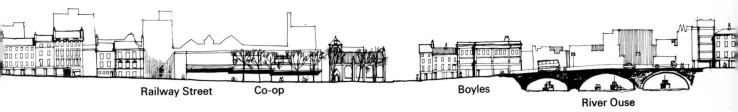

Railway Street   Co-op   Boyles

River Ouse

tackled as an Action Area within the normal processes of planning. Similarly while there are pockets outside the Study Areas such as Ogleforth, or the North Street and Skeldergate Conservation Areas, or the immediate surroundings of the two St. Mary's (Bishophill and Castlegate), or the backyard industry behind Tower Place, where expenditure in the interests of conservation is essential (and has been costed), some of this work too might be regarded as 'normal'.

9.8   On the other hand there are other areas, *not* costed, such as Castlegate and Walmgate, where expenditure on conversion or repair may well be incurred, and of course there are similar cases outside the walls. It is in this sense that the 'total cost of Conservation' in York cannot be precisely isolated. Our hope is that by costing rather more than is strictly attributable to Conservation inside the areas selected for detailed investigation (fig. 203) we have roughly balanced the costs of Conservation outside them.

9.9   A word should now be said about the method of costing. We first set up a house-to-house survey of the Study Areas, using the proforma reproduced on p. 90 and the City Engineer's 'Field Sheets' which contain essential information on site boundaries etc. This survey enabled us to plot:
1   'Non-conforming' uses, i.e. activities prejudicial to the predominant use of the area and therefore requiring relocation.
2   Under-used or mis-used buildings requiring conversion, but not demolition.
3   Buildings for which repair grants could be claimed.

9.10   Site acquisition costs in the case of Category 1 were then assessed by the Valuation Consultants and grossed up for each Study Area. The same was done by the Quantity Surveyors in respect of demolition costs.

9.11   We then prepared our redevelopment proposals for the cleared sites, which (together with ancillary road works) were costed by the Quantity Surveyors and forwarded to the Valuation Consultants and to the Development Consultants so that returns could be estimated.

9.12   In the case of Category 2 and 3 sites in the Study Area (and many sites come into both categories) the cost of works was estimated by the Quantity Surveyors and an average local authority grant of 40 per cent applied to them. The whole of the figures were then analysed by the Development Consultants, who prepared the figures on which Appendix G is based.

9.13   Outside the Study Areas, the following improvements (fig. 205) were costed by a similar process, except that house-to-house surveys were not attempted.

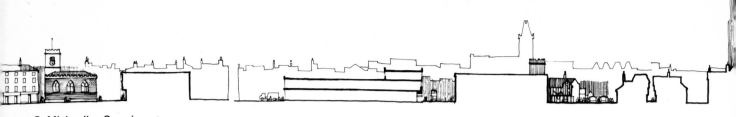

St Michael's Spurriergate New stores Parliament Marks Market C
Church Street and Spencer

Redevelopment surrounding St. Mary's, Bishophill.
All Saints, North Street, Conservation Area.
Skeldergate Conservation Area.
Upper-storey conversions in the Shambles, High Petergate, Goodram-gate, Coney Street, Colliergate, Fossgate and Coppergate.
Complete paving of Stonegate, High Petergate, Coney Street and New Street.
Ogleforth improvements.
The new Minster Close—hard and soft landscape.
Improved settings for All Saints, Pavement and St. Mary's, Castlegate.

9.14   Among civic improvements which we have recommended but do not regard as chargeable to Conservation are the widening of Skeldergate, the Cromwell Road and Walmgate redevelopment areas, the new Exhibition Square, the Parliament Street reconstruction and the new buildings and landscaping in the Castle precinct.

9.15   The most difficult aspect to evaluate has been the annual cost of conversion and repairs. The fact that in the first two years of the Town Scheme the demand for grants has virtually balanced the exiguous supply (and this reflects a national lack of demand) is by no means a happy state of affairs, and it is hard to tell to what extent it has been due to nationwide restrictions and high interest rates, or to a chronic reluctance, even with grant aid, to incur the problems and risks of investing in conversions. Only time can tell, but it is our belief that the big obstacle is environmental, and that if they could be liberated from noise and congestion the attraction of historic buildings for private investment would be transformed overnight. We have therefore resisted the temptation to minimise this component just because at the present time it is in the doldrums.

9.16   But there is an important difference between conversion and repair, which is that the former is optional (pending the flow of demand) while the latter is essential. We have therefore, within the limits of the practicable, separated the two and while charging them both to the cost of Conservation have put conversion, as it were, in brackets and subjected it to certain qualifications which appear below.

9.17   It should be added that the costing exercise has been simpler in principle than in practice, and that the figures which appear in the table on p. 242, and on which Professor Lichfield has based the important report which is printed as Appendix G, reflect the order of magnitude of the operation and not its precise cost. In the rest of this chapter we highlight the main figures and conclusions of this Appendix.

9.18   First, on the net cost side, we have a grand total in capital terms

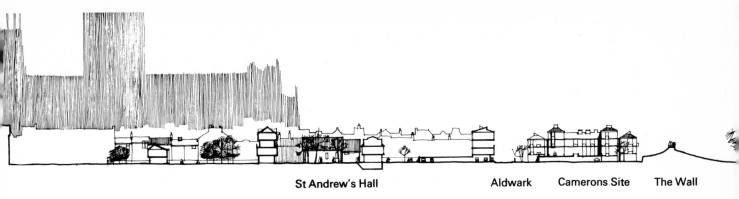

St Andrew's Hall   Aldwark   Camerons Site   The Wall

of £2.1m (see Table p. 242). Assuming, as we think we in fairness can, that redevelopment in the interests of conservation will rank for grant on the same basis as redevelopment in the interests of modernisation, we have anticipated a 50 per cent central government grant for redevelopment and a 40 per cent local authority grant for repairs and conversions. We have then converted capital cost to annual cost and arrive at an annual cost to the local authority of £90,000, which in York is a 6d. rate. If to this we add an allowance of £10,000 p.a. for running a Conservation Section (see Chapter 10), which might well later operate, and be chargeable, sub-regionally, we have a total annual cost of £100,000.

9.19   We may now apply to this annual cost our particular choice of the methods of recouping benefit proposed in Section 5 of Appendix G. We cannot of course apply them all, since they are to some extent alternatives, and our choice among them will be largely a matter of taste—or politics. We here take three examples in order to illustrate the order of magnitude of this recoupment. The first is a percentage charge on hotel bills. Without looking further ahead than the completion of the Viking, this would bring in, at a conservative estimate, £28,000 a year at 5 per cent and £56,000 a year at 10 per cent. The second is a 6d. increase in admission charges to all local 'sights' for which charges are made at present. This, again conservatively, would bring in £22,000. If we take the lower figure on hotel bills, we have half the cost of Conservation recouped by these two charges alone.

9.20   The third is a suggestion not made in Appendix G but one which we believe ought to be seriously considered. It costs the nation at present (through the University Grants Committee) £1,440 to house a student in a new building. In the case in Micklegate already illustrated (para 7.39) it cost £460. The familiar criticism of this form of housing is based on a vision of gloomy digs in a Victorian street, separation from friends and contemporaries, and a grim commuter-style journey to work. Supposing the provision of students' dwellings in the historic (and eventually traffic-free) streets of York were tackled on a big enough scale, none of this criticism would apply. It would be a convenient, gregarious and picturesque life such as has been lived by European students for a thousand years, and we have not the slightest doubt that they would enjoy it.

9.21   Supposing then that the University Grants Committee were authorised to reimburse the City the cost of housing each student in approved reconditioned houses in the heart of York, the number of students that could be so housed would be about 700 at a total conversion cost of £370,000. The annual cost of Conservation to the local authority, already theoretically reduced by the two charges used as examples in para 9.19 to £50,000, would now come down to £13,750, or roughly the product of a penny rate.

206 This reproduction of Baines Plan of 1822
is taken from the 1948 Plan for the City of York
in which the comment was: 'this map of 1822
shows subsequent "unplanned" road improvements in yellow. It seems probable that if such a
plan had been produced at that time, showing
proposals for improvements to be carried out
within the next 120 years, it would have had a
rather cool reception as being unlikely of
achievement. Nevertheless, this great work
was carried out and, over slightly more than a
century, the cost has gone almost unnoticed.'

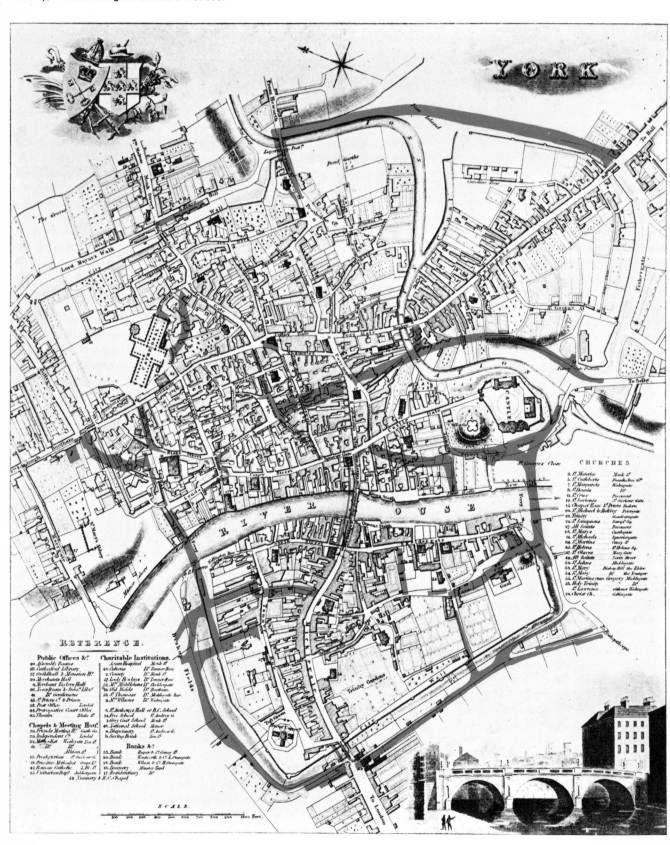

10 Realisation

10.1 We finally in this chapter examine urban conservation in its place as a function of local government, and some of the factors, adverse and favourable, which will decide whether a policy such as we have outlined will be put into effect not only in York but over the country as a whole.

10.2 Conservation is and always has been a part of planning. Cities renew themselves by a twin process of conversion and new construction and public authorities have the duty of first deciding what is the proper balance between the two in their own circumstances and then intervening to whatever extent is necessary to ensure that this balance is maintained. The first eight chapters of this report were an attempt to formulate this balance for the walled city of York. The ninth examined this formulation in terms of costs and returns. It remains to suggest how the job could be done.

10.3 For most planning authorities the first step will be to set up within the planning department an appropriately qualified Conservation Section. It will not be easy to find either the money or the specialist staff for this, and there is much to be said for Lord Holford's suggestion of a national Urban Conservation Service, staffed by officers of the appropriate departments and by working consultants, whose function would be to give technical information and advice to planning authorities and to administer the historic building grant system. This service could later no doubt be decentralised to regions.

10.4 The first duty of the local Conservation Section will be to recommend the boundaries of Conservation Areas. So far, planning authorities have been given no criteria for defining this key concept (just as in the traffic field they have been given no criteria for defining environmental standards). This no doubt has the advantage of giving opinion a chance to crystallise, provided it does so—a process in which reports such as this have a part to play.

10.5 The essence of the matter is that in defining a Conservation Area the Planning Authority is not saying merely 'this is attractive', but 'this is to stay as it is'—because it is, in the words of Civic Amenities Act 1967 . . . 'an area of special architectural or historic interest the character or appearance of which it is desirable to preserve or enhance'. We have already stated our view that this inevitably implies that within Conservation Areas, buildings above a certain standard (which we have defined for York) will not be allowed to decay, and that *this* implies restricting such areas to those the nation can afford to look after. Only the best will be good enough. We have also stressed that the key to success lies not so much in direct aid as in the normal processes of planning: the removal of conflicting uses, the diversion of traffic and the deflection on to other sites of pressures for redevelopment.

205

10.6 Before this prolonged, expensive but inevitable re-structuring can take effect, historic buildings are in for a thin time. Noise and congestion will get worse before they get better, and pressures for the decent removal of what by then will be very shabby and precarious relics of the past will be intensified. It is during this period of stress that the work of the Conservation Section will be of vital importance. Its main duties could be summed up as follows:

a. To define Conservation Areas
b. To survey listed buildings within them and roughly estimate the cost of essential repairs
c To operate an advisory service for owners of listed buildings, covering both technical and financial aspects
d. To control a direct-labour repair squad—for use in urgent cases (It would incidentally be widely in demand by owners of rented houses generally, to whom getting repairs done without intolerable delays is a national problem).
e. To operate the grant system (see para 6.17).

10.7 Meanwhile new development in and adjacent to Conservation Areas will be getting under way, and legislation will be necessary, as in the National Parks, to enable planning authorities to impose special standards (which in York should apply to the whole of the walled city). These should include:

a. A requirement that all new development is architect-designed
b. Firm understanding that in rejecting any but the highest design standards the planning authority will have the Minister's support on appeal
c. Relaxation of the Building Regulations, without reference to Whitehall
d. Exclusion from the General Development Order, 1963*

10.8 Few local authorities will have the specialist architectural staff to operate these services and controls, and in such cases the use of consultants will be necessary at least for some of them.

10.9 We have indicated in Chapter 6 how an Historic Buildings Grants structure might be tied in with the designation of Conservation Areas, and that the principle of the enforced maintenance of our Class A B and C buildings is vital in these areas. We recognise the difficulties of this principle, and in particular the need to ensure at one extreme that public money is not given to those who do not need it and at the other that enforcement action is not taken against those who cannot afford it. The clue to success is detailed knowledge of the individual case and it is here, rather than in an open-handed grant policy, that money is best spent.

10.10 The difficulties should not be exaggerated, nor should the cost. It has been estimated that the national stock of buildings worthy of permanent conservation is something like one fiftieth of the new buildings to be constructed in the next fifteen years, and that the cost to the country of conserving them would be less than half the cost of replacing them. In the case of York, an expenditure of £2m. on city centre redevelopment for a city of 105,000 population is nothing abnormal. We know of two among many cities of similar size, one

*This Order exempts the following from planning control:
Enlargement of a dwelling by 1,750 cu. ft. or 1/10th; or the erection within its curtilage of ancillary buildings.
Erection of fences, gates etc. up to 4 ft. high abutting a highway, or 7 ft. elsewhere.
Erection by Local Authority of small ancillary buildings, lamp standards, kiosks, seats etc.
Works by a Local Highway Authority on land outside, but abutting the highway.
Development by River Boards, drainage authorities, mineral undertakers, all statutory undertakers, the National Coal Board etc.

historic and the other industrial: one has applied for £4½m. loan sanction for central redevelopment exclusive of road works; the other is spending a 9d. rate on similar redevelopment. Birmingham, we are told, spends £1½m. *a year* on the upkeep of its public open spaces. In this sort of context the annual cost of rescuing and conserving for posterity the finest medieval city in Britain may seem modest indeed, even if for the moment one ignores the economics of benefit.

10.11   But the benefits can only be claimed if the job is carried through, and carried through entirely. In conservation as in other fields there are economies of scale, and fatal diseconomies if a project is approached half-heartedly or spread over an excessive time span. The campaign to restore and regenerate the heart of York will bring its benefits if it is handled as a campaign and seen to be so: then private investment will follow the public lead. Conversely if public action is tentative, half-hearted and tedious it will cost the public more.

10.12   But when all has been said on the benefit side, the burden on the ratepayers of York, if the cost of Conservation is expressed in annual terms and shouldered by them, will be heavy, because among our historic cities it is unique in the number and frailty of its ancient buildings together with the savage environmental handicaps—industrial encroachment and traffic congestion—they have to endure. One may admit that York has its own ancestors to blame for this without thinking it right that the sins of the fathers should be visited upon the children to this extent. What encouragement can the central government best give, to get things moving?

10.13   The factor which will settle the issue of speed and decisiveness one way or the other, and with it the credibility of the campaign to regenerate York, is the road programme outside the Walls. This is not a Conservation cost, but its efficient and speedy execution is the essential groundwork for Conservation. If there is anything to be said for a policy of government support for a small number of historic cities of outstanding importance (and in most other European countries the case for such spending has been made), and if York is thought to qualify to be one of them, this support could be most effectively applied in current conditions not by spending more on roads, but by spending it more quickly in these special cases. For York this means specifically, in our opinion, the Fishergate Loop, the Clifton Bridge approaches and the Station—Gillygate distributor.

10.14   Meanwhile, whatever the resulting strain on the existing road system, the process of renewal and improvement already begun must be accelerated, and we recommend the following first priorities:
1   Legislation giving local authorities special powers within Conservation Areas on the lines recommended in Chapters 8 and 10.
2   Traffic restriction and new floorscape in Stonegate and Petergate and the creation of the new Minster Close.
3   Designation of Aldwark and Swinegate as Action Areas and a phased programme for their clearance and redevelopment in that order.
4   Site acquisition and construction of the first of the four multi-storey car-parks.

10.15   As to the last of these items, the order of need of these car parks unfortunately does not tally with their order of easy availability. The order of need we suggest is
Merchantgate
Skeldergate
Monkgate
Gillygate.

It is most desirable that mass parking should initially be provided on the SE rather than the NW side of the city centre, not only in order to exploit the width of Piccadilly but also in order not to intensify the heavy load which any closure or restrictions in Deangate will place on Lendal Bridge and St. Leonard's Place.

10.16 While these first four priorities are getting moving, there should be no delay in the setting up of a Conservation Section and its addressing itself to the tasks suggested in para 10.6.

10.17 These tasks of course concern old buildings; but there must be nothing backward-looking about the operation as a whole. There is no need for one single *pseudo* building within the walled city. On the contrary nothing but the best should be accepted. Bootham School and the King's Manor have shown the way. Equally we do not see York renewed as a museum-piece for schoolgirls and old ladies (though it should make them happy too). Its atmosphere should be the opposite of this. For example the north bank of the Foss opposite the Castle could some day be given over to a Fun Palace providing for every indoor game and water sport and after-dark gaiety ever invented. Through the persistence of its citizens York now has one of the finest new Universities in Europe, and the City-University axis should be the line of advance.

10.18 The heart of York is for all ages, just as it comes down to us from all ages. It may yet be proved that this kind of environment, once it has been restored to the human being on foot, will be more life-enhancing and therefore more efficient than anything we could invent to replace it. J. B. Morell used to describe York as 'The City of our Dreams'—an arresting but ambiguous phrase which expressed potential rather than actuality. We are now within sight of the decisions that could make it a reality.

Christmas Eve 1967

Appendices

A Acknowledgements

The following individuals and organisations have taken part in a great variety of ways in the surveys, analyses, drafting and illustration of this report. I thank them all, and in particular the Planning Department of the City Corporation, led by Mr R. S. Bellhouse, C Eng, MI Mun E, MTPI, Dip TP, City Engineer and Planning Officer, and other departments of the Corporation. Specific help was given by Miss J. Hargreaves and Mr K. Robinson on historical information.

First my own firm:

| **Brett & Pollen** | Harry Teggin, David Taylor, Bruce Sidnell, Harry Hartwell, Pamela Ward, Jonathan Watson, David Gamblin, Michael Gregory. Mary Syms, Christine Forster, Zoe Neal. |

Other Contributors

Bernard Thorpe & Partners Site Valuation	Mr Philip Booth Mr Brian Read
Gerald Eve & Co. Shopping survey and Financial Analysis (Appendix D)	Mr Geoffrey Powell Miss Margaret Thomas Mr John Deyes (Shopping Survey) Mr Edward Reeve (Preliminary investigation)
Davis, Belfield & Everest Construction Costs	Mr W. F. J. Fussell Mr D. J. Pearce
Nathaniel Lichfield & Partners Economics of Conservation (Appendix G)	Professor Lichfield Mrs Honor Chapman
Appendix B	Mr David Lloyd
Appendices C and E	Miss Pamela Ward
York University Design Unit Petergate Study	Mr David Crease and students of Leeds University
Photography	Mr Keith Gibson Sir Martyn Beckett Bt

Advice and Information

York Civic Trust

Royal Commission on Historic Monuments	Mr John Harvey Dr Gee Mr Williams (Condition of buildings in Micklegate) Mr Bassham (reproductions)
York and East Yorkshire Architectural Society: York Chapter	Mr Harry Green Mr George Pace Mr John Hutchinson Messrs Waites and Moorey
York Philosophical Society	Mrs Mackenzie

York Georgian Society	Mr John Hutchinson
The Dean and Chapter and the Minster staff Future Policy	Canon B. A. Smith Mr Bernard Feilden, Architect to the Minster Messrs Cobham & Smith, Solicitors to the Dean and Chapter
The Clergy of York Access to churches and general advice	
University of York Future Policy Social and economic aspects Proposed Art Centre Tourism	The Vice-Chancellor, The Registrar, the Bursar Professors Fletcher, Wiseman, Peacock, Dosser and their departments Bernard Harris, David Chase, Anne Riddell Michael Davenport
Institute of Advanced Architectural Studies Secretarial assistance and advice	Dr P Nuttgens and his staff
The Borthwick Institute of Historical Research Future policy	Mrs R. Gurney and archivist
York Chamber of Trade Shopping and parking	
York Junior Chamber of Commerce York Group for the Promotion of Planning Tourism	
Castle Museum Statistics and policy	The Curator
York Art Gallery Statistics and policy	The Director, first Mr Hess and then Mr Ingamells
Yorkshire Museum Statistics and policy	The Curator
The Ordnance Survey	Mr Beston, Mr Wilkins, Mr Williams
The District Valuer and Valuation Officer	Mr Henderson and Mr Peat
British Rail, N.E. Region Future policy	Mr Hardy, Chief Architect Mr Gilchrist, Estates Dept Mr Stainthorpe, Public Relations
British Travel Association Tourism	
West Yorkshire Road Car Company Future policy	Mr Patey, Chairman Mr Lawrence, General Manager Mr Garforth, Mr Bell
Tourism Survey	Mr John Chance
Alleys and Rights-of-Way	Mr Birkhill
Information and Theses on York	Prof. Anthony Goss
Advice and information on pedestrian streets	Mr A. A. Wood, City Planning Officer, Norwich

Surveys

The following gave helpful information in connection with the detailed surveys:

Ings Property Co.: Mr Philip Rowntree

Mr and Mrs Ford Longman

The York and East Yorkshire Architectural Society: Miss F. Wright

Mr Hoskins (Ogleforth)

The Proprietor, Ideal Laundry in Trinity Lane

York Hotel Proprietors and Members of the York Hotels and Restaurants Assoc.

Camerons Brewery, Mr Relton, Clerk of Works

York Tourist Promotion Board Steering Committee— Mr R. Burn

Redundant Churches Commission—Mr Harvey

Church Commissioners—the staff of Messrs Smith Gorr and Co. represented by Mr Byers and Mr Foster

Charrington (Yorkshire) Breweries, Mr Norton, Company Secretary

Councillor Daley, Civil Defence

York Housing Association

City Planning Officer, Newcastle, and his staff— (comments on revitalisation)

The Gas Board, Davygate—Mr P. Deathe

Yorkshire Insurance Co.—Mr Holston (Property in Aldwark)

Goodramgate Traders—Mr Ron Thompson and Messrs Saville, Robson, Knowles, Reid, Greenwood, Smallpage, Kilvington, Wright and Mein (building in Swinegate and Aldwark).

Students

The following took part in surveys under the direction of Mr David Lloyd and Miss Pamela Ward.

Rosemary Thomas, Gerrard Hill, John Ratcliffe, Francesca Ramsey, Kate McKenna, Frank and Sandra Vigon, Matthew Bowen, David Brown, Colin Casbolt, Guy Christianson, Susan Clark, John Cross, Robert Dingwall, Lesley Edwards, Graham Hunsley, Michael Judson, Roderick MacKenzie, Philip O'Riordon, Gordon Oswald, Christopher Sargent, Margaret Turner, Jill Ward, Richard Williams, Graham Wilson, Caroline Ferrey, Kenneth Hatfield, Paul Disney, David Robertson, Jonathan Benn, Keith Carr, Chris Ryan, Glynn Nightingale, Anthony Benn, Mike Hickling, Mike Miles, Ian Duncan, Vivian Ellwood.

B The townscape of York: a street gazetteer

David Lloyd BA, AMTPI

Aldwark A long street, just inside the walls, much decayed in recent years. Many mixed commercial uses, pleasant but empty houses and cleared sites. Two outstanding historic buildings, Merchant Taylors' Hall and St. Anthony's Hall (the latter at the corner with Peaseholme Green), and also one fine house (No. 17) of c.1700.

All Saints' Lane An important pedestrian alley running hard up against the north side of All Saints' Church, North Street, and giving access to it.

Baile Hill Terrace A leafy row of Victorian houses facing Baile Hill and the Walls, which would repay conversion.

Barker Lane An alley off Micklegate, leading to Toft Green. It has no special character in itself but in its small scale, like St. Martin's and Trinity Lanes, it forms an admirable foil and contrast to the spaciousness and relative grandeur of Micklegate.

Bedern Once the College of the Vicars Choral (whose dilapidated former chapel has only recently been mainly demolished), and in the mid 19 c. a notorious slum. Now a drab thoroughfare entered under an arch from Goodramgate. It has nothing of visual interest save a superb view of the Minster over the low houses which front onto Goodramgate.

Bishophill The area included under this heading comprises the whole southern enclave of the walled city SW of Bishophill Senior and SE of Bishophill Junior. Except for parts of the two Bishophill streets, this area was wholly developed in the mid 19 c. and consists of closely spaced industrial-type terraced houses, mostly small though a few are fairly substantial. Replacement of some of the poorer blocks by flats has already taken place. In Bishophill Junior there is nothing of visual interest save St. Mary's Church with its late Saxon tower, the oldest medieval structure in York. Bishophill Senior has a few old houses forming a dilapidated but still pleasant group at its NW end; one of them, well placed on a curve, is a fine early Georgian mansion which is now a warehouse (and has magnificent ceilings within). The churchyard of the recently demolished Church of St. Mary Bishophill Senior is still a pleasant place. The site is at the brow of a bluff and the tall limes which surround it are local landmarks (like those in the nearby Quaker Burial Ground), especially from across the river. Carr's Lane (qv) bounded on the churchyard side by old stone and brick walls, descends to Skeldergate.

Blake Street An important street topographically, leading from St. Helen's Square in the Bootham direction. It takes a somewhat wavering course which is attractive from the townscape point of view, with the Red House standing prominently at the close of the NW vista. The only two buildings of real distinction fronting the street are the Assembly Rooms with J. P. Pritchett's portico, and his Savings Bank at the corner of St. Helen's Square. Some good early 18 c. shops face the Assembly Rooms.

Bridge Street In its present form dates from 1810, when it was widened in conjunction with the rebuilding of the Ouse Bridge. Tall plain houses of local early 19 c. type on the N side, a more heterogeneous group of buildings, some of earlier origin, on the S side.

Carr's Lane A delightful short-cut leading from Skeldergate up to Bishophill Senior. It climbs (more steeply than any other York thoroughfare) and twists between old brick and stone walls, stone paved and cobbled, and passes the churchyard of the demolished St. Mary Bishophill Senior (see Bishophill) with its tall limes. Downward there is a view, through a gap between the buildings on the far side of Skeldergate, to the towers and turrets of Clifford Street and the spire of St. Mary Castlegate.

Castlegate Once the main approach to the Castle and also part of the main way out of the city south eastwards. But the building of Clifford Street in 1884 relegated it to the status of a minor street, and it is now one of the sadder examples of a once fine York street which has deteriorated through demolition, dilapidation and poor replacement of buildings. In this case the process has apparently gone on since before the Second World War, but the street is still an important and memorable one, and its remaining Georgian houses must be protected and restored.

On the N side is a good row of mainly 3-storey Georgian buildings culminating in the magnificent tower and spire of St. Mary's Church; the S side is scrappier and broken by an unsightly gap, but is still pleasant. Then past the church is the street's most disturbing feature, a cleared site used as a car park next to St. George's Hall, whose ugly side elevation, revealed through the demolition of the adjoining building and plastered over, is the most prominent feature in the street. Opposite and beyond the Hall respectively are Castlegate's two finest houses, early Georgian mansions both by Carr, the effect of which is sadly marred by their surroundings. Then come the climax and the anticlimax—the climax the sudden view of Clifford's Tower on its mound with the 18 c. buildings of York Castle grouped behind, the anti-climax the desolation of the space that stretches between them.

Castle Precinct The immediate setting of York Castle and Clifford's Tower—which next to the Minster are the most visited places in the city—is a sad revelation to the visitor. To explain the present state of the precinct it is necessary to summarise the Castle's history. The 14 c. Clifford's Tower, now a ruin, stands on the site of one of the two mottes thrown up by William I. The later Castle, with its buildings contained within a bailey wall, lay immediately to the SE. These came to be used mainly as a prison and for the Assizes, and were replaced in stages, the former Debtors' Prison in 1701-5, the present Assize Courts in 1773-7 and the former Female Prison in 1780, the latter two by Carr, each fronting one side of a regular courtyard of which the fourth side (towards Clifford's Tower and the city) is open. In the early 19 c. new prison buildings were built, mainly NE of Clifford's Tower, and the whole was surrounded by a high wall. The prison was closed in the 1930's, the early 19 c. buildings and their surround wall demolished, and two of the 18 c. prison buildings converted into the Castle Museum. Most of the site of the demolished prison buildings has become a car park with concrete post-and-wire fences and a visually squalid Civil Defence site beyond. All this is the immediate foreground of the Castle buildings and of Clifford's Tower, the view from the top of which consequently is a bitter disappointment. The unbroken extent of the space is such that the scale of the open sided courtyard and the classical buildings around it is belittled; only Clifford's Tower manages to assert itself over the surrounding desolation.

Chapter House Street A charming cobbled lane in the Minster precinct, bounded by small houses, the flanks of the Treasurer's House and old walls, the choir and chapter house at the end. For variety of colour and texture, subtle juxtaposition of small elements and sudden contrast of small with great, this is unexcelled anywhere in England.

Church Street In its present form this dates from 1830-40. Part of it is a widening of an older street called Girdlergate, but the southern part, into St. Sampson's Square, was an entirely new street. On the SE side, at the N end, are tall 19 c. York town houses; on the NW side all the way along, a smaller-scale mixture of no special distinction. The chief feature of the street is St. Sampson's Church, which though relatively uninteresting in itself (it was reconstructed in 1848, although it still looks medieval outside and has a medieval tower) is a very important feature in the townscape; the tower especially is a notable landmark from the Newgate and St. Sampson's Square directions.

Church Street is straight, and hence untypical of York, but this does mean that a relatively long vista is obtainable from St. Sampson's Square, ending with the buildings round the south end of Goodramgate. It is an important link topographically, and the short narrow streets leading SE (Patrick Pool and Silver Street) bring it into intimate contact with the Newgate market area.

Church Lane A short-cut from Spurriergate past St. Michael's Church, turning at right angles into an alley emerging in Low Ousegate. From the angle a small lane leads to an ancient anchorage by the river—one of the

few remaining public accesses to the river on this side between Ouse Bridge and Lendal Bridge.

Clifford Street The one street in intra-mural York which has a distinctively late Victorian character. It was constructed in 1884 partly over slum land and partly over gardens, a site occupied in the Middle Ages by the Franciscan Friary. Its great landmark is the Law Courts, with its piled-up silhouette of turrets and domes; the next most prominent building is the Technical College with an elaborately balustraded roofline and central gabled feature. These and almost all the other buildings in the street are in dark red brick with terracotta and a few stone dressings. The street, despite the fact that it takes a bold curve, displaying the principal buildings in perspective, is not very successful as townscape; this may be partly due to the lack of relationship between the buildings, their unrelieved heavy colouring, and the many haphazard gaps in the frontage, some of them openings into side roads. It deteriorates at the Nessgate end.

Coffee Yard One of the most alluring of York's alleyways. Entrance is through a small archway into a narrow passage, contained within the structure of a dilapidated medieval house at the angle of Grape Lane and Swinegate. Then a stretch of open footway and another passageway, with a double bend in the middle, through a basically medieval timber-framed building which spans it. Then into a delightful small courtyard, stone-paved and fronted with a variety of small scale domestic architecture of medieval to Georgian date, and in between the back wings of two of the Stonegate town houses, emerging into Stonegate in its central, most handsome part.

College Street Part of the Minster precinct, passing St. William's College and entering Goodramgate under a timbered archway, the last surviving gateway into the precinct, the effect of which has been largely lost by the demolition of the former buildings to the south to construct Deangate (qv).

Colliergate Often overlooked because of the parallel Shambles. Nevertheless, it would be remarkable in any other city, and is all the more important now that so many other attractive streets have been spoiled by insensitive modern intrusions. The character of Colliergate is still largely that of a slightly wavering medieval street with varied but largely Georgian frontages of moderate scale. Shop fronts are nondescript but unobtrusive. The exciting feature of the street is the vista along Petergate as one nears King's Square, crowned by the Minster towers.

Coney Street and Spurriergate Coney Street has since the early middle ages been one of the principal streets of York, perhaps outrivalling in the past even Pavement, Micklegate and Petergate. It led from the site of the old Roman south gate, at the end of Stonegate, to the medieval crossing of the river at Ouse Bridge, and all the houses on its SW side backed on to the river. It was a street of merchants' houses and inns, with the Guildhall at one end and the city's richest parish church close to it. During the last two centuries it has gradually become the city's chief shopping thoroughfare. This has meant a great deal of alteration and rebuilding, especially during the present century, and most of all since the Second

World War. Modern Coney Street has few buildings of individual distinction, apart from the bombed ruins of St. Martin-le-Grand (now sensitively restored) and the Mansion House (actually fronting St. Helen's Square). Nevertheless, the street still retains considerable dignity; many of the frontages above shop level are plain late Georgian or early Victorian with classical proportions; their usual height is four storeys which gives the street a handsome scale; there are as yet few relatively wide stretches of frontage redeveloped as a whole to give a disturbing horizontal emphasis; the effect is still largely one of repeated verticality, with tall, narrow frontages; and the graceful curve of the street gives an interestingly changing perspective. The most unfortunate building is probably a department store, an architecturally poor inter-war building with a horizontal emphasis, standing right at the visual pivot of the street. The medieval timbered and gabled building at the corner of New Street is a precious survival.

Spurriergate is the short continuation, at its SE end, of Coney Street. The transition (actually at the Market Street junction) is not obvious, but Spurriergate on the whole has a meaner appearance, offset only by the pleasant facade of St. Michael's church at the corner of Low Ousegate. The recent shop redevelopment on the opposite corner is one of the worst examples of post-war building on a prominent site in York.

Coppergate This, formerly a quiet little street, curves like a bow from the Piccadilly-Pavement junction to the Nessgate-Clifford Street junction, and takes a continuous stream of traffic. Its few remaining old buildings (e.g. a timbered framed group near the Piccadilly end and the Three Tuns farther along) are minuscule, and it still has some semblance of character thanks largely to these and to All Saints' Church. But it is less memorable than the parallel High Ousegate.

Davygate Topographically important, being the link between St. Sampson's Square and all that lies behind it, and St. Helen's Square. The street has a pleasant gentle curve, but its most prominent building is the recent neo-Georgian Marshall and Snelgrove block (an opportunity lost on so important a site). Some of the Victorian and later buildings have distinct character, notably the neo-Elizabethan brick block partly occupied by Brown's, and the Italianate gas showroom close to St. Helen's Church, which is also a feature in the townscape of St. Helen's Square.

Deangate Deangate was cut in 1903 through one corner of the Minster precinct, linking Minster Yard and Goodramgate. Its effect has been unfortunate, almost disastrous. For its existence has meant that the route from Duncombe Place, along the south side of the Minster and through Deangate into upper Goodramgate and past Monk Bar, has become a main route, taking through as well as city traffic. The precinctual effect of the surroundings of the Minster, (except to the N and E) was shattered by the opening of Deangate, and the effect of College Gate leading into College Street (qv) largely lost.

Dewsbury Terrace A charming Victorian range facing the city walls east of Micklegate, which would repay improvement.

Duncombe Place The townscape in front of the W end of the Minster was transformed during the 19 c. The old gate to the Minster Precinct at Lop Lane (the name of the narrow thoroughfare which preceded Duncombe Place) was finally demolished, after having been long in ruin, in 1827, and the old 'Peter Prison', just within the gate, about 1835. Houses and cottages, mostly small and poor, which had encroached tightly around the W front of the Minster, were demolished between 1824 and 1839 and a block of houses on the SW side of High Petergate, between the site now occupied by the Dean Court Hotel and the row opposite St. Michael-le-Belfrey was demolished in 1860. It was the latter demolition which led to the formation of Duncombe Place, an almost wholly Victorian creation except for the line of its NW frontage, which was that of the old Lop Lane.

Duncombe Place is the last stage in the 'processional way' from the station, over Lendal Bridge and along Museum Street to the Minster, and as such it is outstandingly important in the townscape of the city. None of the buildings which face it, apart from the Minster, is particularly distinguished; the best is probably the modest Georgian Red House. St. Wilfred's Church, whose dark tower is such a prominent foil to the Minster, is not a life-enhancing building; the York Dispensary opposite (1899) is pleasant but undistinguished. The Registry (1860), actually on the SW side of Blake Street, is outstandingly important as it closes the view along Duncombe Place from the Minster, but it is only a moderately impressive building. Also important is the stone classical building of about 1840 facing down the wider stretch, and the W facade of St. Michael-le-Belfry and the excellent South Africa War Memorial (by Bodley) holds its own very well.

Duncombe Place has a very promising shape on the map, but it is disappointing on the ground, partly because of the way in which it is carved up by roadways, dwarf walls and a straight line of trees. The space outside the W facade of the Minster and in front of the entrance to Dean's Park ought to be the climax of the townscape of this part of the city, but it is just an asphalted stretch, partly divided by low railings.

Fairfax Street A bye-law street in the Bishophill area, redeemed by its open land.

Feasegate This commercial street, popular with pedestrian shoppers, curves round attractively from Market Street into St. Sampson's Square, with the choir skyline of the Minster in the distance. It has little or no architecture apart from an interesting Victorian upper storey plate glass facade (the lower storey has been altered).

Fetter Lane A narrow street linking Bishophill Senior/Junior with Skeldergate. It has a pleasant curve and slope, but almost nothing of any visual interest; most of the flanking buildings are commercial and nondescript.

Finkle Street A narrow lane, wholly pedestrian, whose charm is in its shape, and in the splendid view of the Minster looming in the distance. It opens off the N corner of St. Sampson's Square, which funnels into it, and curves round between relatively new buildings in a folksy style, into the at present dreary Back Swinegate.

Fossgate Has lost character in recent years and is now a rather down-at-heel thoroughfare. There is little of architectural value remaining on the SW side save for the entrance to the Merchant's Hall, but the NE side still has charm, with a characteristic York mixture of vestigial timbering, plain small-scale Georgian and exuberant Victorian. It is important as the approach to Walmgate and the whole SE quarter of the walled city.

George Street An old and useful link between Walmgate and Fishergate Bar, with an admirably restored early Victorian terrace on the E side and a plain Roman Catholic 19 c. church by Hansom at its junction with Margaret Street. It is however sadly gappy and in need of renewal.

Goodramgate Goodramgate is still one of the most attractive streets in York, even though it has suffered a brutal intrusion recently. Its scale is smaller than that of some of the neighbouring streets (e.g. Petergate); the buildings are nearly all two-storey or low three-storey, with one excrescence, the Hunter and Smallpage building, rearing over the rest to four storeys. Its old buildings are a happy blend of timber framing, some plastered, some recently exposed, and red and brown Georgian brick; its shop fronts are mostly small scale and unobtrusive. Its shape is endearing, curving at first sharply, and then nearly straightening, then curving away again into the upper reach of the street (described below), which has a different character. Its hidden gem is Holy Trinity Church, behind 'Lady Row' (1316), probably the oldest row of houses in York. The disastrous new building in Goodramgate is unfortunately on the outside of the first curve as one goes northwards. Its upper floor has a row of arched openings of gross scale and its indecisive roof line is a little less high than that of the neighbouring houses. It is monstrously out of sympathy with everything else in the street.

N. of Deangate, Goodramgate carries heavier traffic from Minster Yard towards Monk Bar, whereas southern Goodramgate is by present-day standards still relatively quiet. It is still a pleasant street, with bold curves and then widening in front of Monk Bar; there is much the same variety of architecture as in southern Goodramgate, but the shop fronts are more scrappy, with some crude intrusions, and the subtle charm of the southern part of the street is less evident. The part N of Aldwark on the east side is different again in character, and dates from a mid 19 c. widening (when the second arch of Monk Bar was constructed).

Grape Lane A narrow lane, mainly commercial, leading SW from Petergate. It has some character due to the series of mainly three-storeyed buildings on the NW side, culminating in a four-storeyed brick house of c.1700, after which the scale drops to that of the two-storeyed timber-framed house (in poor condition) containing the arch into Coffee Yard.

Hampden Street See Fairfax Street.

Hungate Originally a winding slummy lane leading from St. Saviourgate to the Foss. Now sawn off by Stonebow and industrialised.

Jubbergate Once a street of some importance in the medieval city, but reduced to insignificance when Parliament Street was driven across its middle.

King Street, Cumberland Street and low Friargate Three parallel streets connect Clifford Street with the King's Staith and the riverside. None has any particular character except what is imparted by the glimpse of the riverside at the bottom.

King's Square and King's Court A key point in the townscape of York. It is the link between Petergate and Shambles, and just off the Church Street–Goodramgate intersection. Its origin, like that of St. Helen's Square, is a churchyard at the haphazard meeting of ways, near the site of one of the Roman fortress gateways (though in this case the space has been created in part by the demolition of the actual church, Holy Trinity, in 1937). It is now, unlike St. Helen's Square, given over largely to pedestrians, with seats on a partly paved area, two or three pleasant trees and an unfortunate rounded rockery. The most conspicuous building fronting the square is now the recently built Refuge Assurance, a dull facade with three broad gables and broad-arched arcading. The rest of the buildings round the square are a pleasant hotchpotch, ordinary Georgian predominating, though there is a recently renovated timber-framed house just on the curve where King's Square funnels endearingly round to the beginning of Newgate and the Shambles (a wonderful piece of small-scale accidental townscape). The NE frontage has been cruelly broken by the demolition of a property on the corner of St. Andrewgate revealing an unsightly view into the derelict area behind. The corner with Goodramgate is made with a most effective tall three-storey Georgian building, and most memorable of all is the marvellous view along Petergate culminating in the Minster towers.

King's Staith and South Esplanade King's Staith, unlike Queen's Staith opposite, is no longer a working quayside. It is a riverside promenade backed by pleasant buildings of domestic scale (one late 17 c. house outstanding), put to miscellaneous uses, including three public houses. It has also in part an attractive cobbled and stonepaved surface. South Esplanade is more frankly an esplanade with solid but unexciting Victorian terrace houses of some scale overlooking the river, the change between house level and promenade level marked by an attractive stone-faced retaining wall. Beyond the Davy Tower (itself a charming feature in its present state, with an 18 c. gazebo built over the medieval base) the promenade emerges onto St. George's Fields.

Kyme Street See Fairfax Street.

Lady Peckitt's Yard Begins invitingly alongside the medieval Herbert House fronting Pavement, and its long 17 c. back-wing. Then the attraction suddenly ends in an indeterminate space in front of recently rebuilt commercial premises.

Lead Mill Lane Contains a handsome early Victorian warehouse with good cornice and pediments.

Lendal A short street of no special distinction; its best building is the set-back early 18 c. Judge's Lodging on the N side. There are some restored Georgian houses opposite. Half the street is destroyed as such because of the long-standing vacant plot on the corner of Museum Street.

Market Street A topographically important thoroughfare forming a busy foot route from Coney Street through to Parliament Street and beyond into the Newgate market area. Its visual aspect is lively and crude; some of the more recent rebuildings (such as the block at the corner of Feasegate with its 'gutted' upper storey) are blatantly ugly.

Merchantgate Minor link in the Piccadilly scheme, feeding into Walmgate; now part of a traffic circus. It has a 17 c. timber framed inn and some gaily painted 18 c. houses; also some hideous backs.

Micklegate West of Railway Street this is one of the two or three finest streets in York, having a character completely different from that of the narrow picturesque streets round the Minster or in the Shambles area. It is broad and dignified—its character is dominantly, though not wholly, Georgian—and (thanks to two or three specially good buildings conspicuously placed) Georgian in a grander manner than any of the other intra-mural streets of York.

From Bridge Street to Railway Street the street has lost character thanks to inappropriate widening and rebuilding. The S side of this stretch is still memorable with the fine early 18 c. range including the Queen's Hotel (with its important interior). It is beyond Railway Street (into which the buses and most of the other traffic turn) that the real character of Micklegate begins to be apparent. It rises and curves sharply out of sight; on the left St. Martin-cum-Gregory is set back, then there are some solid Victorian blocks of some scale in an Italianate Gothic style, followed by some fine Georgian-fronted houses. These are less conspicuous than the line of houses on the outside of the curve, which is dominated by the very fine Georgian town house by Carr (recently St. Margaret's School) placed at exactly the most conspicuous position on the curve. All this stretch of the street is setted, enhancing the scale of the adjoining buildings. As one follows the street round the curve, the rest of its northern frontage opens up, with a varied line of predominantly Georgian fronts, mostly of a consistently modest architectural standard, but including one other major town house by Carr (Micklegate House) also in a prominent position and dominating this part of the N side of the street. At the same time certain features of the S side come into prominence—the projecting trees in the churchyard of Holy Trinity (set back like the smaller St. Martin's) and the outline of the only significant block of pre-Georgian houses in the street, the three-storeyed timber framed houses with over-sailing upper storeys just beyond the church. The rest of the S side is spoilt by an inter-war garage; on the N side simple 18 c and 19 c. houses continue up to the Bar, the effect of which, closing the vista, was partly reduced by the opening of the subsidiary arches on either side of the main arch.

Minster Gates A short but extremely important breakthrough (given over entirely to pedestrians) linking Stonegate with Minster Yard. The fact that its axis is at a slight angle to Stonegate enhances the effect. Mostly plain Georgian houses with some old paned shop fronts all making a properly dignified but modest foreground to the S transept.

Minster Yard The Minster precinct was enclosed in 1285 with four gates, but the gates were all demolished except the small one into College Street by the early 19 c. Houses, many of them small and poor, had encroached upon the precinct especially near the Minster's W front, but these were all swept away by the 1830's (see Duncombe Place). Nevertheless something of a precinctual feeling must have remained until Deangate was built in 1903, enabling heavy traffic to pass along the S side of the Minster.

Off Deangate, E and NE of the Minster, Minster Yard though packed with parked cars retains an appropriate cathedral calm. Here College Green is a grassy space setting off the E end of the Minster, with St. William's College on the N side, but its effect as a space in relation to the adjoining buildings is partly spoiled by the fact that it is fenced off from the roadways bordering it. The Treasurer's House and adjoining buildings hem in the Minster closely, before the breakout into the Dean's Park. This alternation between spaces and buildings is one of the special characteristics of the setting of York Minster.

Monk Bar Court A silent pocket of primitive cottages tucked in behind the Walls W of Monk Bar.

Museum Gardens One of the most beautiful city parks in England. They were laid out in 1827-30 by the Yorkshire Philosophical Society according to the principles of late Georgian picturesque landscaping, and their focal points are the Museum in its serenely Grecian style and the contrasting romantic ruins of St. Mary's Abbey. All the elements of the landscaping as originally conceived are still there; the trees have reached maturity but are not yet past it. There is not very much evidence of recent re-planting. The abbey ruins are a little bare and untidy towards their eastern more fragmentary end.

Museum Street Dates from 1861-2, when Lendal Bridge was built, and is part of the supremely important 'processional way' from the railway station to the Minster. Approaching along Station Road the Minster is grandly visible, but then gradually drops away until, just before Lendal Bridge, the pinnacles of the W towers are lost to view. It is then that the Yorkshire Club building achieves great importance: architecturally only mediocre, but the focal building in the foreground of a famous view.

Other buildings of significance (because of their position) on this route are the two Victorian castellated towers on either side of the bridge and the more substantial medieval Lendal Tower on the opposite side of the road. The continuity of buildings to the S is rudely broken by the empty space at the corner of Lendal, temporarily fenced. Opposite, the handsome 19 c. No. 4 Museum Street is important because it partly closes the view along a section of the street. At the Lendal junction the Minster begins to come into view again and magnificently unfolds as one approaches Duncombe Place.

Nessgate A short and ugly street which has become a confused junction of roads and traffic.

New Street Constructed in 1745-6 on the site of the medieval Davy Hall. Nos. 3–9 are a fine row of mid-18 c. houses. There is nothing else of value except the side elevation of the group of timber framed houses at the corner of Coney Street.

Newgate and Little Shambles Originally these, with Patrick Pool and Silver Street, formed parts of a closely packed area of little houses fronting onto narrow streets. Since the Second World War most of Little Shambles and a small part of the frontage to Newgate have been cleared and a new market place created, in which have been re-established the stalls formerly in Parliament Street and St. Sampson's Square. This is an irregular-sided space, framed by the restored backs of the houses on Shambles and the backs of the commercial premises on Parliament Street, with a strikingly restored half-timbered house as a central feature, and pleasant glimpses along Patrick Pool and Silver Street to St. Sampson's Church. The effect of Marks and Spencer's recent extension is deplorable. Newgate still appears a narrow, picturesque alley and the present restorations and partial rebuildings of old houses at the corners of Patrick Pool have improved its appearance. On the whole the transformation of this area into a market place retaining many of the little buildings around it has been successful. Especially to be commended are the series of small passageways, some passing under old archways, from the market area into Shambles.

Newton Terrace   See Dewsbury Terrace

North Street From Micklegate to All Saints this is now a narrow warehouse commercial thoroughfare of no architectural character. Opposite All Saints its character suddenly changes, thanks to the creation of the riverside open space which has transformed this backwater of York. Facing it, and grouping well with the church with its thrusting slender spire, is a typical York row of 15 to 18 c. houses, the charming restoration of which is an example for emulation elsewhere. The layout of the new garden is open to criticism; but is memorable for the view across the Ouse from it.

Ogleforth A disappointing street to enter after turning the corner from Chapter House Street. Its character is transitional between that of the Minster Precinct and that of Aldwark—in other words it is a mixture of small cottages, some attractive, some shabby, and backstreet commercial premises, with expanding cleared sites. The front of the 17 c. 'Dutch House' has been recently reconstructed.

Ousegate, High A once fine street which has degenerated over a long period, and is now a noisy traffic artery. The W side of the street was largely destroyed by fire in 1694, and some of the fine three-storeyed houses with pilasters and bold cornices built after it still remain, with some less worthy buildings alongside them. The E side, apart from All Saints' Church, is more scrappy. High Ousegate still has the makings of a fine street; it is important topographically, and the houses of c. 1700, grouping with All Saints, are worth conserving.

The corners of Nessgate and Spurriergate illustrate the extremes of good and bad in the effect of architecture on townscape. The bank on the corner of Nessgate is not an outstanding piece of mid-Victorian Italianate classicism, but it is appropriate to its position, and stands well as one comes up from the Bridge along Low Ousegate. The bright red High Victorian Barclays Bank is an unhappy neighbour for All Saints, Pavement.

Ousegate, Low The present character of Low Ousegate dates from c. 1810, when it was widened in conjunction with the rebuilding of Ouse Bridge. The typically tall plain houses of the period till recently predominated; but the present rebuilding of the NW side adjoining the river has changed the street's character.

Patrick Pool A pleasant narrow street, with most of its houses recently renovated or rebuilt, linking Church Street with the Newgate market area.

Pavement This was anciently one of York's two chief market places: the other was St. Sampson's Square (Thursday Market). It was an unusually wide street by York standards, closed at its SW end by All Saints' Church with its tall open lantern tower (said to have been used as a beacon), past which the much narrower High Ousegate continued towards Ouse Bridge; and ending in the opposite direction near the former church of St. Crux (demolished 1887), beyond which the narrower St. Saviourgate led further NE. Its aspect and character have been drastically transformed during the last century and a half. First, Parliament Street with its great width was opened NW from Pavement's S end in 1836. Then Piccadilly, leading SE, was formed in 1912, creating a great cross-road at the southern end of Pavement. Finally, since the Second World War, Stonebow has been opened to continue the line of Pavement at its NE end, curving boldly to the south of St. Saviour's Church, across what had been a slum area. As a result, Pavement has lost the character of an enclosed and self-contained market street and has become part of a series of busy thoroughfares, onto which other much-used roads open. Nevertheless, apart from the fact that as one of the chief streets of York it is necessarily important, it still has good characteristics. From the St. Saviourgate end the view culminates finely in All Saints lantern tower; conversely the view NE, ending in the curious combination of ancient and modern buildings including the recent Stonebow development, with the tower of St. Saviour's and the portico of Centenary Chapel still prominent beyond it, is at least interesting, although the handling of the balustrading of the elevated car park seems unnecessarily brutal. The W side of Pavement is now architecturally nondescript, but the E side is dominated by the striking and well-restored Herbert House, supported on either side by Georgian and Victorian façades of some scale.

Peaseholme Green 20 c. non-townscape. The old inn, St. Anthony's Hall and St. Cuthbert's Church are isolated amid the visual muddle.

Peckitt Street A lane from Tower Street to the river, with pleasant cottages in its E side.

Peter Lane A crack leading from Market Street to High Ousegate, known to the few.

Petergate, High and Low The division between High Petergate and Low Petergate is at Stonegate. Nowadays, however, there is a much clearer break at Duncombe Place, and for the purposes of this survey the streets have been described as Petergate East (Duncombe Place to Goodramgate) and Petergate West

(Bootham to Duncombe Place). The street generally follows the line of the principal thoroughfare of the Roman legionary fortress, but with a pronounced deviation in Low Petergate, south-east of Stonegate.

Petergate East This is one of the most memorable streets in York, until recently virtually unblemished. It is much better to go along Petergate East from SE to NW with the Minster towers always beckoning. They are splendidly visible beyond the long perspective of Petergate seen from King's Square. In this lengthwise vista of the street the distinctive elements are the succession of gables (mainly on the SW side), the contrasting plain brickwork of Georgian fronted buildings (as on the outside of the curve where Petergate finally turns away out of sight) and the west towers rising gloriously just behind those buildings on the curve. Architecturally Petergate displays a large number of 17c. or earlier gabled and timber-framed houses (some rather crudely rendered externally), a few individually fine Georgian houses in deep red brick, and much plain later Georgian work in brown brick. The buildings are tall for the width of the street, and there is an obvious contrast in scale with Goodramgate, which is pleasantly evident as one stands at the junction of the two streets. Few shop fronts in Petergate are offensive and one or two are still wholly or partly Georgian or early Victorian examples of some distinction. Of the two new buildings in Petergate, one has typically panelled curtain walling characteristic of the 1950's, and not wholly inappropriate in its setting, particularly as the panels give it a vertical, not a horizontal, accent; the other is a massive essay in brickwork with substantial concrete sills and a ground-floor colonnade. Here again the design itself is not unattractive, but there is an unfortunate horizontal emphasis which is at variance with the character of Petergate. Taken together, these two buildings appear as a regrettable intrusion into Petergate; one only would have been less than half as harmful (furthermore one of them stands on the site of a recently demolished house which was an outstanding medieval survival behind a Georgian front). The part of Petergate immediately NW of Stonegate has two clear-cut elements, a fine row of early Georgian-fronted terrace houses (earlier behind) and on the corner of Stonegate, a range of timber-framed houses, which group with the 16 c. St. Michael-le-Belfrey opposite.

Petergate West This part of Petergate has not quite the strongly consistent character of Petergate East, and a smaller proportion of the buildings is architecturally important. There is, moreover, one obviously over-restored timber-framed house and more of a 'tourist' atmosphere. Nevertheless this street is unique in York in that it leads direct to the city gateway, Bootham Bar, without the post-medieval widening which has rather spoiled the relationship of bar to street elsewhere. The NE frontage ends in a good range of plain early 19 c. houses curving round to face the Minster.

Piccadilly A 20 c. street, dating from 1912. It has scarcely any positive visual qualities except what are fortuitously given it by the Merchant Adventurers' Hall and its grounds and by the large and commonplace office block near St. Denys's Church. The 'subtopian' effect continues right up to the Pavement/High Ousegate intersection, with its mean traffic roundabout.

Precentor's Court A delightful lane under the shadow of the Minster, but given a somewhat heavy neo-Georgian background by the Purey-Cust Nursing Home, offset by the more delicate Georgian proportion of the old houses around the turn in the street.

Priory Street A consistent Victorian street off Micklegate, with a grandiose Methodist Chapel, an eccentric Presbyterian Church and some well-scaled terraces. The new flats at the end are a come-down.

Queen's Staith A working quayside, with cranes, barge moorings, warehouses, bollards and cobbled surface, and a view across to the less lively King's Staith on the opposite bank of the Ouse. The quayside is attractive in its present unselfconscious state.

Railway Street A dull street constructed in 1843 as an approach to the old railway station. (It was originally called Hudson Street, but the name was changed after the Railway King's downfall).

Rougier Street In its present form the 20 c. equivalent of Railway Street. Nondescript office and commercial blocks erected in the last few years.

Saint Andrewgate The most decrepit thoroughfare in central York, but not entirely a lost cause. The former St. Andrew's Church, secularised after the Reformation and much patched, is still a pivotal feature. To the S the frontages are largely cleared, but there remains one distinctive 18 c. pedimented town house (built and occupied by the architect T. Atkinson), now a warehouse. The middle and northern parts of the street still have some Georgian and early Victorian cottages capable of improvement, enhanced by the street's gentle wavering. The late 19 c. facade of the T.A. Centre is of interest.

St. Helen's Square St. Helen's Square is the heart of York. Here are historic municipal buildings, the edge of the main shopping centre, the beginning of one of the main approaches to the Minster. And the tiny square in a sense epitomises York; it has charm and intimacy, a pleasant haphazard shape, buildings of various periods in harmony with each other and in scale with their immediate surroundings, glimpses of greater buildings and—something which is unfortunately characteristic too—relatively modern development which is not in harmony with the rest and diminishes the attractiveness of the whole, but does not destroy it. The Palladian Mansion House and the restored medieval St. Helen's Church with its charming little lantern, each a characteristic building of its local type, face each other across the square. On the NW side are excellent commercial buildings, one of them, the Yorkshire Insurance building (G. T. Andrews, 1846) outstanding of its kind, perhaps the best early Victorian building in York. The Savings Bank, by comparison, is less appealing but more original (J. P. Pritchett, c.1840). Lesser buildings fronting the square are important because of their positions. That on the corner of Stonegate and Blake Street is a relatively plain late Georgian four-storey building with an excellent Victorian shop front, effective in its position half-framing the view along Stonegate towards the Minster. The one on the opposite corner next to the church is very small fry architecturally but it is effective as a foil to both St. Helen's Church and the view in perspective of Stonegate.

The development which partly spoiled St. Helen's Square was the rebuilding in the 1930's of the whole of the SE side, (including a set-back of the frontage) producing a dull, unexceptionable piece of inter-war neo-Georgian architecture that might be anywhere. St. Helen's Square is now unfortunately a busy traffic intersection, not improved visually by the frigidly symmetrical 'islands' in the middle.

The Square was formed only in 1745 out of the former churchyard of St. Helen's round which some of the converging streets took a crooked course.

Saint Leonard's Place and Exhibition Square The only piece of town-planning in the Regency tradition in York. It was cut through a section of the city wall in 1834-35 to by-pass Bootham Bar, and the stucco crescent is a handsome composition. This leads round to the open space round which are grouped variously the delightful King's Manor buildings with Walter Brierley's 20 c. extension, the Victorian Art Gallery with its ugly but appropriate facade and a section of the St. Mary's Abbey precinct wall with Queen Margaret's Arch. Across the street are the fine early Victorian stucco De Grey Rooms, the gloomy Gothic Theatre Royal and a sideways view of Bootham Bar. This is potentially one of the best townscapes in York; the buildings surrounding the space are a remarkable and varied collection, but at present they do not hang together satisfactorily. This is partly because of the unfortunate division of the space into a busy carriageway, the indeterminate space in front of the Art Gallery, and the fenced-off forecourt to the King's Manor.

St. Martin's Lane An alley off Micklegate, whose small scale is in pleasant contrast to the grandeur of the larger street. It begins by St. Martin-cum-Gregory, with a gloomy terrace of tall Victorian houses overlooking the churchyard, then it becomes a slightly curving alley between buildings and walls, pleasant in shape and scale, till it emerges at the Bishophill Senior/Junior junction.

St. Sampson's Square and Parliament Street St. Sampson's Square was formerly Thursday Market—one of the two old market places in York which, despite its former name, had different markets on several different days for different commodities. It was a small space, not quite rectangular, rather like the market place of a small Yorkshire country town. Only narrow streets, notably Davygate and Feasegate, led into it. In 1836 the whole of this part of York was transformed by the opening of the immensely wide Parliament Street between St. Sampson's and Pavement—really an elongated open market place, intended to supplement, and in a large measure to supersede, the two ancient market places. As a town-planning undertaking in the middle of an ancient city it was bold in scale, but the architectural effect was disastrous. Parliament Street was lined with the three storey plain classical fronts in drab brick which were almost standardised York architecture in the early 19 c, and many of these remain, though in shabby condition. There are no exciting vistas at either end, no towers, distant or near, to catch the eye; only the recession into nothingness of Piccadilly at one end, the nondescript NW frontage to St. Sampson's Square at the other; nothing to break the monotonous roofline of either side

of Parliament Street itself; the one lively building, the hot red bank at the corner of High Ousegate, has had its roofline stupidly simplified and is now dull at roof level.

Saint Saviourgate A sad example of a very attractive York street which has suffered serious architectural assaults in the last few years. Until this happened it was something of an architectural oasis in a quarter of York which, though retaining many buildings of individual interest, had degenerated as a whole into shabbiness. The street retained a consistent architectural character, most of its buildings early 18 c. domestic (in particular the fine range in rich red brick NE of St. Saviour's Church) but enlivened by a remarkable series of churches and chapels. First there was St. Saviour's itself, a relatively dull city church largely rebuilt in 1884 though still medieval in appearance, and retaining its medieval tower, and forming an effective foil to the brick Georgian houses; second there was the Centenary Chapel (Methodist, 1840) with its splendid portico, seen sideways down the street; third the Unitarian chapel, originally built in 1692, set back from the street and not a very conspicuous feature in it but helping to endow it with some character. All these buildings, happily, so far survive, mainly in good order. What St. Saviourgate has lost in the last few years are some Georgian houses opposite St. Saviour's and the Salem Chapel, by J. P. Pritchett, whose fine portico closed the view most admirably down St. Saviourgate. The building which has replaced it is a commonplace office block of five storeys, which might be in any large city, an impersonal termination to the otherwise memorable northward view along St. Saviourgate. The smaller office block which has replaced the demolished houses opposite St. Saviour's is as commonplace, shattering the former relationship between the Centenary Chapel and the surviving Georgian houses farther along the street. And most damaging of all is the return frontage of the one-storey platform of the new complex of buildings in the angle between St. Saviourgate and Stonebow—a piece of architecture crudely designed in the 'New Brutalism' style of the late 1950's and finished coarsely in concrete. As a composition this complex has positive merit, and the form of the main block is carefully considered. But the effect upon St. Saviourgate is harsh in the extreme.

Most of the remaining houses have been, or are being, well restored, as has the Gothic Lady Hewley's Hospital, appealingly set at an angle to St. Saviour's church and the street. The tree in St. Saviour's churchyard conspicuous in the street has a townscape importance comparable to those in the churchyard of Holy Trinity, Micklegate.

St. Saviour's Place Important link between the top end of St. Saviourgate and Peaseholme Green, its N side improved by Ings Property Co. Buried in warehouses on the S side is a forlorn mansion by Carr of York.

Shambles York's most famous medieval street is more remarkable for its cosy human scale than for the quality of its architecture. The approach from King's Square is intriguing: a funnelling of the angle of the 'square' into a ten-foot alley, a twist and then a fork, with Newgate leading onto the right and Shambles beginning sharply on the left. All its reputed romantic quality is here visible; the tall timbered houses leaning over and nearly meeting (in fact, even in York, there are few other streets as narrow as this), and some plainer Georgian fronts to set them off. It is beyond this first stretch that disappointment comes; there is a blatantly sham timbered gable on the left and other poor recent rebuilding which spoils the whole effect of the southern end of the street. On the W the houses have recently been well renovated—how well one can appreciate by going through one of the intriguing little archways into the Newgate market area and seeing the good condition of their backs.

Skeldergate Historically a mixture of old houses and warehouses, those on the NE mostly having some connection with the river. Now it is almost wholly commercial in its NW stretch, with very little that is at all attractive. At Carr's Lane the part of the street that still retains character begins. First there is Dame Middleton's Hospital, with its late Georgian block set back in pleasant tree-shaded grounds with an attractive small later annexe in the foreground. Then there is a row of buildings on the same SW side, beginning with a fine early Georgian town mansion, and including an excellent fruit warehouse fitting well into the group. Opposite are ordinary commercial buildings, but at the south end of the street, just up the river from Skeldergate Bridge, is the finest warehouse building in York, mid-Victorian, built of brick with massively framed openings and an attractive roofline, not overwhelming in scale.

Skeldergate has one of the most crudely designed minor buildings in York; a new public house with 'wavy' boarding as on a garden shed, a sort of parody of the traditional straight weatherboarding of Essex or Kent.

Silver Street A short link from Church Street, past St. Sampson's Church, to Newgate.

Spen Lane A decayed street in the Aldwark quarter, with one pleasant restored house and a view of the Minster rearing grandly over the roof of the old converted church building of St. Andrew's (desecrated after the Reformation), the near-at-hand small building setting off the distant great one in a memorable way, and the imminent squalor contrasting with the distant magnificence. A pleasant little alley leads past the east end of the church into St. Andrewgate.

Station Road and Tanner's Moat Except for the survival of the city wall, this corner of York has been transformed in various stages since the beginning of the Victorian era, with the building of the old station, the opening of Lendal Bridge and of Station Road as the approach to it, the building of the present station just beyond the wall with the hotel near it, the erection of the grandiose NER headquarters building at the beginning of this century and finally the intrusion of the stodgy new Yorkshire Insurance building at the corner of Rougier Street and the unbecoming garage building opposite it. If it were not for the city wall this part of York would seem like part of some large 19 c. and 20 c. commercial city. However, Station Road is important as the first stage within the wall of the 'processional way' to the Minster, continuing along Museum Street and Duncombe Place. For this reason the appearance of the buildings fronting Station Road and Tanner's Moat (which runs parallel, descending, behind a retaining wall, to the riverside) is of great importance. Tanner's Moat is ramshackle, especially since the top of the once exuberant Horse Repository has gone.

Stonebow Stonebow is York's mid 20 c. street and there could hardly be a more telling contrast than between the visual chaos of the buildings on its SE side and the harmony and seemliness of some of the nearby older streets which remain relatively undisturbed. But the street has now acquired some positive 20 c. character with the completion of Stonebow House; the effect of this on St. Saviourgate and Pavement may be cruel but there is no doubt that seen from Stonebow, without the contrast of older, gentler buildings, the effect of this deliberately brutal piece of multi-storey concrete-built development is impressive.

Stonegate Stonegate is, on the whole, the most attractive street in York and the one which epitomises the city's character. It is almost straight (this is uncharacteristic) being on the line of the cardinal street of the Roman fortress, but there are enough variations in the lines of its frontages (and of course sufficient variety in the treatment of the skylines of its facades) to avoid the slightest monotony. Furthermore the view is closed northward superbly by the Minster chancel rising obliquely beyond the low buildings at Minster Gates. The buildings in Stonegate have a typical York variety. A surprising number are basically medieval, but many have plain, three-storeyed Georgian brick fronts. Others are visibly medieval and romantically oversailing or gabled— particularly the splendid series on the SE side towards the St. Helen's end and the range on the opposite side up to the corner of Petergate. One late medieval house has a Victorian Tudor front with florid bargeboards and other elaborate details (a type rare in York and more characteristic of Chester) which adds character to its part of the street. There are some very fine shop fronts, both Georgian and Victorian—this street seems more free than any other in York from crude modernisation. It is very much a 'tourist' street, but it carries this role with dignity and sensitivity.

Swinegate and Little Stonegate Narrow streets of no architectural character almost entirely given over to gloomy industrial and warehouse premises. This is disappointing, since they form part of the topographical framework of a vital part of York, between Stonegate, Petergate, Church Street and St. Sampson's Square, with two intriguing pedestrian ways, Finkle Street and Coffee Yard, connecting with them, as well as a third, leading into Petergate.

Tanner Row and Toft Green As separately named streets Tanner Row runs from North Street to the railway offices, and Toft Green from there to the city wall near Micklegate Bar. But the real break in character is at Rougier Street, and for the purpose of this survey the combined street is considered in two parts, NE and SW of Rougier Street.

Tanner Row NE of Rougier Street A still pleasant narrow thoroughfare, one of the few where houses and commerce are mixed up without disagreeable effect. The houses (mainly on the SE side) are a pleasant mixture of Georgian and earlier timbered styles, part of the same block which has a frontage onto North Street next to All Saints' Church. The commercial buildings are mostly on a small scale; but there is one ugly gap.

Toft Green, with Tanner Row SW of Rougier Street The very beginning of this street, from Rougier and Railway Streets has the nondescript character of those two thoroughfares, but it soon assumes a distinctive character which is unique within the walls of York. This is Railway York—comprising the old station of 1840 and the former headquarters (1907) of the North-Eastern Railway, now the regional offices of British Railways. Here, as near the Minster, one can get the sense that York is a metropolis—the metropolis of railways as well as of the Church in northern England. The headquarters block is not great architecture, but it has definite character in a somewhat debased and inflated 'Norman Shaw' style; it is the only 20 c. building in York which successfully brings off big-city scale. The old station is now somewhat overwhelmed by the later railway offices especially the NE facade (of 1853) which contained the old hotel, but the character of G. T. Andrews distinguished facade on the Toft Green side can still be readily appreciated. Toft Green itself, past the station and opposite it, is a nondescript service road to Micklegate. It then runs, under the inside of the mound of the wall, to Micklegate Bar.

Tower Place A secluded and much sought-after row of late Georgian cottages facing St. George's Field.

Tower Street Now a one-sided street forming part of the fringe of the desolate Castle Precinct. It has some pleasant late 18 c. and early 19 c. houses.

Trinity Lane A lane leading from Bishophill to Micklegate. At the Bishophill end its character has been sadly degraded by the demolition of the buildings and walls which once fronted it, revealing ill-used and untidy plots of land, only partly compensated by the Saxon tower of St. Mary Bishophill Junior. On the SW side there remains a pleasant rambling Georgian house now used as a laundry. The Micklegate end is still attractive and bounded by houses and walls and shaded by a few trees, and its most conspicuous feature is the well-restored late medieval house on the SW side with its very striking and unusual traceried porch (brought from elsewhere). Then the view is closed by part of the end of one of the grand 18 c. houses in Micklegate, and alongside the tree-shaded Trinity churchyard, the pedestrian emerges into Micklegate, the grandeur of that street enhanced for him by his attunement to the small, intimate scale of the lane.

Victor Street A bye-law street in Bishophill, wider than most and enhanced by a late Victorian warehouse with yellow brick enrichment and a late 17 c. house in need of reconditioning.

Walmgate An important street, and until Piccadilly superseded it the principal entry into the medieval city from the east. Never as distinguished as Micklegate, and lacking its topographical advantages, it is now sadly gappy. The street passes through three zones on its way into the heart of the city. The first is a zone of pre-war and post-war municipal housing, of which the most recent example immediately adjoins Walmgate Bar, whose Elizabethan timber upper floor structure, projecting from the original gateway, looks rather lonely in this spacious 'new town' environment. The middle belt begins with the medieval Bowes Morell House on the left and St. Margaret's Church on the right, both sadly in need of better settings. This section contains a few 18 c. and 19 c. cottages of character, and a set-back terrace of new shops, but is of very little interest by York standards and is likely to be progressively rebuilt. On the right, long medieval plots extend to the Foss, mostly filled with a jumble of workshops, of which two are of some architectural value. The third belt is marked by St. Denys's Church, with a good 18 c. range opposite it, and the street ends at Foss Bridge with the handsome early 19 c. Wilson's Hospital on one side and a ramshackle commercial building on the other. Here trees, a 17 c. timbered inn set back, and one or two simple 18 c. houses have the genuine feel of inner York.

Whipmawhopmagate From being a small, short street, this is now a confused medley of traffic and pedestrians, as chaotic architecturally as it is functionally —even though it is at or near the convergence of some of York's most memorable streets.

C Life in the walled City

Pamela Ward

Blossom Street at 3 a.m. is silent, lifeless, disturbed only by the occasional taxi, a cycling workman, the hoot of a diesel train and the rustle of discarded chip papers. Supposing the workman to be joining a late shift at the Cocoa works, it is a key to York's activities. The city apparently dies at night; pleasures are not highbrow, and tend to finish early; in contrast to the Minster and Georgian streets the majority of *people,* workers in the traditional industries, chocolate and railways included, traders, and their premises, are unassuming, unpretentious, small scale, in fact still medieval—a gentle way of saying that once you live in it York no longer retains, except in certain lights at certain times, the dignified aura of an historic city of international significance. It is a scruffy, friendly, blunt, unambitious place and lacks the 'culture' and intellectual consciousness one might expect. If its fabric has lasted this long, it is probably the work of a few keen individuals, similar to those who fight for it today, rather than of the unseeing and apathetic affection of the man in the street.

Anyway the man in the street at 3 a.m. is more likely to be going to work than enjoying himself. I know of only one place where one can be publicly sociable in the small hours, and that is the all-night buffet on platform 14—the resort of those unfortunate enough to be changing trains at that hour, and recommended to students as a place for sobering up prior to waking the landlady. Late trains, mail, parcels and newspapers are shunted about until the early morning trains liven the place up with the first loads of workers/commuters.

It is estimated that more than 3,700,000 passengers use the sixteen platforms in the course of a year. There are 2,200 train movements through the station every day—on average 100 per hour. The total area owned by British Rail exceeds that of the city within the walls. The city has recently become a Motorail terminal, and is to become the headquarters for the Northern and Eastern regions now amalgamated.

Traffic entering the city in the morning is at its worst at about 8.30 a.m. and on the Blossom Street/Micklegate route. It is busy in both directions for a good hour before that, with reps., Flowers Transport lorries and commercial vehicles of all sizes going in both directions, to and from the West Riding and Leeds, but between 8 a.m. and 9 a.m. it is choked with incoming workers for factories the other side, offices and shops, and some school children, from the Leeds direction, and the vast suburban housing areas of Dringhouses and Acomb.

York Workers York Employment Exchange figures for the York area (Shipton, Haxby, Strensall, Flaxton, Scrayingham, Full Sutton, Stamford Bridge, Bugthorpe, Escrick, Acaster, Copmanthorpe, Askham Richard, Long

Marston, Linton, Newton-on-Ouse) for June 1965 give a total of 38,891 men and about 25,500 women, based on the number of insurance cards held in the area. Women in 1962 worked 26% in chocolate, 18% in professional services, 16% in the distributive trades; men 16% in chocolate, 13% in construction, 15% in railways and transport.

Rowntrees Workers Despite a tradition of not travelling, and two-thirds of the women working part-time, a proportion of Rowntrees 8,500 employees are noticeable crossing the city each day. York-West Yorkshire run 13 special buses, though on normal routes through the centre, to the main suburban residential districts—Acomb, Clifton, Burton Stone Lane, New Earswick, Tang Hall, Fulford—to arrive at the works at 7.30 a.m. and 1.30 p.m. leaving at 12.30 p.m. and 4.30 p.m. Three or four more arrive at 8.30 a.m. carrying office staff, and again at 2 p.m., leaving at 5.30 p.m. A special train still brings people from Selby after stopping at York Station (only 60 still come from Selby) and to be at Rowntrees at knocking-off time is to be surrounded by a mass of cars and bicycles in addition. There is of course no public transport for men on night shifts, and about 50% regularly use bicycles day and night, especially in summer.

Students and School Children About 700 children actually attend school within the walls, but many more have to cross the city because of the bus routes. A shorter working week means that morning and evening school children coincide with workers heavily loading the buses at peak hours, when twice as many buses are necessary. Children walking to school use the Museum Gardens as a short cut to schools in the Bootham area, meeting workers coming the other way. Regularly on Wednesday mornings the girls in blue from the Mount School walk in crocodile down Micklegate to join the Bootham boys in an assembly at the Friends' Meeting House. They are conspicuous in the town in pairs and groups afterwards. Otherwise children in uniform in the city centre are usually school parties on day trips or York schools attending the Castle Museum for a series of lectures.

Technical School or College students (600 full-time, 2,000 evenings) are identified by their black and white scarves, moving between Clifford Street and Priory Street between classes and lunch. Art school students (700) sit around Exhibition Square at lunch time, or join University students and workers lazing, lunching or working in Museum Gardens.

University Students are not confined to the campus

at Heslington, despite its detached air. A surprising number live in Acomb and have to traipse through the city each day. Clifton is popular for student accommodation, being on the 9A bus route which goes through to the University, albeit by a very roundabout route, and is convenient for those working in King's Manor from choice or preference. There are now just enough students at the University and browsing round the town for books and odd items for York to begin to feel a university town. Student bicycles do not yet compete with those of industry, and an intellectual looking type on a bicycle in Coney Street is likely to be a lecturer brought up in Cambridge. The only students the public are really aware of are those who walk in silent protest marches occasionally, and these they condemn for time-wasting and creating a disturbance, while condoning the traffic chaos caused by Father Christmas. Fewer still are heckled while expressing their views on Racialism and similar subjects in King's Square.

Traffic Whether it is students, workers or school-children, or later shoppers coming into or through the city, Micklegate is always the place where traffic congestion, generated elsewhere, builds up in the peak hours. The traffic from the west is stopped by a police-man on the Mount, by a lollipop man on Blossom Street, by traffic lights at the Queen Street junction, by buses coming from Railway Street and depositing passengers at Ouse Bridge, and by the police or a warden at Nessgate junction. Other entrances and exits are busy at peak hours, Bootham—Gillygate gets a bit congested, especially when lunch hour and the end of a Rowntree shift coincide, but no block is so easily created and protracted as one involving Micklegate. A bus unloading old-age pensioners at the foot of the Shambles at lunchtime can in minutes block the roundabout and so Coppergate, the Nessgate junction and most of Micklegate. A long bus leaving Railway Street to go up Micklegate to rest in Toft Green obviously blocks the top of Micklegate, but can in busy periods jam traffic through to the shopping area in a reverse process.

In the rest of the town, it is likewise generally a large vehicle which causes a jam; cars alone flow fairly well. Large lorries delivering to the iron-works in Little Stonegate have to reverse into the street from Stonegate, having first waited for other delivery vans such as British Road Services to come out. Large vans climb onto the narrow pavements of Coney Street, Petergate (which has furniture shops) and Stonegate. Ironically, one has the impression of most delivery vans blocking the road when the streets are most crowded with shoppers, presumably to keep the shops well-stocked for shopping peaks—except at Tesco's where the smart young manager bawls out of the window of his office to unfortunate drivers that no branches of Tesco ever take deliveries on Fridays and Saturdays. Occasionally Bellerby's vintage Rolls-Royce van slides discreetly past, heading for the stores in Grape Lane.

Shoppers Bootham, Gillygate, Walmgate, Micklegate have a series of small shops including newsagents and tobacconists, cafes and shoe and electrical repair shops with a particularly small-town or village-like atmosphere. Many open early, close late and are open on Sundays, and during the week have regular, daily customers, many known by name and treated as friends. Shoppers and business people walking into town rather than enduring the complications of the bus system and

traffic jams, call for their daily paper or cigarettes, drop their shoes for repairs, exchange comments with the proprietor on the state of the weather and degree of traffic queue before proceeding to the town centre. Early in the morning, the smell is of fresh cakes and bread baked on the premises ready for office girls going out for cakes for the coffee break; by lunch-time fish and chips predominate, and this mingles first with evening traffic fumes after a hot heavy day and with the smell of beer after opening time.

Central shopping streets are practically deserted on Mondays, many of the key shops remaining closed. Wednesday afternoon means even more deserted streets, and tourists mystified that York has very little open even in summer. Thursday, Friday and Saturday become progressively more terrifying for pedestrians and frustrated drivers, Coney Street becoming virtually impassable on Saturdays. Groups of friends congregate outside the main stores, overflowing into the road; clusters of fathers wait with children outside Woolworth's, and York's teenagers seem to regard the street as the place to meet their friends, or loll about against shop fronts watching. Friday shoppers strain the taxi services, while those on Saturdays depend on family outings with hundreds of private cars to bring home the bulk of the week's shopping.

The Market begins mid-week and is most extensive on Saturdays, selling crockery, drapery, flowers, fruit, vegetables, meat, fish and so on. On weekday mornings when the streets are deserted before 8 a.m. the market area is full of stall-holders' delivery vans and general bustle and banter. The market cafe opens at 8.10 a.m, supplying bacon, cakes and rolls and cans of tea or coffee to take away if there is no time to eat on the premises. Long distance lorry drivers use the cafe as a break when passing through York, or to have a snack before going to a friend's for a few hours' sleep. Between eight thirty and nine trading begins. A notice warns that it must cease in the evening immediately the market bell is rung.

Lunchtime swells the crowd in the streets with workers soon after the Minster has sonorously struck noon—one of the few noises apart from unsilenced motorbikes which one notices above the general traffic racket. Eating lunch in town is often part of the main shopping trip of the week for families and friends. There are Chinese restaurants, an Indian one, Wimpy-type cafes, chain store and department store restaurants, scruffy cafes, Terry's in St. Helen's Square, with cosy waitresses and an interior like the Lusitania, or a self-service alternative at Betty's. If a member, or with one, you can lunch spaciously at the Yorkshire Club—or at the City Club which admits men only. For curry cheaply or good sandwiches, a genial crowd of regulars mixed with a few tourists meets in the crush of Young's two bars. As soon as the weather makes it remotely possible, people eat outside. The Museum gardens are beach-like with crowds on hot days, the river walk less popular. Children traditionally picnic with litter on the Eye of Yorkshire, the round plot of grass in the Castle Precinct, and children and visiting families fill the formal part of St. George's Field, making trade brisk for the ice-cream cart. King's Square is a popular centre for workers eating or collecting lunch. The fish and chip shop at the end of Petergate quickly has a queue, and pigeons fill the square to pick over the leavings. You can sit here and watch the stream of visitors to the Shambles and listen to anyone passing through who has anything to say which he feels must be said publicly. On the Micklegate side of the river, a few picnickers sit on the walls by Lendal Bridge, and bus conductors and drivers drift into the often noisy social club on Toft Green.

At any time on a fine day, people sit in these same places and watch, and also round All Saints Pavement, St. Sampsons, St. Cuthberts and Stonebow seats and gardens, the paved area in Davygate, and round the walls. Where it is busy rather than pleasant, one usually finds older people resting, and old men with nothing to do.

Civic Pageantry If the Lord Mayor is receiving at the Mansion House, or leaving on an official visit, St. Helen's Square has a few moments of excitement, but it has to be something really grand before many people notice, and this does not happen very often. The normal comings and goings of the Lord Mayor justify the comment of a visiting schoolboy—is it a funeral? Special visitors are taken ceremoniously to see the Civic Plate and have tea in the Mansion House, and Guildhall occasionally has concerts.

The Merchant Taylors Company processes from its hall once a year in May, with robes, to and from All Saints Pavement. At the Beginning of the Assize four times a year there is a procession from the Judge's Lodging in Lendal to the Guildhall for the reading of the Commission. The Judges then drive in daily procession to the Castle under police escort.

The fire brigade provides occasional diversions on South Esplanade with hose and pump drill, and the same area is used by the Sea Cadets for small boat activity as an extra to their weekly meetings in Micklegate, where they are frequently seen in clumps on the pavement.

The Minster has its own congregation, probably between 100 and 200, with 50 of them regulars. The clergy consist of the Dean and three residentiary canons, with two vicars choral, and the new master of the Choir School (30 day boys) who is himself in Orders. The Dean leads the Minster, the Mother Church of the whole Northern Province. The Administration of the Minster is not connected with that of the Diocese, the Archbishop being known as Visitor to the Minster. There are four Chapter meetings each year involving the Dean and the 30 canons. The office of the Dean and Chapter has between forty and forty-five on its payroll including 24 employed in the stoneyard, women in admin., vergers, cleaners, library staff and minster police.

The rehabilitated glassworks now provide a fascinating opportunity to inspect medieval stained glass taken down for restoration.

City Churches All Saints Pavement, St. Michael le Belfrey, St. Helen's and St. Michael Spurriergate are still active in contrast to the 'redundancy' of others. All Saints Pavement has village-like choir practice on week nights, and experiments with lunchtime readings or addresses on political/religious/philosophical subjects sometimes involving local MPs. It has an annual patronal festival on St. Peter's Day, and connections with the Merchant Taylors. The Methodists in St. Saviourgate have meeting rooms manned during the day, and providing cheap meals and working facilities for

students. The Society of Friends in Clifford Street have possibly the largest meeting north of the Euston Road, with up to 500 attending, including many children from the Quaker schools.

The City in the Evening York pubs do a brisk trade from opening time and the end of business hours during the mass exodus: regulars drop in for a quick drink or an unvarying couple of bottles of Guinness on the way home—interesting characters without fail in, for example, the Three Tuns in Coppergate, the Bay Horse on Blossom Street, and the Ouse Bridge Inn.

'The White Horse and the Market Tavern, the Lendal Bridge, the Coach and Horses and the others, are at weekends packed to capacity with young people from York and the villages outside, flash girls, farm workers, hard men and rockers. The rock pubs are all things to all men. A rumble is the easiest. An air of frustrated violence fills the already crowded bars and a spilled drink, a casual glance at an unknown girl, a "joke" is enough excuse for a fight.

'Walking down Coppergate between eleven and twelve on a Saturday night can be frightening and, occasionally, dangerous.' *

The rowdyism continues up Micklegate where it wears itself out in doorbell ringing and the consumption of chips, with consequent litter. The smarter crowd meets in the two inns in Stonegate, or in Youngs.

Central York has two cinemas, and constant complaints are that there are no decent films. Three cinemas have closed in as many years, one now thriving on Bingo and holding meetings of the City Film Society. At the King Street Hall there is Bingo and wrestling with occasional dog shows on Saturdays. Sessions finish around nine o'clock, when women throng the bus queues. There are occasional concerts in the Guildhall, or the Tempest Anderson Hall, with attempts by some to provide for more in St. George's Hall. The Theatre has pretty good audiences for most of its varied programme. It has put on some Shakespeare, nearly all the Pinter plays, at least two by Wesker, and such popular pieces as 'Out of the Crocodile', 'Rattle of a Simple Man', 'Alfie', 'The Masters', 'The Rivals', 'O What a Lovely War', 'No, No, Nanette', 'Chase me Comrade', 'The Killing of Sister George', 'The Birthday Party' and 'The Widow's Paradise'. The two performances best attended by students last year were 'Dracula' and a comedy thriller 'Love or Money', rather than the more serious plays put on for their benefit.

Members of the rep company and students foregather at Peter Madden's, where something and chips is available late at night after the end-of-performance drink at the York Arms in Petergate.

Clubs There are three working men's clubs within the Walls, compared with about thirty registered in the city as a whole: St. Clements in Queen Victoria Street, Vickers Instruments in Bishophill, and York British Legion at 61, Micklegate. A few doors away in Micklegate the new 55 Club has drinking and gaming for a maximum of 40 members at any one time in a Georgian atmosphere. It is about the third attempt at something of this sort in this building. An Old World Club is about to open in Stonegate where the Raceways failed as did several teenage clubs of different kinds before. The new manager is to try low stake gaming, with drinking, diners and dancers in the basement. People complain

*Quote from 'Eboracum', a former student magazine

about the lack of entertainment and good food in York in the evening, but few manage to cater for it successfully and consistently. Tiffanys has had two changes of policy since it opened last year, and is now going to try providing proper meals instead of snacks in Wimpy decor; children go to listen to pop records on Saturday afternoons. The Society Club in Bootham is the only club with consistent management and a reputation for the best food in York. It provides excellent dinners for a few at a time, and has other 'facilities' for members in other rooms.

If you have nowhere to go, you can join the rockers with their *huge* motor bikes and black leather congregating in King's Square, walk the deserted streets disturbed only by an occasional peacock squawk, avoiding the noise of pop and rock round Nessgate, and see the river at its best on a still night along South Esplanade: subtle lighting of the warehouses opposite, with a glow from the Cock and Bottle which does not reveal its day-time ugliness, and once past the pubs only an occasional tramp scuffling along under the wall.

D York as a shopping centre

Gerald Eve & Co.

Extent of Shopping Hinterland

1   York is the traditional market, shopping and service centre for an extensive area of middle Yorkshire (fig. 207). The nearest centres of comparable or superior function are at Leeds, 24 miles to the south-west and Harrógate, 22 miles to the west, these centres limiting the extent of York's shopping attraction in these directions. But in other directions distances to competing centres are much greater with Darlington and Kingston-upon-Hull respectively 48 and 38 miles distant and a smaller centre at Scarborough 41 miles to the east, so that York's shopping attraction extends correspondingly further in these directions.

2   Studies of local accessibility and analysis of data from the Board of Trade 1961 Census of Distribution and Other Services have indicated an area (shown on fig. 207) from which most potential shoppers use York central shopping area frequently and regularly. Towards the outer edge of and in some instances beyond this area are several small market towns such as Malton and Selby with facilities sufficient to meet regular shopping needs generated by shoppers living nearer to them than to York. For 'occasional' purchases of clothing and major consumer durables, population in these outlying areas and small towns generally use York in preference to any other centre. It is possible therefore to identify an inner 'regular' hinterland for which York is more accessible than any other shopping centre, large or small, and an outer hinterland with more strongly developed local facilities but for which York is the preferred 'occasional' shopping centre. Both hinterlands are shown on fig. 207.

3   Two other features of York and its hinterland should be noted. Firstly, much of the area, and particularly York itself and areas to the west have reasonably easy access to a major regional centre in Leeds, and there is some outflow of consumer durable spending in this direction. Secondly, the city of York has a considerable tourist attraction which brings spending into the town, albeit into a different type of shop, e.g. shops selling souvenirs, pottery, cafés, etc.

Shopping Hinterland Population

a) *Recent Trends*
4   York County Borough administrative area had a mid-1966 estimated population just over 106,000 persons and has changed little in size since 1951. But if to this is added population in those parts of adjoining rural districts which have been accommodating the city's

more recent growth then the 1966 population of 'Greater York' was probably nearer 145,000 persons. Beyond this were some 30,000 population living in the remainder of the inner hinterland area (noted in paragraph 2 and illustrated on fig. 207) giving York a total 'close-support' shopping population of about 175,000 persons. The outer hinterland contained an additional 75,000 persons likely to use York for some of their shopping, mainly for consumer durables, to give a total estimated 1966 shopping population of about 250,000 persons.

5   Between 1951 and 1961 population in the wider hinterland including York grew by about 6,200 from an estimated 239,000 in 1951 to 245,000 in 1961. But growth was concentrated in the inner hinterland and mainly within the limits of 'Greater York'. In fact population of the latter area grew by about 9,500 persons while that of the remainder of the inner hinterland declined by about 2,200 and the outer hinterland by 1,100 persons. As far as can be established in the absence of detailed local population estimates this trend is continuing with the volume of growth in 'Greater York', if anything, increasing.

b) *Future Trends*
6   In the absence of detailed local growth forecasts, we have for the purposes of this study assumed that the current growth rate in 'Greater York' continues. Much of the increase will continue to be accommodated within 'Greater York' but provision is being made for some of it to be accommodated in certain villages further afield in the inner hinterland area where the prevailing declining population trend will then be reversed. By 1981 we have assumed that the population of 'Greater York' will grow from 145,000 as estimated for 1966 to 157-160,000 and that the remainder of the inner hinterland's population will grow from about 30,000 as estimated for 1966 to at least 40,000 and possibly to 50,000. We have assumed no change in the 'occasional' hinterland population.

7   The future growth of trade in York and in particular its central area will be largely in response to future population growth in 'Greater York' and the remainder of the inner hinterland as described above.

The Central Shopping Area

a) *Retail and Service Shop Floorspace*
8   York central shopping area is substantial and varied in character. A floorspace survey undertaken in April 1967 showed about 1,315,000 sq. ft. in retail and

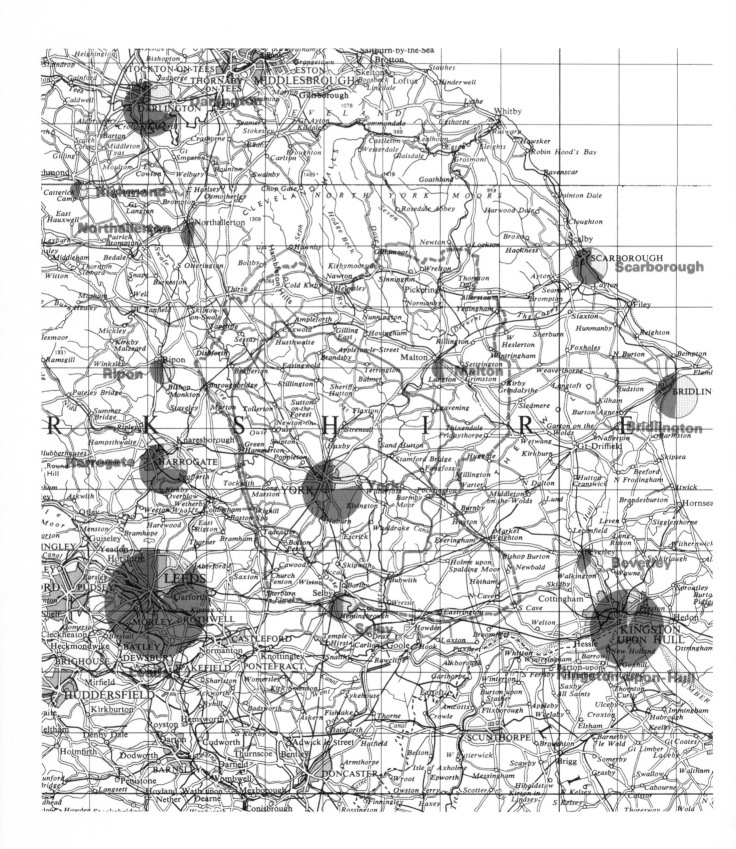

207 Regional setting for shopping

Regional Centres e.g. York : circles are proportional to volume of Central area sales in 1961. Sub-regional centres e.g. Selby : circles are proportional to volume of Town sales in 1961

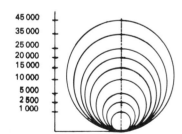

45 000
35 000
25 000
20 000
15 000
10 000
5 000
2 500
1 000

⊙ **Sales through shops selling mainly food etc**

● **Sales through shops selling mainly consumer durables**

—— **Hinterland for regular shopping visits to York**

‐‐‐‐ **Hinterland for occasional shopping visits to York**

service shops in use in the main central shopping area north-east of the River Ouse so that York is clearly one of the major shopping centres outside the conurbations, comparable in size in our experience with Cheltenham, Southport or Maidstone. (There was also nearly 50,000 sq. ft. of vacant space, but nearly 20,000 sq. ft. of this was vacant awaiting redevelopment. Genuinely vacant space at about 2.2% of total in use and vacant was at a lower than average level in our experience).

9   There was in addition some 284,000 sq. ft. of shop space in use south-west of the river in Bridge Street, North Street and Micklegate. Only at its northern end between the Ouse Bridge and North Street is this shopping development even 'fringe-central' in type, the remainder of the Micklegate shopping being more local in character. (For the record, the Board of Trade included the whole of Micklegate within the central shopping area as defined for the 1961 Census of Distribution and Other Services).

10   Summarising, the central shopping area (1,315,000 sq. ft.) and the 'fringe-central' stores in the Bridge Street/North Street area (185,000 sq. ft.) total 1,500,000 sq. ft. retail and service shop floorspace in the centre as a whole.

11   Within the centre thus defined it is possible to distinguish areas of differing shopping function. These are :

Zone (i)   Spurriergate/Coney Street linked by Market Street and Feasegate to Parliament Street and the south side of Daveygate.
The area contains nearly 40% (about 591,000 sq. ft.) of the total 1,500,000 sq. ft. in use noted above. Its shopping frontages contain nearly three quarters of the national multiple traders represented in the whole centre, three out of its six department stores and all its large variety stores. They also contain two thirds of the total floorspace in shops selling mainly clothing, shoes etc. Nearly all shops (95% of total floorspace) are concerned with retail rather than service trade. All these features establish this zone as the intensive 'core' of York's shopping centre and the principal supplier of shopping needs generated by town and hinterland population.

Zone (ii)   Stonegate, Petergate, the Shambles and linking streets.
This area contains about one fifth (nearly 318,000 sq. ft.) of the total floorspace in use in the centre, but shops are smaller (average size about 1,600 sq. ft. compared with 3,700 sq. ft. in zone (i)). There is one departmental but no large variety store, and there are few national multiples. But there are a number of specialist shops selling clothing, jewellery, antiques, silver, china and pottery etc, and these form an important part of York's wider regional and tourist attraction.

Zone (iii)   'Fringe areas' including Goodramgate, Fossgate, Piccadilly, Bridge Street, North Street, part of Micklegate, etc.
These areas contain mixed shopping uses with more food shops (including supermarkets)

than in zones (i) and (ii). Shopping is less 'central' in character, there are no large variety stores, and the two department stores, though large, are of the type normally found only in 'fringe-centre' locations. There were more vacant shops (19) in this zone than in the other two combined (10).

(b) Recent Trends in Shop Development

12   Shop development applications approved and implemented since 1958 have resulted in a net gain of at least 170,000 sq. ft. of floorspace i.e. about 11% of the 1,500,000 sq. ft. in use in the centre and its fringes at April, 1967. About 143,000 sq. ft. of this net gain occurred in the Coney Street/Parliament Street area (zone (i)), the quantity of shop floorspace in this zone having grown by nearly 32% since 1958 compared with an increase of 13% for the centre as a whole.

13   In terms of actual new building (including both replacement and net addition) nearly 306,000 sq. ft. (52%) of the total of nearly 591,000 sq. ft. in zone (i) is of post-war age and concentrated mainly in Spurriergate, the south-eastern end of Coney Street, Market Street, Feasegate and the north side of Parliament Street. The location and expansion of large stores, Marks & Spencer (Parliament Street) British Home Stores, Boots (both with access from Coney Street and from Market Street/Feasegate) and F. W. Woolworth (on the south side of Coney Street alongside other major national multiple shops) has fostered strong pedestrian flows along the line provided by these streets.

14   Over the same period since 1958 there has been no net increase in the Stonegate/Petergate sub-division of the centre (zone (ii)) and very little rebuilding. In view of the picturesque character of much of this shopping area and its value to York's tourist attraction this is hardly surprising.

15   The remainder of the net addition (27,000 sq. ft.) to central floorspace took place in zone (iii) mainly in streets fringing zone (i). Total post-war new building (including redevelopment) amounted to about 80,000 sq. ft., nearly 18% of the total stock in this zone at April, 1967. Food supermarkets in Goodramgate, the Stonebow and Piccadilly figured largely in this new building.

16   At the time of our survey there were three major planning consents not implemented. One which has been outstanding for some years concerns the re-development of Rowntrees Department Store involving a net addition of 25,000 sq. ft. of shop floorspace. The site is a restricted one giving rise to servicing and car parking problems.

17   The second consent covering the re-development of the Tower Cinema (New Street) and adjoining warehouse, office and shop properties leading through to Daveygate and St. Sampson's Square is now in course of implementation. New shop floorspace in this scheme amounts to about 51,000 sq. ft. (26,000 sq. ft. ground floor), and almost the whole of it will constitute net addition of space to the centre and to the main multiple trading area (zone (i)) as defined at paragraph 11. The site is a little way off the line of the main pedestrian flow noted earlier as passing from Parliament Street through Feasegate/Market Street to Coney Street, and the ultimate success of this new development will depend on its success in creating another such pedestrian flow-line. (Although New Street already links Daveygate and the western end of Coney Street it is not at present a shopping street and will be only partially changed on completion of the scheme).

18   The third consent covers a disused garage and motor showroom and three small vacant shops on the north side of Daveygate. The major use in the redevelopment will be offices and the amount of shop space proposed (6,570 sq. ft. ground floor) is much less than the original 17,750 sq. ft. (including a service garage).

19   Summarising, new shop floorspace under construction or included in outstanding planning consents totals a minimum of 57,000 sq. ft. and a possible but unlikely maximum of nearly 83,000 sq. ft.

Forecast of future shop floorspace demand in York central shopping area

20   Future demand for shop floorspace will depend on a number of factors. These are summarised in the following paragraphs. Since the bulk of central area shop floorspace is occupied by retail trades, paragraphs 21-26 deal with demand arising from this source. Paragraph 27 deals with future demand arising from service trades. Paragraphs 28 and 29 summarise demand arising from both sources, and set against this the amount of new building under construction or in the pipeline.

21   We have assumed that the extent of the inner regular shopping hinterland is unlikely to change since York is nearer than any other comparable centre to this area. We have also assumed that the extent of the occasional hinterland and the proportion of total potential spending drawn from this area remain the same, but this assumption may prove over-optimistic should existing traffic and car-parking conditions persist or worsen, in which case Leeds and Harrogate for example could gain ground in the western part of York's hinterland. It is likely that the existing limited net outflow of spending on consumer durables towards Leeds from York and at least the western parts of its hinterland will continue. Finally we have assumed that York maintains its tourist attraction.

22   The population increase forecast for the hinterland were discussed in paragraph 6. Briefly, we have assumed that population in 'Greater York' together with the inner hinterland will grow from 175,000 to about 200-210,000 by 1981.

23   We have taken account of national trends in retail spending since the date of the last Board of Trade Census of Distribution and Other Services in 1961, and on the basis of these have assumed that retail sales will have grown by 2% per annum over the period 1961-81. Within this overall growth, sales of food, sweets, tobacco and newspapers will increase at a slower rate than sales of consumer durables.

24   Within 'Greater York' we have assumed that the development of new peripheral housing areas will tend to strengthen out-of-centre shopping, mainly for food and other convenience goods. A large part of such needs

generated by the town and inner-hinterland population living outside the immediate neighbourhood of the central area are already met locally. In particular, shopping facilities at Acomb are gradually building up to district centre scale, serving growing western housing areas. But the bulk of consumer durable purchases are made in the central shopping area, and we have assumed this this situation will continue.

25   On these assumptions we estimate that retail sales in York central shopping area (as defined by the Board of Trade) will grow from nearly £14 millions as at 1961 to about £22.5 millions (at 1961 prices) by 1981.

26   The whole of this increase will not justify additional shop floorspace. Continuing modernisation of shop premises (including more rebuilding with minor extensions etc.) and modernisation of trading methods will enable the existing amount of floorspace to take some share of the increase, and at least a part will be attributable to increasingly affluent shoppers buying better quality and more expensive items than at present. We estimate that trading on floorspace existing at April 1967 could be expected to intensify to absorb up to £20 millions of the 1981 retail sales forecast so that by this date increased population and spending alone will justify net additional floorspace to handle about £2.5 millions of retail sales, mainly of consumer durables. We estimate that £2.5 millions of additional sales would justify a net addition of about 75,000 sq. ft. of shop floorspace including sales and non-sales uses.

27   The present proportion of service (about 13%) to retail (87%) shops in the centre is likely to be maintained, and a demand for about 15,000 sq. ft. (sales and non-sales) is likely to arise on this account.

28   Summarising paragraphs 26 and 27, we estimate total 1981 demand for additional floorspace at about 90,000 sq. ft. including sales and non-sales uses, and that since new space will be concerned mainly with selling consumer durables there will be pressures for most of it to be accommodated within zone (i) of the central area.

29   Within this zone some 51,000 sq. ft. of new floorspace is being built at present and 6,000 sq. ft. of new space is included in the outstanding planning consent on the north side of Daveygate and immediately adjoining zone (i). This leaves an unsatisfied demand of 33,000 out of the total estimated demand of 90,000 sq. ft.

30   So far we have considered only the calculated net additional floorspace justified by increased population and spending. But the scale of York's shopping activity is such that national multiple retailers not already established in the centre will seek representation in order to compete for a share of this very substantial trade. To compete successfully such traders will only consider locations within or immediately adjoining the existing peak shopping frontages in zone (i), and large enough to accommodate a large shop or store unit of a size appropriate to their activities. The forces which have made for the renewal of so much of zone (i) still operate and will continue to do so.

31   Sites within zone (i) not already renewed and able to meet the locational requirements noted in paragraph 30 are limited. Existing frontages along the south side of Parliament Street appear to provide the most suitable area in which renewal is in any case likely to occur, and an opportunity for adding to floorspace exists by bringing the building line forward to reduce the width of Parliament Street.

32   In conclusion we should emphasise two points. Firstly the achievement of the level of central area sales which we have forecast for 1981 will depend partly on the improvement of the existing centre to reduce traffic congestion and improve servicing and provision of car parks.

33   Secondly the conclusions which we have reached regarding future shop floorspace will be valid only so long as the assumptions on which they are based prove to be sound. The rate of population growth in York and its close hinterland are obviously critical to a calculation of this kind.

E Tourism

A Pilot Survey: August 1967

1 365 people were questioned, selected at random, between 5 pm and 7 pm in the area immediately round the Castle Museum and in S. George's Field car park; in the Shambles, King's Square, Petergate and Stonegate; in the area immediately surrounding the Minster; and in the shopping streets and Micklegate.

2 The 12 leaders of school parties, and 23 people on business, shopping, visiting friends, or for any other reason, were omitted from the analysis in the first instance, leaving 330 to consider in relation to tourism and sight-seeing.

3 The 330 with their accompanying parties represented a total of 1,257 visitors, 1,087 from the U.K. and 170 from abroad. The proportion of adults to children in parties (usually from 1 to 5 members) where one person was questioned was about 11/2 for both visitors from the U.K. and visitors from abroad. It appears that York is not considered an interesting resort to bring children; despite the Castle Museum's popularity with school parties, or perhaps because of it, there is not even a noticeable increase in the proportion of children with adults interviewed in that area, though the time of day might be a factor here.

4 In the street interviews, comment was not solicited, but often given. Of 98 spontaneous comments, 14 expressed general approval for the city as a whole, with a particular aspect specified by several others. Comments, however, were on the whole criticisms. There were 27 complaints about the lack of signposting, both to enter the city and to find car parks, public conveniences, hotels, information and tourist attractions once inside the walls. A further 10 thought there should be more street maps and information readily available. Most people had found adequate parking eventually, only 4 of the commenting group feeling there should be more. 18 people regretted the late opening and early closing or non-opening of garages, shops, restaurants and the Information Centre. Many of the 365 people questioned had only just arrived (5-7 pm) and the information centre had closed at 5-30 pm. One used the police station; others depended upon stopping people in the streets. It was difficult to know where to eat or where to stay, particularly at weekends, and 7 people complained of a lack of restaurants in a reasonable price range. 13 people deplored the amount of traffic, some suggesting it should be kept out of the centre, especially with a view to making the area round the Minster a pedestrian area. 9 commented on the amount of litter.

5 Guests in hotels did not fill in enough questionnaires to make a valid analysis possible. Of 39 valid hotel questionnaires, 32 contained the statement that the visitor or his party had come to visit the city because of its overall historic character, rather than for any one particular feature, 24 mentioned the Minster particularly, 10 the Walls, 13 the Castle Museum, 13 the scale and atmosphere of the place as a virtue, 5 the Gardens and Parks, another 5 the shops. 2 came because of the library; 3 had enjoyed the river; 4 people (all Northerners or from Midlands industrial areas) commented on the cleanliness, and 10 (mostly Americans) on the friendliness of the people and the high standard of hospitality. The same people deplored the lack of signposts most of all, and were equally indignant about parking facilities, lack of bus tours and services within the city, and of information.

Table 1	Number of Visitors & Size of Parties	Place of Origin		
		U.K.	Abroad	Total
	Total Number of parties	262	59	321
	Total Number of adults	769	149	918
	Total Number of children	148	21	169
	Total Number of people	917	170	1,087
	Average Number of adults per party	2.93	2.36	2.86
	Average Number of children per party	0.56	0.36	0.53
	Average size of party	3.50	2.88	3.39

Table 2	Length of Stay			
	Total Number of parties staying 0 nights (day visitors)	224	22	246
	Total Number of parties staying 1 night	19	23	42
	Total Number of parties staying 2 nights	9	4	13
	Total Number of parties staying 3 nights	3	5	8
	Total Number of parties staying 4 nights	1	0	1
	More than 4	6	5	11
	Total Number of parties	262	59	321
	Average Number of nights spent in York	2.63	2.76	2.71
	Total No. of nights	100	102	202

Table 3	Method of Travel			
	Number of parties arriving by car	175	35	210
	train	35	10	45
	bus	49	12	61
	no answer	3	2	5
	Total number of parties	262	59	321

Table 4 **Attracted by**	Place of Origin		
	U.K.	**Abroad**	**Total**
Historic buildings	221	57	278
Shops	33	5	38
A good centre	25	2	27
Others	11	0	11
Total	290	64	354
No Answer	9	0	9

Table 5 **Have been or will go to Minster**			
Yes	205	56	261
No	57	3	60
Don't know	—	—	—
Total	262	59	321
Museum			
Yes	164	39	203
No	98	20	118
Don't know	—	—	—
Total	262	59	321

Table 6 **Organised Group**			
Yes	20	8	28
No	242	51	293
Total	262	59	321
Average number in organised groups	41.75	23.5	36.54
Number in organised groups	835	188	1023
Number of groups	20	8	28

Table 7 **Part of Larger Tour**			
Yes	50	45	95
No	212	14	226
Total	262	59	321
Toured surrounding countryside			
Yes	40	22	62
No	222	37	259
If 'yes' by			
car	30	16	46
bus	8	5	13
train	2	1	3

Table 8 **Been to York Before**	Place of Origin		
	U.K.	**Abroad**	**Total**
Never	54 groups	41 groups	95
Once	29 „	8 „	37
More than once	141 „	4 „	145
Total	224 „	53 „	277

Table 9

Average daily expenditure for overnight visitors

*average party here=2.5 U.K. and 2.83 abroad (cf Table 1)

Average Expenditure (per day per party) on: (in shillings)	Parties from U.K. (38 answered)	Parties from Abroad (37 answered)
Meals	16.21	27.62
Pubs	1.32	4.51
Museums	2.58	1.81
Boats	0.76	0.61
Shops	17.5	24.14
Garages (Parking and Petrol)	—	3.81
Entertainments	0.71	—
Postcards, ice-cream etc.	3.39	5.68
Total average daily expenditure per average party	42.44	67.72
Average expenditure per party per day on hotels	88.33	132.2
Total average day/night expenditure per average party	130.77	199.92

Table 10

Average daily expenditure for day visitors (in shillings)

	U.K. (224 parties answering)	Abroad (22 parties answering)
Meals	20.78	8.21
Pubs	2.35	0.32
Museums	3.49	2.22
Boats	0.91	—
Shops	36.62	8.27
Garages (Parking and Petrol)	2.05	0.13
Entertainments	0.24	—
Postcards, Ices etc.	4.03	1.97
TOTAL average expenditure per average day visiting party	70.47	21.12

F Journey purpose to all zones

Journey purpose to all Zones as recorded at Tadcaster Road on Thursday 26 August 1965
(Extract from City Engineer's Report, October 1965)

(i) All Through Traffic

Purpose	Pleasure	Shopping	Work	Miscellaneous	Trade
Vehicles	55.9	—	11.8	1.3	31.0
Occupants	74.1	—	7.6	0.9	17.4

(ii) All Non-Through Traffic

Purpose	Pleasure	Shopping	Work	Miscellaneous	Trade
Vehicles	28.9	4.4	39.1	1.3	26.3
Occupants	40.1	5.8	30.4	1.0	22.7

(iii) Class 'A' Vehicles—Through

Purpose	Pleasure	Shopping	Work	Miscellaneous	Trade
Vehicles	67.6	—	14.3	1.7	16.4
Occupants	79.9	—	8.9	1.2	10.0

(iv) Class 'A' Vehicles—Non-Through

Purpose	Pleasure	Shopping	Work	Miscellaneous	Trade
Vehicles	35.2	5.9	32.4	1.6	24.9
Occupants	48.2	7.5	24.4	1.2	18.7
Average Vehicle Occupancy	2.52	2.34	1.38	1.35	1.38

Note 1—All values except Average Vehicle occupancy are expressed as percentages.
Note 2—Class 'A' vehicles group consists of cars and light goods.

G Economics of conservation

Nathaniel Lichfield & Associates

1.0 Obsolescence, Renewal and Conservation

In presenting the history and current scene of Central York, chapter 1 of this Report shows how the existing buildings, places and streets are the accumulation of centuries of piecemeal growth and change. In doing so it also shows how, at any given time in the history of the centre, socio-economic pressures drive towards the adaptation of the urban fabric to contemporary needs by the removal of what is currently considered to be obsolescent in the light of those needs.

Just what is obsolescence at any particular time is difficult to define, since any particular structure or environment can be found lacking in contemporary terms due to a variety of contributory factors. For convenience these factors can be considered under five headings:

(1) Structural obsolescence, where the fabric of the building has reached the point of being unable to offer adequate physical shelter.

(2) Functional obsolescence, where the building has such internal defects in arrangement and sanitation as to impede efficient use.

(3) Locational obsolescence, where the building is no longer sited in an appropriate relation to the external linkages and communications which influence its use.

(4) Environmental obsolescence, where the conditions in the immediately adjoining area (incompatible neighbours or traffic) render the use of a building unacceptable to its occupants in its current use, or, in the extreme case, any occupants for any use.

(5) Economic obsolescence. All these conditions of obsolescence are remediable by the expenditure of money, whether inside the building as in (1) and (2), or outside as in (3) and (4). This money will not be spent unless it can be adequately compensated by the returns to be obtained from more effective use of the building, and thereby greater occupational value, in either its current use or some other use. If the expected returns would not be sufficient then the building is also economically obsolete. There is also a special case of economic obsolescence where a building may have some or even none of the other four obsolescence factors, but where the potential value of the site for a new building, again in the same or a new use, is sufficiently high to justify its redevelopment. This might be called site obsolescence.

In the context of this Study, many buildings or groups in York, which ought to be preserved for architectural or historic reasons, have one or more of the first four categories of obsolescence just described, and are also subject to economic and site obsolescence. For instance much of Central York is structurally obsolete, and much is environmentally obsolete due to the traffic, industrial and warehouse use adjoining residential.

Today we call the continuing process of adapting the obsolescent urban fabric to contemporary needs 'urban renewal'. The process of urban renewal is made up of different degrees of adaptation of the obsolete urban fabric in accordance with some overall town and regional plan. The extreme is comprehensive redevelopment, whereby large or small areas of buildings and their associated public facilities are swept away and rebuilt to a new and contemporary pattern. Next comes piecemeal redevelopment, where isolated structures are redeveloped but the limited scale of rebuilding does not permit of significant change in the local environment; alternatively there is piecemeal adaptation in the environment, for example by the provision of a car park, street widening, tree planting or small open space. Then comes reconditioning, the adaptation or rehabilitation of structures, whereby the shells of the buildings remain but are adapted internally for some new use or for the continuation of the old use on more efficient lines.

It is this last element in the urban renewal process which is called conservation. There is only a thin dividing line between such conservation and complete preservation which is usually defined as the process of maintaining the structure despite the lack of an economic use.

Conservation is common practice in any town, but it takes on special features in historic towns because the retention or replacement of the structures is dictated, not by current considerations relating to their economic obsolescence but by the over-riding desire to preserve the fabric for future generations. Thus the need to conserve and preserve the essential fabric and features which are thought to be of long term value act as constraints on the general process of urban renewal. In a historic town the constraints are so strong that we talk of urban conservation rather than renewal.

2.0 Economics of Urban Renewal and Conservation

From what has been said on economic obsolescence, it follows that renewal by both redevelopment or rehabilitation will take place under market forces where the entrepreneur, whether occupier, owner or other development agency, can foresee that measure of return on his investment which compensates for the trouble and risk involved. While the principle is clearly of most relevance in the private sector it also has its application in the public sector, for example: roads, car parks, open spaces and public buildings. Here the developing agency cannot always measure the return in terms of a direct financial profit but will consider that the returns by way of services or indirect benefits to the community compensate for the investment, even though there is a direct financial loss.

On these principles the public and private sector working side-by-side, sometimes in harmony and sometimes quite separately, can together achieve the renewal of any central area. It is against this generalised picture that it is necessary to pick out the essential differences which apply in historic towns.

The obvious one is that, although listed buildings might be economically obsolete, they are retained even though some degree of obsolescence is perpetuated. Thus the redevelopment of obsolescence, that would otherwise occur through the realisation of higher site values, is frustrated. This could mean a slackening in the general economy : obsolete structures like obsolete plant can make for inefficiency in output. Occupiers, whether residents or business people, hesitate to use these structures for either modern living or business if they can find some better alternative elsewhere, perhaps in another town. But if the buildings are located on prime sites, as happens with shops in historic buildings, then competitive supply cannot find a well-located outlet so that the city is compelled to continue its functions in buildings which are, by definition, obsolete.

On the other hand, the site values which cannot be realised might conceivably be reaped in other locations : conceivably because they will only be reaped if the alternatives are suitable. If in fact there are other suitable locations, then a competitive supply of accommodation is generated which clearly undermines the market value of the old.

This gives rise to 'too little demand' : given a certain demand in the economy of a town for the structures, given the stabilisation of their supply through the efforts of conservation and preservation, and given the disinclination of people to take obsolescent buildings if they can avoid doing so, it follows that the demand for those that are to be preserved can be less than their supply. The consequence is the difficulty of finding beneficial occupiers and accordingly the difficulty of maintenance. In York this situation could exist in relation to both commercial and residential uses.

However, in considering and assessing this demand, attitudes of occupiers of buildings are not always related simply to the efficiency of utilisation and location. It is common experience that occupiers also value those qualities of buildings which are associated with their aesthetic and historic backgrounds (for example, prestige, atmosphere, uniqueness) and this appreciation also colours the demand. In point of fact, as such buildings become rarer in number owing to demolitions, these qualities can be expected to be all the more highly prized, a feature which could well be of great significance in the future. But it is also very relevant today that whereas current occupiers might not prize a historic building sufficiently to preserve it, other occupiers could, either because of differing scales of values or higher incomes. Thus conservation might be achieved by facilitating the occupation of historic buildings by potential as opposed to current occupiers.

Finally, in assessing demand the influence of regional and local planning cannot be overlooked. For one thing supply is controlled, and this alone can help to canalise demand onto the conserved structures. For another, potential demand can be steered under government influence; for instance the University Grants Committee could provide grants for conversion of buildings to student rooms as well as for building new halls of residence. Such influences can be powerful if positively used, but they are not necessarily decisive in creating all the demand at appropriate prices that will be necessary for successful implementation of conservation.

3.0 Financial Analysis of Conservation Proposals

In formulating his proposals the Consultant has had some regard to considerations of economic viability, but he does not maintain that the proposals are financially or economically feasible in the sense that they have been tested against the likely available resources and future demand for accommodation. Indeed, this is not the prime intention. Rather, the purpose of the study, as stated in paragraph 1 of the terms of reference, is to bring out 'the implications of a conservation policy for the historic core of York'. One of the consequences of the study will thus be the possibility of examining the economic implications of specified proposals identifying what is 'desirable to preserve'.

In registering and assessing these economic implications of conservation, one important consideration should not be forgotten. The correct background for considering any investment is not simply the expenditure and return that will arise from a project, but their comparison with that which would arise if some other course of action were to be followed. In Central York, if no public expenditure at all was undertaken in the walled city, it would inevitably deteriorate, not only in appearance and environment but also in its ability to function as the centre of the sub-region. Some expenditure would prevent deterioration and socio-economic decline. Accordingly, even if there were no policy of conservation, the City would necessarily have to spend money on a minimum of public facilities, in particular on measures for dealing with the circulation of local traffic (assuming that non-local traffic would be dealt with by works outside the walls), for the accommodation of parked cars and for the servicing of premises away from the shopping and business streets.

In other words, the true cost of conservation could be taken to be the net expenditure (cost minus return) over and above the inevitably minimum measures that would need to be undertaken for York to 'compete on level terms with its neighbouring cities', whether as a conserved centre or otherwise.

As Chapter 9 of the Report shows, the cut-off point is arbitrary. There are many borderline instances and, more important, if conservation were in fact abandoned, then the 'minimum planning measures' would necessarily be different from those adopted in a York to be conserved. Indeed, perhaps the true cost of conserving York can only be assessed by forecasting what would happen in the centre were there no historic buildings to be conserved. But this approach would be unreal in the context of this study, since the purpose of the study is to consider the implications of conserving York against a background of agreement on the necessity of doing so. In other words, the conservation of Central York is a constraint upon the possible alternatives.

In this Report there is no attempt to assess the financial cost and return of the 'minimum planning measures' but only the financial implications of the 'desirable' conservation proposals. Chapter 9 of the Report sets out the approach that has been adopted towards the financial analysis, and Table 1 shows the order of the financial cost and return to the City of implementing the proposals for each of the three study areas and also for certain specific projects and general reconditioning of graded buildings outside the study areas. The Proposals are described in the main body of the Report. In Table 1, columns 2-7 relate to those proposals involving redevelopment and makes the distinction between building costs and external site works including improvements to the environment; and column 8 to those for reconditioning of established structures and, for areas outside the study areas, environmental improvements particularly to the street and car parking system such as paving of streets, hard and soft landscaping, improvements to the setting of buildings including the cost of removal of some non-conforming users.

3.1 Redevelopment

For appropriate parts of the Proposals the city could initiate conservation by purchase for comprehensive redevelopment under the 1962 Town and Country Planning Act or under the corresponding measures in the new Bill to be introduced in 1968. This initiation would cover redevelopment of large and small areas, piecemeal redevelopment or environmental improvement. Where isolated pockets of redevelopment fall outside a 'comprehensive redevelopment area', the powers will depend on whether or not a municipal function or general development is envisaged. Or it might be that private enterprise would undertake the project on a freehold site in its ownership.

Table 1 shows that the total acquisition costs would be just over £1 million and external site works and building costs a further £1.7 million totalling some £2.7 million. Column 5 shows that about half the total would be in Aldwark and about a quarter each in Swinegate and Micklegate. The detailed valuations show that a major part of the cost is on non-conforming industrial uses.

In order to test the financial outcome of the comprehensive redevelopment for the three study areas, the realisation values under three alternative possibilities are given in column 6. The first assumes that all the building would be carried out by the City Council and individual freeholds sold in the open market. This is shown to give a total realisation of £1.5 million, about half in Aldwark, nearly 30% in Swinegate and less than 20% in Micklegate The overall financial loss would thus be about £1 million, with about £500,000 in Aldwark, £200,000 in Swinegate and £360,000 in Micklegate. Much of this is to be explained by the net loss on writing down industrial uses to residential.

The next alternative envisages letting the residential property at rack rents, subject to rent regulation, and selling off the resultant investment to an institution at a commercial rate of return. Here the realisation is much lower, totalling only about £1 million with a loss of £1.5 million. The third alternative envisages that the property would be built and let by a housing association, which was not concerned with making a profit, the capital realisation would then be much as in the first alternative.

All these methods envisage that the authority or housing association would carry out the total construction. If instead the authority were to convey the cleared land for redevelopment, valuation shows that their net capital loss on the land transaction would be much the same as in column 7, with variation depending on the precise method adopted for disposal.

For areas other than the Study Areas the financial outcome has only been tested for the first alternative: that of freehold sale, as this would be the most appropriate form of realisation in the circumstances for these areas. The total realisation would be about £86,000 giving an overall financial loss of £44,000.

In short, even taking advantage of the most favourable form of development to themselves, the City Council is liable to show a loss over the whole period of the conservation of the order of £1 million in capital terms. However, this figure does not reflect the benefit of any redevelopment grants which will be available under the Local Government Act—1966 Section 7. Since at the time of writing the regulations for the grant are not available, it is not possible to forecast what the Exchequer grants would be; but it could well be up to 50%. In other words the ultimate deficit on the authority would be £500,000. This loss of course would not be felt immediately, but would be spread over the total period of the works (say, ten years) and then be financed out of loan. The works have not been costed in sufficient detail to permit of a year-by-year programme reflecting loan charges and revenues but it would appear from the figures that if the ultimate liability were some £500,000 in capital value, the ultimate financial burden in annual terms would be say £40,000.

3.2 Reconditioning Structures

It is assumed that the relevant buildings will be listed and subject to Building Preservation Orders, in whole or part. For these the powers of enforcement and compulsory acquisition, as reinforced by the Civic Amenities Act 1967, can be used. Column 8 shows the actual costs of reconditioning, by conversion, repair or restoration, the listed buildings in the Study Areas, and also those outside the study areas, to which reference is made in the last paragraph of 3.0, together with the cost of other environmental improvements including the cost of acquisition and removal of some non-conforming users whose sites would not be redeveloped for any financially profitable use. The total cost would be £1,000,000 of which about half would be in the Study Areas and half outside. These figures have been compared with the values of the properties after reconditioning, but the present value of these properties has not been assessed so that the total input of capital is not known. In all cases the after value is somewhat less than the costs of reconditioning, thus showing that under conditions as far as they can be foreseen in York at the present time, private owners cannot be relied upon to carry out the whole of the reconditioning under market forces. But nonetheless they would certainly be interested in particular buildings, and a study of sample properties has been made to show the possibilities. Table 2 shows the results.

The Table shows, as might be expected, that the cost and return analysis for different properties will vary considerably. In some the owners can be expected to put the properties in good order and maintain them there, even without the benefit of grants, and in others even the established grants would not induce them to do so if they are motivated by financial considerations.

In order to make sure that these graded buildings would be reconditioned by private owners the City would need to bear part of the financial cost. The net cost of reconditioning has not been determined for the reason

Table 1: **Costs and Returns to the City from Conservation Proposals**

1	2	3	4	5	6	7	8
Area (a)	Acquisition Costs (b)	External Site Works (c)	Building Costs (d)	Total, Columns 2, 3 and 4	Realisation of Freeholds (e)	Capital Loss on Redevelopment	Reconditioning and environmental improvements (f)
STUDY AREAS ALDWARK	£ 441,000	£ 52,000	£ 825,000	£ 1,318,000	£ 837,000[1] 587,000[2] 864,000[3]	£ 481,000[1] 731,000[2] 454,000[3]	£ 159,000
SWINEGATE	186,000	35,000	402,000	623,000	426,000[1] 284,000[2] 430,000[3]	197,000[1] 339,000[2] 193,000[3]	119,000
MICKLEGATE	326,000	38,000	261,000	625,000	267,000[1] 174,000[2] 284,000[3]	358,000[1] 451,000[2] 341,000[3]	221,000
STUDY AREAS TOTALS:	953,000	125,000	1,488,000	2,566,000	1,530,000[1] 1,045,000[2] 1,578,000[3]	1,036,000[1] 1,521,000[2] 988,000[3]	500,000
OUTSIDE THE STUDY AREAS	54,000	6,000	70,000	130,000	86,000[1]	44,000[1]	498,000
TOTALS	1,007,000	131,000	1,558,000	2,696,000	1,616,000[1]	1,080,000[1]	1,000,000

NOTES:
- (a) See Report: Chapter 9.
- (b) On basis Land Compensation Act, 1961: market value, including fees and disturbance.
- (c) Site works such as street works, lighting, landscaping to be borne by City Council.
- (d) Including clearance, fees, interest on capital during construction.
- (e) [1]Sale of individual freehold properties, at open market value.
  [2]Private developers, letting of properties at rack rent subject to rent control, at capital value.
  [3]Housing Association, letting of properties at rack rents, capital value.
- (f) Includes acquisition costs for removal of certain non-conforming users.

SOURCE: Gerald Eve and Co. based on figures supplied by Bernard Thorpe and Partners and Davis, Belfield and Everest.

Table 2: **Cost and return of reconditioning sample properties**

Example	Capital Cost[1]		Realisation Value	Net Position[2] (A)	Net Position[2] (B)
(1) Conversion of a warehouse to residential use of two superior flats to let at a net rent of £200 p.a.	Acquisition Construction	£1,000 £4,150			
	Total, say	£5,000	£5,000	break even	£800 gain
(2) Conversion of a warehouse to residential use of 7 flats of about £1,000 sq. ft. to let at net rent of £150 p.a.	Acquisition Construction	£6,250 £16,700			
	Total, say	£23,000	£13,000	£10,000 loss	£7,200 loss

NOTES:
[1] Including fees interest and contingencies.
[2] Column A shows the position without the benefit of Discretionary Improvement grants under the Housing Act 1964; Column B the position with the grant.

mentioned but the cost to the City might be about 40% of the construction cost. Of the total cost of £1 million in column 8 £0.7 million is for conversion, repair or restoration of buildings: the remaining £0.3 million being for environmental improvements. Depending on increasing interest being shown in the private sector if the City were to contribute 40% of the cost of conversion the total annual cost would be about £50,000.

3.3 Redevelopment and Reconditioning

Summarising and bearing in mind high interest rates and relatively short periods for loan sanctions the annual financial cost to the City could be about £130,000 if the Exchequer redevelopment grant were not obtained, or £90,000 if it were forthcoming: both figures assume a 40% contribution towards the cost of conversion. These figures would result in either a 9d or 6d rate to the City based on the 1966 Rateable Value.

3.4 Initial Works and Maintenance Thereafter

Initial expenditure on conservation does not solve the problem for by definition the intention is to conserve conditions as far into the future as possible. During this period cost of maintenance will be higher for the older buildings both because of their more delicate fabric and because some of those which are at present in good condition and do not need attention will inevitably deteriorate. Values of the property may not be maintained or rise, although it is to be expected that once conservation is carried out the very scarcity of these properties, and the unique conditions within the Walled City, will help to keep values at a high level.

But since a continuing interest is needed in the property, it follows that the opportunities would be better if the City Council were to continue to have an interest as landlords. Bearing this aspect in mind, it would appear from Table 1 that the third method of realisation, a housing association, would be the best since the City Council could ensure that the revenues from the property would continue to be spent on maintenance and upkeep. If the properties were sold off as in basis 1, or passed to an investing institution as in basis 2, the prospects for upkeep would probably not be as high.

4.0 Cost Benefit Analysis of Conservation Proposals

Cost-Benefit Analysis

The financial analysis just described presents only the financial costs and returns to the public and private bodies responsible for implementation although, by implication, the figures also introduce financial effects on other groups. For example, insofar as there is a net loss to local and central government, this burden will be met by City ratepayers and national taxpayers; and insofar as returns to present owners reflect the sale or ground rent price of land to be made available after clearance, or sale or rental return from the buildings after restoration, the financial costs to future occupiers are established.

But even this implied inclusion of other groups in the financial analysis leaves out of the account many other parties who are involved directly or indirectly in the process, and also many other costs and benefits of a social and economic character. In other words, the financial balance sheet does not give a comprehensive picture of the socio-economic repercussions of planning policies for conservation. To provide this it is necessary to make a wider cost-benefit analysis.

In the popular sense, cost-benefit analysis is simply conventional economic analysis aimed at selecting which of alternative investment or operating expenditures would show the best relation of cost and return. As such it could be applied in a conservation study simply to alternative proposals for the restoration of an historic building, whereby different amounts and arrangements of expenditure are compared with the differing rental values that could be obtained. But the term has come to have a wider application: that of investment by public bodies where the returns from the services they provide cannot be measured in terms of market prices (for example, highways, education, or health) and where, since the investment is by a public body, the indirect as well as the direct consequences of the investment must also be considered.

In applying the analysis to the field of planning, development and renewal, special features arise. For one thing, investment and operating expenditures in a city are so diverse in character that both private and public sectors, and many different and inter-related forms of investment must be considered together. For another, since the decision is a planning one in the broadest sense, many of the repercussions are intangible (the value to the nation of rebuilding York Minster) but nonetheless should not be excluded from the balance sheet even though they cannot be measured in money terms. These considerations have led to the formulation of a particular application of cost-benefit analysis in the planning field, known as the planning balance sheet.

While an actual planning balance sheet for all the conservation proposals for York could be attempted, this would be outside the scope of the study *. Instead a brief description of the technique is presented to illustrate how it would be applied to one specific element of the proposals for York: the transformation of Stonegate into a pedestrian street. This illustration will help to amplify what has been said above about the limitations of the financial analysis and also identify the parties who would obtain the benefits of conservation, and so give a lead to the possibility of recouping some of this betterment from them.

Approach to the Analysis

As indicated the essential reason for the analysis is to consider all the sectors of the community who would be affected by the alteration of Stonegate, and not merely those who would have a financial stake. In this sense the community includes not only the residents of York but also others who have an interest, such as the tourists, and the lorry drivers who deliver goods to the shops. Thus the first step is to enumerate all the interested parties. This is achieved by distinguishing, as sectors, groups with common objectives, such as current occupiers of shops and houses, pedestrians, motorists, and so on. This enumeration is clarified by regarding the proposals in an economic framework, that is to say, regarding the process of achieving conservation, or indeed any other planning policy, as basically one of the investment of resources (including limitation of invest-

*For an example of the application to historic buildings, see Nathaniel Lichfield, 'Cost Benefit Analysis in Urban Redevelopment, Research Report No. 20', Real Estate Research Programme, University of California, Berkeley, 1962

For an example of the application to central area renewal, see Lichfield, 'Cost Benefit Analysis in Urban Redevelopment: A Case Study: Swanley', *Urban Studies,* 1966

ment) aimed at providing occupational and environmental services which are consumed both by the occupiers of the buildings, whether continuing or visiting, and those who circulate in the spaces between. Furthermore, since planning proposals constitute real estate development and renewal, producers include current property owners, whose assets are used in the process, and the consumers the corresponding current occupiers.

The relevant sectors of the community are thus grouped into producers/operators on the one hand and consumers on the other. On this approach the following grouping shown on the table below is related specifically to Stonegate, and each sector can be taken to include not only our generation but also those of the future.

From this classification, the costs and benefits of the proposals for conservations to each group can be traced through by visualising that the alteration of Stonegate has been completed and then forecasting the difference in the repercussions compared with the present situation *.

The method broadly follows the lines of general social accounting technique by collecting all the costs and benefits into a specially designed Accounts Table. Producers/Operators and Consumers are kept separate on each side of the table but are paired as far as possible. Each linked or associated pair of producers/operators and consumers are considered to be engaged in a transaction whereby the former produces services for sale to the latter. These transactions are not confined to goods and services exchanged in the market. They extend as well to indirect costs and benefits. An example of the former is the loss to a business which is to be displaced from Central York as a non-conformer to the extent that the proprietor is not fully compensated for disturbance. An example of the indirect benefit is

that to an owner whose property is enhanced in value through the clearance of industry from adjoining land.

Costs and benefits are isolated by enumerating the assumed objectives of each sector and, where possible, they are measured in money terms. This is usually fairly easy for producers' costs and benefits, but not for those of consumers, because many are intangible in that they have no market price. For example, pedestrians walking in safety and also experiencing the amenity of beautiful and interesting groups of buildings while traversing the streets. These elements are measured in non-money terms as far as possible (for instance relative numbers of people) but even where quite immeasurable they are included in the balance sheet by means of symbols.

The end result is thus a comprehensive picture of the implications of conservation to all the interested parties. As such the planning balance sheet provides a background against which the decision of whether or not to conserve, and also how much to do, can be taken. The decision is not easy, nevertheless, because due to the non-measurables, there is no single money rate of return to provide a conclusive answer. Accordingly it involves the weighting by judgement of the relative importance of various groups and their objectives.

The Stonegate Study
Elsewhere in this Report, Stonegate has been described as one of the prettiest luxury shopping streets in the world and is perhaps the finest remaining comprehensive example of historic York. In the main the shops cater for local and tourist shoppers in specialised trades, such as antiques and boutiques. The street is narrow, being only about twenty feet wide and at present is one-way from south to north for traffic. Apart from delivery vans climbing onto the pavement to park and interfering with pedestrians during the day, one of the worst hold-ups to traffic is from large lorries delivering to the ironworks in Little Stonegate, into which they have to reverse from Stonegate.

Stonegate forms the north-west boundary of the Swinegate study area. The condition and listing of the buildings in Stonegate is set out elsewhere in this

*While, as indicated in Section 3 above, the datum for comparison should be the situation which would arise if York were not conserved, the current situation can be taken for this analysis.

PRODUCERS/OPERATORS	**CONSUMERS**
1.0 York City Council as the Conservation Authority	2.0 The Public Using Stonegate 2.1 Pedestrians — Shoppers — Visitors (national and international) 2.2 Motor Traffic — Commercial — Private
3.0 Landowners	4.0 Occupiers of Land and Buildings

considered together :

3.1/4.1 Commercial — Shopkeepers
 — Office
 — Restaurant and Club Owners

3.2/4.2 Residents

| 5.0 York City Council as Local Authority
5.1 Municipal Costs
5.2 Municipal Revenue
7.0 Central Government
7.1 National Costs | 6.0 Ratepayers

8.0 National Taxpayers |

Report: in the main most of them are listed and in good condition. The proposal is that it should be closed completely to traffic during the day becoming a paved pedestrian street. Deliveries to the shops in Stonegate will take place on weekdays between the hours of 5 am and 10 am in the morning. Little Stonegate will be bollarded and become a service cul-de-sac with access out of Swinegate. The new bus route from Fishergate Bar to Bootham Bar will pass along the restricted Davygate at the bottom end of Stonegate whilst Low Petergate at the top end will also become a pedestrian street.

A few of the buildings in Stonegate are in need of conversion, or repair, to bring them up to a good standard of condition, and this will be carried out also.

Each of the Stonegate sectors enumerated above is now examined in turn. Much of what follows has already been described in the body of the Report, this reiteration merely marshals the arguments within the framework of the planning balance sheet. The Accounts Table (omitted here) is normally accompanied by a written text, and it is this description of the Table which is included: being an analysis of the repercussions on the various sectors of the community in terms of the difference in costs and benefits of the conserved Stonegate compared with current conditions.

1.0 York City Council as the Conservation Authority

The overriding responsibility of a Local Authority within the overall welfare context is financial: that of minimum net cost consistent with the standard of environment to be achieved. The financial benefits and costs to the City (and costs to Central Government) have already been discussed in the financial analysis. The capital costs directly attributable to the conservation of Stonegate are as follows:

Buildings	: Conversion Repair	£27,000
Street	: Closure, paving, bollards, street, furniture, etc.	£ 3,250
	TOTAL	£30,250

Assuming, for the sake of this analysis, that the City Council would pay, under the Local Authorities (Historic Buildings) Act 1962, for 40% (arbitrary figure) of the cost of conversion and repair of the buildings by way of grants, its total capital cost would be £14,050: approximately £1,120 per annum in terms of an annual loan charge at 7% over 30 years. They would receive no direct financial return for this investment, but if each of the 50 shopkeepers in Stonegate were to contribute to the cost of paving, it would cost each one £65 and reduce the annual cost to the City to £850 per annum.

2.0 The Public using Stonegate

This sector is restricted to those people using the street; people occupying the buildings and the public once they enter the buildings are considered separately.

2.1 Pedestrians in Stonegate include both shoppers and others with business in the buildings along the street and also visitors from the rest of the country and abroad who, whilst incidentally buying things in the shops or eating in the restaurants, have come to York to see the medieval City. They would benefit from the exclusion of motor traffic in being able to traverse the street at a fast pace if they wish to gain time or at a more leisurely walk to view the shops and restored buildings and precinct; they would be able to walk in safety avoiding the sudden conflicts with traffic which happen at present, as for instance when emerging from Coffee Yard into Stonegate; and they would be able to enjoy the amenity of the narrow medieval street without the noisy, noxious, visible intrusion of cars and delivery vans and the depression of decaying buildings.

2.2 Motor Traffic in this context comprise commercial vehicles delivering to and carrying from the shops, and private motorists. For the benefit of their trip purposes they would have some increase and some decrease in costs.

Commercial delivery vans would save time on their trips by being able to unload close to the buildings without pedestrian interference and by being able to reach Stonegate more quickly along roads within the walled city which are open purely to commercial traffic in the less crowded hours. But they would have the added cost of enforced delivery during evening, night or early morning—greater, lesser or the same cost as at present depending on whether Stonegate is the only destination or whether a round trip could be rationalised to fit in with the new delivery times—and of penetrating the walled city only in certain places to reach Stonegate.

Private cars would be able to reduce their journey time costs by being able to find a parking space, at a money charge, in the new multi-storey car parks at Monkgate and Gillygate (from which the walking time to Stonegate is about four minutes) without having to cruise around to find an odd corner in which to park. But they would lose the facility of being able to drop passengers or stop for a few minutes close to their destination, although there would be a direct bus service to Stonegate from Gillygate. It is difficult to assess whether the total journey time would be any the less, because this latter disadvantage would offset the former advantage. These factors would apply to all private motorists whether they were workers, shoppers or visitors. But residents adjoining Stonegate and throughout the walled City would have the advantage of privileged freedom of movement within the Centre on issue of a windscreen licence, along all roads not actually closed to traffic.

Finally, the rationalisation of traffic movement within the walled city in general should give greater safety and consequent savings in accident costs.

3.0/4.0 Current Landowners and Occupiers of Land and Buildings

These producers and consumers are considered together as their benefits and costs derive from the same causes even though they may be distributed unevenly between them.

In order to implement conservation proposals there is bound to be a certain amount of permanent and perhaps premature displacement by removal of non-conforming users and so on. But in the properties adjoining Stonegate there would be no permanent displacement, so that there will be no such costs to displaced owners.

The majority of owners and occupiers in Stonegate would derive benefits from conservation whilst they would have to bear some of the costs. In terms of capital cost of conversion and repair, owners will have the residue of the capital cost, after they have received grant from the City Council, of £16,200. However, the conversion of the buildings will enhance their value.

Commercial occupiers such as the shopkeepers and clubowners will have additional costs of having staff available to receive deliveries after opening hours and possibly also the capital cost of £65 per shop for paving. But on the other hand, it is likely that an increase in trade would be experienced in Stonegate, particularly for the predominating antique shops and boutiques which rely to a large extent on browsing shoppers. Therefore there would be benefits to retail occupiers, and the increase in the numbers of people using pedestrian streets could also lead to an increase in the trade of the restaurants and clubs. Such trade would also be increased from the new residents of the new houses in Swinegate and Grape Lane. As such the extra investment involved would be likely to give a high financial return.

Residents living over the shops would again have mixed benefits: during the day the noise of traffic would be removed, but would be transferred to the early morning, which might possibly be more of a nuisance. The accessibility of these dwellings for private motorists has been considered above in item 2.2.

5.0/6.0 York City Council as Local Authority and Ratepayers

It is unlikely that the municipal costs of the day-to-day cleaning, collection of refuse and lighting of Stonegate would increase. As to revenues: if the value of properties along Stonegate improves due to increased turnover in shops, there would be a corresponding increase in rateable values. Thus the net revenue position should improve, except that ratepayers as a whole in York will be financing the annual loan charges of £1,120 on the capital cost as set out in item 1.0 above. This has, however, already been counted under item 1.0.

7.0/8.0 Central Government and National Taxpayers

The analysis has assumed that there would be no contribution to this capital cost from Central Government. If there were to be a contribution then the national taxpayer as well as the local ratepayer would also bear a share of the cost as assessed under item 1.0.

Summary and Conclusion

From this outline of the analysis the following provisional conclusions can be drawn: provisional in the sense that the analysis is included primarily to illustrate the method.

Producers/Operators: the City Council as Conservation and Local Authority would be involved in net costs of £14,050 (£1,120 per annum) which might be shared with Central Government (1.0, 5.0, 7.0) and the current owners of property (3.0/4.0).

Consumers: pedestrians would benefit (2.1), motor traffic would have both costs and benefits but would appear to gain overall (2.2), commercial occupiers would benefit (3.1/4.1) but residents might not owing to day time gains being offset by early morning disturbance (3.2/4.2).

In brief, the net financial cost of the alteration of Stonegate would attract net benefits to most sectors of the community which would not be all directly reflected in higher property values, and would also bring some disbenefits. It is not possible to say just where the actual balance would be because many of the relevant factors, for instance increased trade, have not been sufficiently probed; although it would seem that benefits would go a long way to offset costs. But the analysis does show that financial costs and returns give only a limited picture, and demonstrates a way of assessing the other costs and returns to the community from conservation.

5.0 Conservation and Betterment

The betterment issue in conservation is in principle no different from that in planning generally. In essence, the case for recoupment of betterment by public bodies is said to arise for two reasons. First, although land values may fall in certain localities, in general they rise in real as opposed to inflationary terms from the growth in population, activities and wealth. After allowing for some return to the entrepreneurial skill of the developer, the resultant financial profit to the land owners can be said to be 'unearned'. Secondly, and more specifically, central and local government by planning policies and vast public expenditure canalise values on to specific sites, but they are normally unable to recoup such enhanced values, whereas they often have to pay compensation for any diminution of value. The contrary argument that the betterment created results in increased tax and rateable value, ignores the fact that such increases really only result in redistribution of tax burden and therefore income.

Against this general background, betterment arising from conservation policies has special features which lead to the justification of some recoupment additional to that which is normally levied. Firstly, it is financially costly to public authorities: in the nature of the exercise, the financial costs falling on public authorities tend to be heavy in relation to financial return and the benefits from conservation are not directly reflected, as in redevelopment in non-historic towns, in enhanced site values which can be tapped by means of capital gains, income tax or local rates. Secondly, the benefits of conservation are intended to accrue not only to a much wider public than that of the city concerned (nationally and internationally) but also to later generations in the sense that the national heritage is being conserved for posterity.

However, the possibilities for the collection of betterment open to Local Authorities in the normal process of planning are somewhat limited. Very briefly, local authorities can recoup on their expenditure only when buying land for development, either as a set-off in certain cases against the cost of acquisition or by capturing, from their new development, some of the enhanced values that they have created. The Land Commission also levies a 40% charge on increases in development value, however caused. But this betterment goes directly to the Commission and Treasury and there is no specific provision for it to be transferred to local authorities, although there has been indication that some indirect subvention might be given.

Therefore, additional measures for betterment collection by local authorities from conservation are needed. As foreshadowed in describing the kind of cost-benefit analysis which could be made of conservation proposals, the following suggestions for sources of betterment are related to the benefits illuminated in the analysis which come from conservation, and which would not be tapped by local or central government under existing legislative and administrative provisions. The suggestions are made in relation to the consumers, for these are the sections of the community which directly enjoy the benefits of conservation.

The Public using the Town

Pedestrians and Motor Traffic

No recommendations are made in relation to these sectors, since it would not be practicable to levy betterment from them.

Visiting Public

This sector relates to the visitors from outside the city, either from the United Kingdom or abroad who, by definition, come to spend some time in the city, possibly staying overnight. Insofar as they do stay overnight, they would be paying for hotel accommodation and accordingly a special tax could be charged for their accommodation or meals, as is done for tourists abroad. The percentage of tax would be clearly noted on the bill, and the proceeds passed to the City. In practical terms, it would not be possible to differentiate in the hotels between the tourist/visitor and the other kind of hotel visitors, so that in effect all hotels would be charging somewhat higher prices. Thus hotels in York would be put at a price disadvantage with hotels elsewhere. If this was felt to be a deterrent to visitors, then the alternative would be to impose the tax but expect the hoteliers to pay it, thus ultimately levying the tax from the landowners; or for the British Travel Association to contribute direct to the City by way of an annual grant due to York's somewhat unique locational and intrinsic value to tourists.

In addition to the hotel accommodation, the visitors would be spending money in the shops, restaurants, and particular tourist attractions. Expenditure in shops could be taxed by the measures described below. Additional taxes could also be levied at the point of entry to the specific attractions to visitors such as the Minster or Castle Museum. Where charges are already made, they might be increased and a percentage channelled to the City. In addition, any means of transportation specific to visitors (such as coaches) could have a special tax levied at their authorised parking place.

Land Owners and Occupiers not displaced

One effect of conservation proposals is to shift potential land values from areas subject to such proposals to other areas in the City, and perhaps elsewhere. For example, where non-confirming uses are bought up to improve the environment, a demand is generated by these for new development on open land or redeveloped sites; and the very preservation of particular historic buildings prevents the exploitation of their sites for new development, and thus edges the frustrated development on to other land. Conservation proposals thus stimulate increases in land values elsewhere. The authority could recoup some of the betterment so created by purchase of such other sites and then re-accommodate the displaced or frustrated uses. Where it does not do so, the Land Commission would recoup some of the increase by the betterment levy. This suggests that there is a case in a conserved City for asking the Land Commission to divert to the Local Authority some of their revenue from the levy. This would be a major new principle and would require either fresh legislation or Government Direction to the Commission; alternatively the argument could be used for increase in Government contribution to historic cities on the lines indicated below.

A specific example of betterment which is more easily definable than most arises on sites close to those directly affected by conservation proposals, where the authority do not intend to purchase: for instance houses adjoining non-conforming industry which is removed, or historic buildings which benefit from environmental measures. Here the authority recoup by buying at pre-conservation value and selling at the higher value. Such purchase would however clearly be difficult to implement in practice, instead the prospect is open for a special improvement tax on such properties where increases of value can be established. The special improvement tax has a long history in betterment proposals and an understandable logic, although in practice it is difficult to assess and enforce. The tax could be either a capital levy (overlap with capital gains taxation would need to be avoided) or a special rate imposed annually for a number of years.

While it might be possible to define betterment of a specific site, it is much more difficult to define the betterment which will arise generally in an area from conservation: removal of non-conforming uses could clearly upgrade the residential quality of a whole sector of the City. When this consideration is taken with another—the general increase in trade and prosperity through the spending of tourist/visitors in the shops and business premises—the possibility arises of a special rate on the whole of the area thought to be affected: in this context perhaps the whole of the walled City. In addition to the general rates for this area, a special rate could be imposed and identified separately on the rate demand. The history of such rates in this country is a long one, but generally speaking it has been applied to rural areas where a specific improvement (such as the protection of a sea wall) clearly should not be charged to ratepayers as a whole since it is for the benefit of a definable few. The principle suggested here is an extension of this idea, in that conservation should be paid for by the local community who would benefit rather more possibly than the rest of the community. The incidence would naturally be somewhat arbitrary, for the diffusion of benefits would not be equal; but then so is the incidence of taxation by local rates generally.

Central Government and National Taxpayers

But the benefits of conserving York should be paid for not only by those who actually visit it, but also by the country as a whole. This is already an accepted principle in that the central government contributes subsidies of various kinds to the maintenance of the national heritage and the principle would merely be extended so that extension of grants would be made out of general taxation not simply to specific buildings, but to whole historic cities. The approach can be justified on the argument that each generation is the beneficiary of a tradition which it is obliged to hand on into the far-distant future. It is true that each generation has its own valuation of the national heritage, and of different segments of it (historic buildings versus landscape), and may not be prepared to spend much of its current resources in long term conservation, but each government should take the view that since central York is irreplaceable, there is the obligation of passing it on for future generations who might value it very highly.

The form of central government subvention on behalf of generations yet unborn could take many forms. It might be in the nature of the specific grants now paid towards historic buildings. It might be by a special provision in the general grant formula for historic towns. Or it might be a percentage grant on revenue deficiencies for approved conservation proposals, as mentioned earlier, the kind of revenue grant that is currently allowed for redevelopment proposals in central areas, under the Local Government Act, 1966, Section 7; as there surely should be no differentiation between the authority that runs into losses by redevelopment for contemporary needs, and the authority that does so by conservation for future generations.

6.0 Summary and Conclusions

Section 2 of this Appendix reviews the economic considerations bearing on conservation in central York, and Section 3 measures those considerations in terms of the total financial cost of the conservation proposals in this Report to all agencies and the financial returns which can be expected to flow directly to property owners, both the City and private, within the three study areas. In brief the cost (some £2.7 million) exceeds the direct final returns (some £1.6 million) producing a shortfall of some £1.1 million on redevelopment even if the City implement on the financially most favourable method of realisation to them. Added to this is the net cost of reconditioning existing structures and environmental improvements, £1 million, giving a total capital cost of about £2.1 million.

This shortfall cannot be described simply as the 'cost of conservation' in York for the reason given in Section 3: the 'true cost' of conservation is the sum required for conservation proposals over and above the sum which would be needed anyway for planning central York simply to renew it in accordance with contemporary requirements. For reasons also given in Section 3, it has not been practicable in this Report to assess this 'true cost'. But even if this had been practicable, it might well have shown that there would still be a financial shortfall. This would not have meant that conservation in general is not financially viable. It would only mean that it is not so in York today, where for historical reasons the cost of conservation works is large compared with the value of the conserved property, mainly because the cost is aggravated by the substantial amount of non-conforming uses which have grown up within the walls; and values are diminished by the slack demand that appears to exist for the rehabilitated accommodation, especially for the higher value commercial uses.

The valuations in Section 3 therefore need interpretation along these lines if their significance for conservation is to be explored. However, the facts are still there: the proposals in the Report would involve the City Council under current financial arrangements in a net cost of some £1.1 million on redevelopment, together with £1 million on reconditioning. As Section 3 shows not all of this cost would necessarily fall on the City Council and the annual cost to them could be about £90,000 depending on the share taken up by Central Government and Private Owners. This however needs putting into perspective in two ways. First, while the sum is in itself large it is by no means large compared with the net costs falling on to other Authorities over the country for renewing centres which are not to be conserved: in some instances the cost is many millions. Second, as the cost benefit analysis in Section 4 shows, while the net financial cost would fall on to the City and owners of listed buildings, under current financial arrangements, there are many diffused financial benefits which would accrue to other sectors of the community,

for example the hoteliers, the shopkeepers and the national economy in tourist earnings. If these financial benefits were credited in the balance sheet the shortfall would be reduced, and perhaps turned into a surplus. In other words, while there would be financial cost to the City there might be no financial cost to the community as a whole. In addition, the cost benefit analysis shows that the community would have some benefits which would not be reflected in financial returns. Again, it has not been practicable in the study to measure these side effects, although it could be done. Instead Section 5 indicates those beneficiaries from which it might be possible to levy some of the betterment which would arise from conservation and how this might be achieved. Just what the betterment would be, and whether it would be worth the administrative and political cost of its collection, are matters that have not been explored.

But whether or not the betterment were collected, the issue is made clear. Under present financial arrangements conservation in York would involve the City in a financial loss, but others in a gain for which they would not be charged. It can be argued that this situation is no different from renewing any 'non-historic' centre. But there are special considerations in York, and the other historic gems of this country, which are very well recognised. The works of renewal/conservation are aimed at conserving essential urban scenes bequeathed to us by the genius of previous generations; these scenes are becoming scarcer as renewal clears them away, for they are irreplaceable; there is a strong compulsion for any civilised community to pass on its heritage to future generations in at least the condition in which it was inherited; and finally, it is this heritage which attracts visitors not only from the country as a whole but from the world, who bring with them a not insubstantial element of our export trade.

All these special considerations point in one clear direction. The conservation of York cannot be only a local responsibility. It must be shared by the nation as a whole. This principle is well recognised as for example in the arrangements for special grants and subsidy. But what is not established is the share of local and national responsibility in meeting the 'true costs of conservation'.

The analysis points the way to a resolution in York. It provides an overall cost of imaginatively renewing and conserving York for future generations and the export trade. It shows that the cost is not forbidding. It shows who benefits, locally and nationally. It shows that present financial arrangements would not allocate the costs according to the benefits. It points to a basis for such an allocation which would be acceptable and practicable. It thus provides the financial basis for coordinated action.

H Terms of reference

1   The Consultant is asked to study and report on the implications of a conservation policy for the historic core of York.

2   The area which is to be the subject of this study is the area within the City Walls, the 'action areas' to be defined by the Consultant after consultation with the Ministry of Housing and Local Government and the York City Council.

3   The primary object of the policy will be to preserve and, where possible enhance, the architectural and historic character of the area, in order to maintain its life and economic buoyancy.

4   The study should identify in detail the particular features—buildings, groups of buildings, street patterns, street scenes, spaces and other aspects of the selected area—which it is thought desirable to preserve, and should explain the reasons for the choice. It will also be necessary in some cases to consider the suitability of these buildings or group of buildings to fulfil their present function or their adaptability where necessary to some other function.

5   The study should take account of the various practical problems which conservation is likely to encounter, including:
(a)   motor traffic and car parking, covering both long-term solutions and interim remedial measures; for this purpose the Consultant may assume the completion within a period of years of an Inner Ring Road and the provision of central and peripheral car parks as shown on the existing or proposed central area plans together with outline traffic managements schemes which are being considered by the York City Council;
(b)   commercial pressures on the area, and how they can be met without damaging its character, or alternatively how they can be accommodated elsewhere; for this purpose and as an aid to his study the Consultant will be supplied with copies of planning applications approved or under consideration relating to shopping, office and similar development.

6   The study should deal with:
(a)   the preservation of listed buildings in the area, including the economics of restoration and maintenance, or where necessary, conversion to new uses. This will involve some consideration of the existing or proposed land uses within the area and of the amounts of accommodation likely to be required for different purposes in the future.
(b)   the measures to be taken for environmental improvement in the area.
(c)   the means to control any necessary new development, to ensure that it is sympathetic to the environment both in design and quality.
(d)   the total cost of conservation, including the public expenditure required and the programming of this expenditure, especially against the likely programming of relevant development outside the area, and other possible sources of revenue.

7   It will not be possible to consider the problems of the conservation area in isolation from the rest of the town and the Consultant will need to relate his proposals for that area to the current planning proposals for the town as a whole in consultation with the City Planning Officer; but if he finds it impossible so to relate his proposals in any instance he should say so and why.

8   Similarly, while the study will necessarily be carried out within the framework of existing legislation, the consultant will be free to suggest any changes in the law which seem to him to be necessary to secure an effective conservation policy.

9   The Council will make available to the Consultant by arrangement with the City Planning Officer any relevant existing survey information or other material in their possession. The Consultant should also take into account any conservation measures already being prepared or carried out by the local authority or other bodies (e.g. the York Civic Trust).

10   The intention is that the results of the study and recommendations should be presented in the form of a final report with supporting maps and diagrams not later than October 1967, the report to become the property of the Ministry and the Council to whom all publication rights will be surrendered.

11   The clients will be jointly the Minister of Housing and Local Government and the York City Council.